Ranger Brown's Narrative

Description of the Narrative

A plain narrative of the uncommon sufferings and remarkable deliverance of Thomas Brown of Charlestown, in New England; who returned to his father's house the beginning of Jan. 1760, after having been absent three years and about eight months.

Containing an account of the engagement between a party of English, commanded by Major Rogers, and a party of French and Indians, in Jan. 1757; in which Captain Spikeman was killed; and the author of this narrative having received three wounds (one through his body) he was left for dead on the field of battle, and details of how he was taken captive by the Indians and carried to Canada, and from thence to the Mississippi; where he lived about a year, and was again sent to Canada, during all which time he was not only in constant peril of his own life; but had the mortification of being an eye-witness of diverse tortures and shocking cruelties, that were practised by the Indians on several English prisoners; one of whom he saw burnt to death, another tied to a tree and his entrails drawn out, &c &c.

The Trials of a Ranger

As I am but a youth, I shall not make those remarks on the difficulties I have met with, or the kind appearance of a good God for my preservation, as one of riper years might do; but shall leave that to the reader as he goes along, and shall only beg his prayers, that mercies and afflictions may be sanctified to me, and relate matters of fact as they occur to my mind.

I was born in Charlestown, near Boston in New England, in the year 1740, and put an apprentice by my father to Mr. Mark White of Acton, and in the year 1756, in the month of May, I enlisted into Major Rogers's Corps of Rangers, in the company commanded by Captain Spikeman.

We marched for Albany, where we arrived the first of August, and from thence to Fort Edward. I was out on several scouts, in one of which I killed an Indian. On the 18th of Jan. 1757, we marched on a scout from Fort William Henry; Major Rogers himself headed us. All were volunteers that went on this scout. We came to the road leading from Ticonderoga to Crown Point, and on Lake Champlain (which was froze over) we saw about fifty sleys; the major thought proper to attack them and ordered us all, about sixty in number, to lay in ambush, and when they were near enough we were ordered to pursue them. I happened to be near the major when he took the first prisoner, a Frenchman: I singled out one and followed him: they fled some one way and some another, but I soon came up with him and took him. We took seven in all, the rest escaping, some to Crown Point, and some returned to Ticonderoga: When we had brought the prisoners to land the major examined them, and they informed him that there were thirty-five Indians and 500 regulars at Ticonderoga.

It being a rainy day we made a fire and dried our guns. The major thought best to return to Fort William Henry in the same path we came, the snow being very deep; we marched in an Indian file and kept the prisoners in the rear, lest we should be attacked: We proceeded in this order about a mile and a half, and as we were ascending a hill, and the centre of our men were at the top, the French, to the number of 400, besides thirty or forty Indians, fired on us before we discovered them: The major ordered us to advance. I received a wound from the enemy (the first shot they made on us) through the body, upon which I retired into the rear, to the prisoner I had taken on the lake, knocked him on the head and killed him, lest he should escape and give information to the enemy; and as I was going to place myself behind a large rock, there started up an Indian from the other side; I threw myself backward into the snow, and it being very deep, sunk so low that I broke my snowshoes (I had time to pull em off, but was obliged to let my shoes go with them) one Indian threw his tomahawk at me, and another was just upon seizing me; but I happily escaped and got to the centre of our men, and fixed myself behind a large pine, where I loaded and fired every opportunity; after I had discharged six or seven times, there came a ball and cut off my gun just at the lock. About half an hour after, I received a shot in my knee; I crawled again into the rear, and as I was turning about received a shot in my shoulder. The engagement held, as near as I could guess, five and a half hours, and as I learnt after I was taken, we killed more of the enemy than we were in number. By this time it grew dark and the firing ceased on both sides, and as we were so few the major took the advantage of the night and escaped with the well men, without informing the wounded of his design, lest they should inform the enemy and they should pursue him before he had got out of their reach.

Captain Spikeman, one Baker and myself, all very badly wounded, made a small fire and sat about half an hour, when looking round we could not see any of our men; Captain Spikeman called to Major Rogers, but received no answer, except from the enemy at some distance; upon this we concluded our people were fled. All hope of escape now vanished; we were so wounded that we could not travel; I could but just walk, the others could scarce move; we therefore concluded to surrender ourselves to the French: Just as we came to this conclusion, I saw an Indian coming towards us over a small rivulet that parted us in the engagement: I crawled so far from the fire that I could not be seen, though I could see what was acted at the fire; the Indian came to Captain Spikeman, who was not able to resist, and stripped and scalped him alive; Baker, who was lying by the captain, pulled out his knife to stab himself, which the Indian prevented and carried him away: Seeing this dreadful tragedy, I concluded, if possible, to crawl into the woods and there die of my wounds: But not being far from Captain Spikeman, he saw me and begged me for God's sake! to give him a tomahawk, that he might put an end to his life! I refused him, and exhorted him as well as I could to pray for mercy, as he could not live many minutes in that deplorable condition, being on the frozen ground, covered with snow. He desired me to let his wife know (if I lived to get home) the dreadful death he died. As I was travelling as well as I could, or rather creeping along, I found one of our people dead; I pulled off his stockings (he had no shoes) and put them on my own legs.

By this time the body of the enemy had made a fire, and had a large number of sentries out on our path, so that I was obliged to creep quite round them before I could get into the path; but just before I came to it I saw a Frenchman behind a tree, within two rods of me, but the fire shining right on him prevented his seeing me. They cried out about every quarter of an hour in French, All is well! And while he that was so near me was speaking, I took the opportunity to creep away, that he might not hear me, and by this means got clear of him and got into our path.

But the snow and cold put my feet into such pain, as I had no shoes, that I could not go on: I therefore sat down by a brook, and wrapt my feet in my blanket. But my body being cold by sitting still, I got up, and crawled along in this miserable condition the remainder of the night.

The next day, about 11 o'clock, I heard the shouts of Indians behind me, and I supposed they saw me; within a few minutes four came down a mountain, running towards me: I threw off my blanket, and fear and dread quickened my pace for a while; but, by reason of the loss of so much blood from my wounds, I soon failed. When they were within a few rods of me they cocked their guns, and told me to stop; but I refused, hoping they would fire and kill me on the spot; which I chose, rather than the dreadful death Captain Spikeman died of. They soon came up with me, took me by the neck and kissed me. On searching my pockets they found some money, which they were so fond of, that in trying who could get most, they had like to have killed me. They took some dry leaves and put them into my wounds, and then turned about and ordered me to follow them.

When we came near the main body of the enemy, the Indians made a live-shout, as they call it when they bring in a prisoner alive (different from the shout they make when they bring in scalps, which they call a dead-shout). The Indians ran to meet us, and one of them struck me with a cutlass across the side; he cut through my cloaths, but did not touch my flesh; others ran against me with their heads: I asked if there was no interpreter, upon which a Frenchman cried, I am one: I asked him, if this way they treated their prisoners, to let them be cut and beat to pieces by the Indians? He desired me to come to him; but the Indians would not let me, holding me one by one arm and another by the other: But there arising a difference between the four Indians that took me, they fell to fighting, which their commanding officer seeing, he came and took me away and carried me to the interpreter; who drew his sword, and pointing it to my breast, charged me to tell the truth, or he would run me through: He then asked me what number our scout consisted of—I told him fifty: He asked where they were gone? I told him, I supposed as they were so numerous they could best tell. He said I told him wrong; for he knew of more than one hundred that were slain; I told him we had lost but nineteen in all: He said, there were as many officers. On which he led me to Lieutenant Kennedy. I saw he was much tomahawked by the Indians. He asked me if he was an officer: I told him, he was a lieutenant: And then he took me to another; who, I told him, was an ensign: From thence he carried me to Captain Spikeman, who was laying in the place I left him; they had cut off his head, and fixed it on a pole.

I begged for a pair of shoes, and something to eat; the interpreter told me, I should have relief when I came to Ticonderoga, which was but one mile and a quarter off, and then delivered me to the four Indians that took me. The Indians gave me a piece of bread, and put a pair of shoes on my feet.

About this time Robert Baker, mentioned above, was brought where I was; we were extremely glad to see each other, though we were in such a distressed condition: he told me of five men that were taken. We were ordered to march on toward Ticonderoga: But Baker replied, he could not walk. An Indian then pushed him forward; but he could not go, and therefore sat down and cried; where upon an Indian took him by the hair, and was going to kill him with his tomahawk: I was moved with pity for him, and, as weak as I was, I took his arms over my shoulders, and was enabled to get him to the fort.

We were immediately sent to the guard house, and, about half an hour after, brought before the commanding-officer, who, by his interpreter, examined us separately; after which he again sent us to the guard house. The interpreter came and told us, that we were to be hanged the next day; because we had killed the seven prisoners we had taken on the lake; but was afterwards so kind as to tell us, this was done only to terrify us. About an hour after came a doctor, and his mate, and dressed our wounds; and the commanding-officer sent us a quart of claret. We lay all night on the boards, without blankets.

The next day I was put into the hospital, (the other prisoners were carried another way) here I tarried till the 19th of Feb. and the Indians insisted on having me, to carry to their homes, and broke into the hospital; but the sentinel called the guard and turned them out; after which the commanding officer prevailed with them to let me stay till the 1st of March, by which time I was able to walk about the fort.

As I was one day in the interpreter's lodging, there came in ten or twelve Indians, with the scalps they had taken, in order to have a war-dance: They set me on the floor, and put seven of the scalps on my head while they danced; when it was over, they lifted me up in triumph: But as I went and stood by the door, two Indians began to dance a live-dance, and one of them threw a tomahawk at me, to kill me, but I watched his motion and dodged the weapon.

I lived with the interpreter till the first of March, when General Rigeav[1] came to the fort with about 9000[2] men, in order, as they said, to make an attempt on Fort William Henry. Their design was to scale the walls, for which purpose I saw them making scaling-ladders. The day before they marched the general sent for me and said:

"Young man, you are a likely fellow; it's pity you should live with such an ignorant people as the English; you had better live with me."

I told him I was willing to live with him. He answered, I should, and go with him where he went. I replied, Perhaps he would have me to go to war with him: He said that was the thing; he wanted me to direct him to Fort William Henry, and show him where he might scale the walls. I told him I was sorry that a gentleman should desire such a thing of a youth, or endeavor to draw him away from his duty. He added, he would give me 7000 *livres* on his return. I replied that I was not to be bought with money, to be a traitor to my country and assist in destroying my friends. He smiled, and said "In war you

---

1 Rigaud, the brother of the Marquis de Vaudreuil, Governor of Canada.
2 There were actually only about 1600.

must not mind even father nor mother". When he found that he could not prevail with me, by all the fair promises he made, he ordered me back to the fort; and had two other prisoners brought before him, to whom he made the same proposals as he had to me; to which they consented. The next day I went into the room where they were, and asked them if they had been with the general; they said they had, and that they were to have 7000 *livres* apiece, as a reward. I asked them if that was the value of their fathers and mothers, and of their country? They said they were obliged to go. I said the general could not force them; and added, that if they went on such a design they must never return among their friends; for if they did, and Baker and I should live to get home we would endeavour they should be hanged. At this time a smith came and put irons on my feet: But the general gave those two men who promised to go with him, a blanket, a pair of stockings and shoes. They were taken out of the guard-house, and marched with the French as pilots. The general did not succeed; he only burnt our battoes, &c, and returned to Ticonderoga.[3] The poor fellows never had their reward, but instead of that were sent to the guard-house and put in irons.

Soon after this I was taken out of irons, and went to live with the interpreter till the 27th of March, at which time the Indians took me with them in order to go to Montreal, and set me to draw a large sled with provisions, my arms being tied with a rope. By the time we got to Crown Point, I was so lame that I could not walk. The Indians went ashore and built a fire, and then told me I must dance; to which I complied rather than be killed. When we sat off again I knew not how to get rid of my sled, and I knew I was not able to draw it: but this fancy came into my head: I took three squaws on my sled and pleasantly told them I wished I was able to draw em. All this took with the Indians; they freed me of the sled, and gave it to other prisoners. They stripped off all my cloaths, and gave me a blanket. And the next morning they cut off my hair and painted me, and with

---

3. March 18-19, 1757.

needles and Indian ink pricked on the back of my hand the form of one of the scaling-ladders which the French made to carry to Fort William Henry. I understood they were vexed with the French for the disappointment.

We travelled about nine miles on Lake Champlain, and when the sun was two hours high we stopped; they made a fire, and took one of the prisoners that had not been wounded, and were going to cut off his hair, as they had done mine. He foolishly resisted them, upon which they prepared to burn him; but the commanding officer prevented it at this time. But the next night they made a fire, stripped and tied him to a stake, and the squaws cut pieces of pine, like scures,[4] and thrust them into his flesh, and set them on fire, and then fell to pow wawing and dancing round him; and ordered me to do the same. Love of life obliged me to comply, for I could expect no better treatment if I refused. With a bitter and heavy heart I feigned myself merry. They cut the poor man's cords, and made him run backwards and forwards. I heard the poor man's cries to heaven for mercy; and at length, through extreme anguish and pain, he pitched himself into the flames and expired.

From thence we travelled, without anything worthy of notice happening, till we came to an Indian town, about twenty miles from Montreal. When we were about a gunshot from the town, the Indians made as many live shouts as they had prisoners, and as many dead ones as they had scalps. The men and women came out to meet us, and stripped me naked; after which they pointed to a wigwam and told me to run to it, pursuing me all the way with sticks and stones.

Next day we went to Montreal, where I was carried before Governor Vaudreuil and examined. Afterwards I was taken into a French merchant's house, and there I lived three days. The third night two of the Indians that took me came in drunk and asked for me; upon which the lady called me into the room, and as I went and stood by the door, one of them begun to dance the war-dance about me, designing to kill me; but as he

---

4. Skewers.

lifted up his hand to stab me, I catched hold of it with one of mine, and with the other knocked him down, and then ran up garret and hid. The lady sent for some neighbours to clear the house of her guests which they did. It was a very cold night, and one of the Indians being excessive drunk, fell down near the house and was found in the morning froze to death. The Indians came to the house, and finding their brother dead, said I had killed him; and gathering a number together with their guns, beset the house and demanded me of the lady, saying I should die the most cruel death. The lady told me of it, and advised me to hide myself in the cellar, under the pipes of wine; which I did. They searched the house and even came down cellar, but could not find me. The lady desired a Frenchman to tell the Indians that he saw me without the city, running away: they soon took after me, every way. The merchant pitying my condition, covered me with a blanket and carried me in his conveyance about five miles, to a village where his wife's father lived, in order to keep me out of the way of the Indians. When the Indians that pursued me had returned, and could not find me, they concluded that I was concealed by the merchant; and applied to the Governor that I might be delivered to them in order that they might kill me for killing their brother; adding, by way of threatening, that if I was not delivered up to them they would turn and be against the French. The Governor told them he had examined into the matter, and found that I did not kill the Indian nor know anything about it; but that he froze to death. On this they said they would not kill me, but would have me to live with them. The Governor then informed them where I was, and they came and took me with them to Montreal again, and dressed me in their habit.

On the 1st of May we set off to go to the Mississippi, where my Indian master belonged, and two other English prisoners with them. For several days the Indians treated me very ill; but it wore off. We went in bark canoes, till we came to Lake Sacrament,[5] the first carrying-place. We continued our journey till we

---
5. Lake George.

came to the Ohio, where General Braddock was defeated. Here they took one of the prisoners, and with a knife ripped open his belly, took one end of his guts and tied to a tree, and then whipt the miserable man round and round till he expired; obliging me to dance, while they made their game at the dying man.

From hence we set off to go to an Indian town about 200 miles from the Ohio, where we arrived in fifteen days, and tarried three. The third night one of the Indians had a mind to kill me; as I was standing by the fire he ran against me to push me into the flames, but I jumped over, and escaped being burnt; he followed me round and round, and struck me several times with his head and fist; which so provoked me that as he was coming at me again I struck him and knocked him backwards. The other Indians laughed, and said I was a good fellow.

The next day we set off for the Mississippi, where we arrived the 23rd of August, having passed over thirty-two carrying-places from our leaving Montreal. When we came here I was ordered to live with a squaw, who was to be my mother. I lived with her during the winter, and was employed in hunting, dressing leather, &c., being cloathed after the Indian fashion.

In the spring a French merchant came a trading in bark canoes, and on his return wanted hands to help him; he prevailed with my mistress to let me go with him to Montreal. When we came there, and the canoes were unloaded, I went into the country and lived with his wife's father, and worked at the farming business for my victuals and cloathing; I fared no better than a slave. The family often endeavoured to persuade me to be of their religion, making many fair promises if I would. Wanting to see what alteration this would make in their conduct towards me, one Sunday morning I came to my mistress, and said, "Mother, will you give me good cloaths, if I will go to Mass?" She answered "Yes, son, as good as any in the house". She did so, and I rode to church with two of her daughters; in giving me directions how to behave they told me I must do as they did. When we came home I sat at the table and ate with the family, and every night and morning was taught my prayers.

Thus I lived till the next spring, when my master's son-in-law, that brought me from the Mississippi, came for me to return with him, as he was going again there to trade. I refused to go, and applied to the Governor. I was then put into gaol, where I tarried five weeks, living on bread and water and horse-beef. When some prisoners were going to be sent to Quebec, in order to be transported to Old France, I went with them. Here we laid in gaol six weeks. But happening to see one of my master's sons, he prevailed with me to go back with him and work as formerly; I consented, and tarried with him till the 8th of September.

There was at the next house an English lad, a prisoner; we agreed to run away together, through the woods, that so, if possible, we might get home to our friends. But how to get provisions for the way, we knew not; till I was allowed a gun to kill pigeons, which were very plenty here. I shot a number, split and dried them, and concealed in the woods. We agreed to set off on a Sunday morning, and were to meet at an appointed place: which we did, and began our journey towards Crown-Point. After we had travelled twenty-two days, fifteen of which we had no provision except roots, worms and such like, we were so weak and faint that we could scarce walk. My companion gave out, and could go no further; he desired me to leave him, but I would not. I went and found three frogs, and divided them between us. The next morning he died. I sat down by him, and at first concluded to make a fire, as I had my gun, and eat his flesh, and if no relief came, to die with him; but finally came to this resolution: To cut off of his bones as much flesh as I could and tie it up in a handkerchief, and so proceed as well as I could. Accordingly I did so, and buried my companion on the day I left him. I got three frogs more the next day. Being weak and tired, about 9 o'clock I sat down, but could not eat my friend's flesh. I expected soon to die myself; and while I was commending my soul to God I saw a partridge light just by me, which I thought was sent by providence. I was so weak that I could not hold out my gun; but by resting, I brought my piece to bear, so that I killed the partridge. While I was eating of it, there came two pigeons, so near, that I killed them both. As I fired two guns, I heard a gun at a distance: I fired again, and was answered twice. This roused me; I got up and travelled as fast as I could towards the report of the guns; and about half a mile off, I saw three Canadians. I went to them, and pretended to be a Dutchman, one of their own regulars, that was lost in the woods. They brought me to Crown Point; upon which I desired to see the commanding officer. He knew me again, and asked me how I came there. I told him my story and what difficulties I had met with. He ordered me to the guard-house, and to be put in irons. About an hour after he sent me a bowl of rice.

After I had been at Crown Point ten or twelve days, the commanding officer sent me back, under a guard of twelve soldiers to Montreal, in a battoe, and wrote a letter (as I afterwards understood) to my master not to hurt me.

When I came to the house, one of his daughters met me at the door, and pushed me back, and went and called her father. At this house there was a French captain, of the regulars, billeted; he was a Protestant. He hearing my voice, called me to him and asked me where I had been. Upon my telling him he called me a fool, for attempting a thing so impossible. My master coming in, took me by the shoulder, and threatened to kill me for stealing his gun when I ran away. But the good captain prevented him from using any violence. The captain asked me if I had been before the Governor; I told him I had not; and he then advised my master to send his son with me (who was an ensign among the Canadians). When we came to a small ferry, which we were to pass, I refused to go any further; and after a great deal of do, he went without me. On his return, he said he had got leave of the Governor, that I should go back to his father and work as formerly. Accordingly I lived with him till the 19th of November; and when Colonel Schuyler was coming away, I came with him to Albany.

Here I was taken sick, and some of the Light Infantry promised me if I would enlist, that they would provide for me; and having neither friends nor money, I was obliged to consent. They ordered me a bed, and care to be taken of me. Five days after, they put me on board a sloop, and sent me to Kingston, and put me into a hospital, where I was three months.

The regiment remained here till May, when we went to Albany, from thence to Fort William Henry, and then to Ticonderoga and Crown Point; both of which places surrendered to General Amherst.

On Sept. 19th, went pilot of a scout to Cachanowaga,[6] with Lieutenant McCurdy, and on our return, as we were on Lake Champlain, turning a point of land, and under great way, we discovered in a large cove a French brig,[7] but it was unhappily too late for us to make our escape. We were pursued and taken prisoners (being seven in Number), and the next morning sent to Nut [8] Island; where we were stripped by the Indians, and dressed after their manner. From thence we were conducted to Montreal and examined before the Governor; after which we were ordered to prison. I applied to the Governor, and told him that I had been a prisoner there two years, and had lived with such a farmer, and desired liberty to go to him again; upon which he sent for my master's son, and being informed of the truth of what I related, consented.

I tarried with the farmer till November 25th,[9] when by a flag of truce 250 English prisoners came to Crown Point, where I rejoined my regiment.

After repeated application to General Amherst I was dismissed, and returned in peace to my father's house the beginning of January, 1760, after having been absent three years and almost eight months.

---

6. Caughnawaga.
7. At that time the French had several armed vessels on Lake Champlain.
8. Isle aux Noix.
9. 1759.

The Adventures of
Robert Eastburn

Introduction

Robert Eastburn, whose *Faithful Narrative* is one of the valuable, because one of the undoubted, original authorities relating to the war that destroyed the French power in North America, was captured by a force of French soldiers and Indians on a wagon road that crossed the divide between the Mohawk River and Wood Creek, just north of the modern city of Rome, New York. He was carried thence to Canada, where he was adopted into an Indian family, and where he remained, part of the time with the Indians, and a part with the French, for something less than two years.

It will add to the interest of the narration of his experiences to know that Eastburn was born in England in 1710 (see *Memoirs of the Reverend Joseph Eastburn*)) but was brought to America by his parents when he was four years old. There after his home was in Philadelphia. His parents were Quakers, but in 1739, Robert was won over to the Presbyterians by the preaching of George Whitefield,[1] and when Whitefield organized a congregation, Robert became one of its deacons.

---

1. Franklin, in his autobiography, says of Whitefield: "In 1739 arrived among us from Ireland the Reverend Mr. Whitefield, who had made himself remarkable there as an itinerant preacher. He was at first permitted to preach in some of our churches; but the clergy, taking a dislike to him, soon refused him their pulpits, and he was obliged to preach in the fields. The multitudes of all sects and denominations that attended his sermons were enormous, and it was matter of speculation to me, who was one of the number, to observe the extraordinary influence of his oratory on his hearers, notwithstanding his common abuse of them, by assuring them they were naturally half beasts and half devils. It was wonderful to see the change soon made in the manners of our inhabitants. From being thoughtless or (continued overleaf)

To those who are acquainted with the history of the American frontier during the eighteenth century, the fact that Eastburn was a Christian is of peculiar interest. For when captured by the French invaders he was one of a party of men who were on their way to the frontier post of Oswego to engage in the Indian trade; and no men, as a class, have been so utterly degraded and deeply cursed by their trade as those who have dealt with the aboriginal inhabitants of the earth. With them a thought of fair dealing was an evidence of weakness; the ability to overreach the savage was their constant boast.

Nevertheless, because some were strictly honest, according to their light (Quakers and Moravians traded with the Indians), and because as a class the traders were most energetic, enterprising, and courageous, it seems likely that the story of their work and adventures should make the most interesting of the chapters of the American annals that have not yet been written.

Thus, it was the work of the Indian traders chiefly their anxiety to preserve and extend the fur-trade that caused all the long series of French and Indian raids on the British-American frontier during the period so graphically described by Parkman in his *Half Century of Conflict*. And the first stroke delivered on the American continent, in what is known as the "Seven Years War" the war during which Eastburn was captured was struck by Charles Langlade, a French trader, with a party of Ottawas and Ojibways, who attacked the American traders and the Indians who were gathered at Pickawillany (near the modern Piqua, Ohio), June 21, 1752. To show the courage and enterprise of Robert Eastburn as a trader, it is necessary to go over the events that, in America, preceded and led to the Seven Years War.

Under the treaty of Utrecht (April 11 , 1713), and that of Aix-la-Chapelle (October 7, 1748), the British had the right to

---

indifferent about religion, it seemed as if all the world were growing religious". Under Whitefield's influence a church one hundred feet long by seventy feet broad was erected and paid for before dedication. It was "vested in trustees, expressly for the use of any preacher of any religious persuasion who might desire to say something to the people of Philadelphia."

trade with the Indians of the interior of North America, regardless of the claims of France to that territory. That every British trader would have made haste to exchange a pint of rum, or six cents worth of red paint, for a beaver-skin at every opportunity, regardless of treaties, may be admitted; but the fact is they had the legal right to do it.

In pursuit of the profits thus to be obtained, the traders—particularly those of Philadelphia—thronged through the passes of the Alleghanies, after the treaty of Aix-la-Chapelle. In 1749, it is said (Parkman) that three hundred of them led their packhorses into the wilds of the Mississippi Valley. Governor Dinwiddie, of Virginia, said of them that "they appear to be in general a set of abandoned wretches," and Governor Hamilton, of Pennsylvania, concurred in that opinion. But whatever their morals they fearlessly threaded the forests of the region beyond the mountains, met and fought the rival traders of the north, went to the Indian villages wherever to be found, and in time established a station on Sandusky Bay, although the French had a station at Detroit and another on the Maumee River, in northern Ohio.

Commandant Raymond, in charge of the French post on the Maumee, wrote, at about this time:

> All the tribes who go to the English at Pickawillany come back loaded with gifts. If the English stay in this country we are lost. We must attack and drive them out.

The Indians that had settled around Detroit were invited to make the attack, but they were found to be "touched with disaffection;" and it was then that Charles Langlade came from the upper lakes and destroyed Pickawillany.

In the meantime the French had taken a formal "renewal of possession" of the Ohio country by sending Céloron de Bienville to bury certain lead plates in the Ohio watershed, and to nail tin plates, on which the French royal coat of arms had been painted, to a number of trees all of which acts were duly attested by a notary public carried along for the purpose. The attack upon Pickawillany having proved as futile as the expedition of Céloron—

though an Indian chief called "Old Britain" was boiled and eaten by Langlade's Indians—measures that were to prove strikingly effective for a time, were adopted by the French.

An expedition was sent by way of Erie, Pennsylvania, to the headwaters of the Alleghany River, where a post was established (1752), and named Le Bœuf. It stood where Waterford, Pennsylvania, is now found. In the spring of 1753, they moved forward to the site of the modern Venango, and there prepared to descend to the junction of the Alleghany and Monongahela in the year after that.

It was now that Governor Dinwiddie, alarmed at what he deemed an invasion of Virginia, and at the prospect of a transfer of the horrors of the French and Indian border warfare from the frontier of New England to the borders of his own colony, sent the youthful George Washington to make a formal demand that the French leave. Legardeur de St. Pierre, commanding the French, replied, "I do not think myself obliged to obey."

Accordingly Dinwiddie raised three hundred raw recruits, and sent them to occupy the favourable site for a fort that Washington had seen, meantime, at the forks of the Ohio. William Trent, a trader, and a gang of back woodsmen went with them, and on an unnamed day in April, 1754, these backwoodsmen began building a fort where Pittsburg now stands.

Their work was apparently in vain. On April 17th, five hundred Frenchmen, with eighteen cannon, came down the Alleghany River, under Captain Claude Pecaudy de Contrecoeur, and drove them away.

Washington's attack on the French force under Ensign Coulon de Jumonville (May 28,) followed, and that is usually called the beginning, in America, of the Seven Years War. Then by finesse, rather than by force of arms, the French, under Coulon de Villiers, drove Washington from Fort Necessity (July 4, 1 755). Though as yet not formally declared, the great war was well on.

In the meantime (on February 20, of this year), the "trusty and well-beloved Edward Braddock," with two regiments of British soldiers, arrived at Hampton, Virginia. An intercolonial conference was held at Alexandria, beginning on April 14, to consider measures for the prosecution of the war, at which Governor William Shirley, whom Eastburn mentions, was present.

The plans made here included attacks on Acadia, Crown Point, Niagara, and Fort Duquesne, as the post at the forks of the Ohio was called. Shirley "and Dinwiddie stood in the front of the opposition to French designs;" to Shirley was assigned the work of capturing Niagara, and he was placed next in rank to Braddock, in the command of the British forces in America. Braddock himself undertook the task of marching through the wilderness to Fort Duquesne.

How Braddock, with 1,373 picked men, reached Turtle Creek, eight miles from Fort Duquesne, on July 7, crossed the Monongahela on the ninth, and was overwhelmed by an inferior force of French and Indians on the site of the modern village of Braddock, Pennsylvania, a little later, need not be told here in detail. The important fact is that the French triumph was complete and seemingly decisive. They not only held control of the fort at the forks, but through the shameful retreat of the British to Philadelphia, the French were left in undisputed control of the passes of the Alleghanies.

That the British confirmed their control of Acadia, in this season, by expelling certain French families from the territory; and that the forces under William Johnson checked the French under Baron Dieskau at Lake George, afforded the people of Pennsylvania and Virginia no consolation. For the evil that Governor Dinwiddie had foreseen was upon them. The horrors of the French and Indian wars that, for half a century, had desolated the frontiers of New England, now loomed over the Alleghanies.

"If you consider it necessary to make the Indians to act offensively against the English, his Majesty will approve of your using that expedient," said a letter dated September 6, 1754, from the French colonial minister to Governor Duquesne, of Canada. Duquesne thought that expedient necessary. Captain Dumas succeeded Contrecoeur in the command of Fort Duquesne, and on July 24, 1756, wrote to the minister, saying:

M. de Contrecoeur had not been gone a week before I had six or seven different war parties in the field at once, always accompanied by Frenchmen. I have succeeded in ruining the three adjacent provinces, Pennsylvania, Maryland, and Virginia, driving off the inhabitants and totally destroying the settlements over a tract of country thirty leagues wide, reckoning from the line of Fort Cumberland.

And the Reverend Claude Godfroy Coquard, S.J., in a letter to his brother, said in reference to the work of these war parties (*N.Y. Col. MSS.*, vol. 10., p. 528):

The Indians do not make any prisoners; they kill all they meet, men, women, and children. Every day they have some in their kettle, and after having abused the women and maidens, they slaughter or burn them.

On one occasion a band of these Indians swooped down to within sixty miles of Philadelphia. A company of the harassed settlers, in their desperation, came in from the frontier, bringing with them the mutilated bodies of murdered friends and relatives, which they displayed at the doors of the Assembly chamber, while they bitterly cursed the opponents of an active war against the savage intruders.

It was in the midst of the red aggressions of the war parties sent out by Dumas that Robert Eastburn, a deacon in the First Presbyterian Church of Philadelphia, left home with a party of traders (among them being his own son, a lad seventeen years old), and travelled away into the wilderness, bound to Oswego, the most advanced post of the American frontier the one nearest to the triumphant French to engage in the fur-trade with such Indians as he might find in that region. And he did that, too, when he knew that Oswego would be in imminent danger of attack while he was there, and that there was no small probability that his party would be intercepted while he was on the way, as, indeed, actually happened.

Robert Eastburn was, in fact, one of the many heroes of commerce, now well-nigh forgotten. It was characteristic of such a man to take his gun and join the soldiers, when a squad was sent out to hunt the enemy. And no one is surprised to learn that he was cool enough to bring down two at one shot, when the enemy were found.

The story of the fight in which Eastburn was captured is told, with some variations in the statements of facts, in volume 10 of the *New York Colonial Manuscripts*. The account most nearly accurate is that in *Journal of Occurrences in Canada from October, 1755, to June, 1756*. Parkman has the most interesting modern account in his *Montcalm and Wolfe*.

At the opening of the campaign of 1756, the French held Ticonderoga, as well as Fort Duquesne, and all the borders of the Great Lakes, except the one post of Oswego. While yet the snow lay deep upon the ground in the northern part of New York, they learned from the Indians of the Iroquois tribes, who were more or less friendly to them, that the English contemplated sending an expedition, by way of Oswego and Lake Ontario, to attack Niagara, while another expedition would try to reduce Ticonderoga and Crown Point. The Indians also told the French that in pursuance of the English intention to attack Niagara, immense quantities of provisions had been sent forward toward Oswego, while the winter roads were good, and that many of these supplies were piled up in the storehouses at the carrying-place between the Mohawk and Wood Creek.

Accordingly Vaudreuil, who had meantime become governor of Canada, not only did what he could to strengthen Ticonderoga and Niagara, but he planned a counter-stroke for the destruction of the forts and stores at the Mohawk Wood Creek carrying-place. He also planned an attack on Oswego, but that was to come later.

To raid the carrying-place, Vaudreuil sent Joseph Chaussegros de Léry, a distinguished Canadian officer (Vaudreuil was partial to the Canadian officers), with three hundred and sixty-two picked men soldiers, rangers, and Indians from Montreal to the mission of Oswegatchie (now Ogdensburg), and thence by trails through the woods to the head of the Mohawk Valley. After great hardships, due to a lack of provisions and the rigour of the weather (March is a harsh month in the Adirondack region), this force arrived on the road leading from Fort William, at the head of navigation on the Mohawk, to Fort Bull, at the head of navigation on Wood Creek, at 5:30 o'clock on the morning of March 26, 1756. As it happened, they found there a party of twelve teamsters, including an unnamed negro, who were on their way with provisions and traders goods to Fort Bull. These they attacked, and killed or captured all the party except the negro.

The negro escaped to Fort William and gave the alarm. The French, on questioning their prisoners, under threat of torture, learned that only a small garrison—thirty men—held Fort Bull, and De Léry determined to attack it. Nearly all the Indians in the party objected to this attack, being well satisfied with the plunder obtained from the teamsters, but De Léry, with a little brandy to rouse their courage, persuaded a dozen of them to go with him, and the rest of them to guard the road from Fort William, and then he marched to the attack.

As De Léry approached Fort Bull, some of the Indians whooped, and thus gave the alarm to the garrison, who closed their gate in time to shut out the French, but the French, by dash forward, were able to secure positions at all the loopholes and prevent the garrison using them. De Léry then called on the garrison to surrender, but in spite of the advantages the French had secured, and in spite of inferior numbers, the heroic band replied with muskets and hand grenades. The fight lasted for an hour. At the end of that time the French succeeded in chopping down the gate, and as it fell, they rushed in and massacred every person they could find. Two or three escaped death by hiding. The stores were destroyed and the fort was burned.

In the meantime Captain Williams, commanding at Fort William, had sent out a scouting party. Behind this party marched Deacon Eastburn, bearing a musket that had been carefully loaded and primed. And what the result of that movement was, Eastburn shall tell for himself.

John R. Spears

Preface

The author (and subject) of the ensuing narrative (who is a deacon of our church, and has been so for many years) is of such an established good character, that he needs no recommendation of others, where he is known: a proof of which, was the general joy of the inhabitants of this city, occasioned by his return from a miserable captivity! Together with the readiness of diverse persons, to contribute to the relief of himself, and necessitous family, without any request of his, or the least motion of that tendency! But, feeing the following sheets, are like to spread into many places, where he is not known, permit me to say, That upon long acquaintance, I have found him to be a person of candour, integrity, and sincere piety; whole testimony, may with safety, be depended upon; which give his narrative the greater weight, and may induce to read it with the greater pleasure; The design of it is evidently pious, the matters contained in it, and manner of handling them, will, I hope, be esteemed by the impartial, to be entertaining and improving: I heartily wish it may, by the divine benediction, be of great and durable service. I am thy sincere servant, in the Gospel of Jesus Christ.

Gilbert Tennent
Philadelphia
Jan 19, 1758

Author's Introduction

On my return from my captivity, I had no thoughts of publishing any observations of mine to the world, in this manner; as I had no opportunity to keep a journal, and my memory being broken, and capacity small, I was disinclined to undertake it; but a number of my friends were pressing in their persuasions, that I should do it; with whose motion I complied, from a sincere regard to God, my King, and Country, so far as I know my own heart: The following pages contain, as far as I can remember, the most material passages that happened within the compass of my observation, while a prisoner in Canada; the facts therein related are certainly true, but the way of representing some things especially, is not so regular, clear, and strong, as I could wish; but I trust it will be some apology, that I am not fo much acquainted with performances of this kind, as many others; who may be hereby excited to give better representations of things, far beyond my knowledge.

Robert Eastburn
Philadelphia
Jan. 19, 1758

Robert Eastburn's Narrative

About thirty tradesmen, and myself, arrived at Captain Williams's Fort,[1] (at the carrying place) in our way to Oswego, the 26th of March, 1756; who informed me, that he was like to be cumbered in the fort, and therefore advised us to take the Indian-House for our lodging. About ten o'clock next day, a negro man came running down the road, and reported, that our slaymen were all taken by the enemy; Captain Williams, on hearing this, sent a serjeant, and about twelve men, to see if it was true; I being at the Indian-House, and not thinking myself safe there, in case of an attack, and being also sincerely willing to serve my King and country, in the best manner I could in my present circumstances, asked him if he would take me with the company? He replied, with all his heart! Hereupon, I fell into the rear, with my arms, and marched after them; when we had advanced about a quarter of a mile, we heard a shot, followed with doleful cries of a dying man, which excited me to advance, in order to discover the enemy, who I soon perceived were prepared to receive us: In this difficult situation, seeing a large pine-tree near, I repaired to it for shelter; and while

---

1. This fort stood where Rome, New York, now stands. It was erected by Captain William Williams, of Sir William Pepperell's regiment, to guard the south, or Mohawk, end of the carrying-place between the Mohawk River and Wood Creek, in the route from Albany to Oswego. It was a palisaded enclosure with, presumably, a two-story, loopholed log-house at each of two corners, to give the garrison a commanding view of the enemy, in case of attack. The fort was destroyed by the English after the French captured Oswego, and a little later Fort Stanwix was built in its place, from plans drawn by James Montresor, director of engineers and lieutenant-colonel in the British army in 1758.

the enemy were viewing our party, I having a good chance of killing two at a shot, quickly discharged at them, but could not certainly know what execution was done, till sometime after; our company likewise discharged, and retreated: seeing myself in danger of being surrounded, I was obliged to retreat a different course, and to my great surprise, fell into a deep mire, which the enemy, by following my track in a light snow, soon discovered, and obliged me to surrender, to prevent a cruel death. (They stood ready to drive their darts into my body, in case I refused to deliver up my arms.) Presently after I was taken, I was surrounded by a great number, who stripped me of my cloathing, hat, and neckcloth (so that I had nothing left but a flannel vest, without sleeves) put a rope on my neck, bound my arms fast behind me, put a long band round my body, and a large pack on my back, struck me on the head (a severe blow,) and drove me through the woods before them: It is not easy to conceive, how distressing such a condition is! In the meantime, I endeavoured with all my little remaining strength, to lift up my eyes to God, from whom alone I could with reason expect relief!

Seventeen or eighteen prisoners, were soon added to our number, one of which informed me, that the Indians were angry with me, and reported to some of their chiefs, that I had fired on them, wounded one, and killed another; for which he doubted not they would kill me. Here upon I considered that the hearts of all men are in the hand of God, and that one hair of our head cannot fall to the ground without his permission: I had not as yet learned what numbers the enemy's parties consisted of; there being only about 100 Indians who had lain in ambush on the road, to kill or take into captivity all that passed between the two forts. Here an interpreter came to me, to enquire what strength Captain Williams had to defend his fort? After a short pause, I gave such a discouraging answer (yet confident with truth) as prevented their attacking it, and of consequence the effusion of much blood; a gracious providence, which I desire ever to retain a grateful sense of;

for hereby it evidently appeared, that I was suffered to fall into the hands of the enemy, to promote the good of my countrymen, to better purpose than I could, by continuing with them; verily the Almighty is wise in council, and wonderful in working.

In the meantime, the enemy determined to destroy Bull's Fort,[2] (at the head of Wood- Creek) which they soon effected, all being put to the sword, except five persons, the fort burnt, the provision and powder destroyed; (saving only a little for their own use) then they retired to the woods, and joined their main body, which inclusive, consisted of 400 French, and 300 Indians, commanded by one of the principal Gentlemen[3] of Quebec; as soon as they got together (having a priest with them) they fell on their knees, and returned thanks for their victory; an example this, worthy of imitation! an example which may make profane pretended Protestants blush, (if they are not lost to all sense of shame) who instead of acknowledging a God, or Providence, in their military undertakings, are continually reproaching him with oaths and curses; is it any wonder, that the attempts of such, are blasted with disappointment and disgrace!

The enemy had several wounded men, both French and Indians among them, which they carried on their backs; besides which, about fifteen of their number were killed, and of us about forty: it being by this time near dark, and some Indians drunk, they only marched about four miles and encamped; the Indians untied my arms, cut hemlock boughs, and strewed round the fire, tied my band to two trees, with my back on the green boughs, (by the fire) covered me with an old blanket, and lay down across my band, on each side, to prevent my escape, while they slept.

---

2. Fort Bull was a mere palisade wall around store-houses. It was garrisoned by thirty men from Shirley's regiment. De Léry attacked it with two hundred and sixty-five men.

3. The commander was Joseph Chaussegros de Léry, an active Canadian officer, who saw service at Fort Duquesne and Crown Point. He is not to be confounded with Gaspard Chaussegros de Léry, chief engineer of Canada, who was called "a great ignoramus."

Sunday the 28th, rose early, the commander ordered a hasty retreat towards Canada, for fear of General Johnson;[4] in the meantime, one of our men said, he understood the French and Indians designed to join a strong party, and fall on Oswego,[5] before our forces there, could get any provision or succours; having, as they thought, put a stop to our relieving them for a time: When we encamped in the evening, the commanding-officer ordered the Indians to bring me to his tent, and asked me, by an interpreter, if I thought General Johnson would follow them, I told him I judged not, but rather thought he would proceed to Oswego (which was indeed my sentiment, grounded upon prior information, and then expressed to prevent the execution of their design.) He farther enquired, what was my trade? I told him that of a smith; he then persuaded me, when I got to Canada, to send for my wife, for said he, you can, get a rich living there; but when he saw that he could not prevail, he asked no more questions, but commanded me to return to my Indian master: Having this opportunity of conversation, I informed the general, that his Indian warriors had stripped me of my cloathing, and would be glad he would be good enough to order me some relief; to which he replied, that I would get cloaths when I came to Canada, which was cold comfort to one almost frozen! On my return, the Indians perceiving I was unwell, and could not eat their coarse food, ordered some chocolate (which they had brought from the carrying-place) to be boiled for me, and seeing me eat that, appeared pleased. A strong guard was kept

---

4. Sir William Johnson. On learning from the Indians that the enemy had come to the carrying-place, he hurried reinforcements up the Mohawk, but arrived too late to intercept them.

5. Near the end of the seventeenth century Governor Bellomont, of New York, suggested that the French might be barred out of the Iroquois country by building a fort where Oswego, New York, now stands, but nothing was done in the matter until Governor Burnet built a "stone house of strength" there, with his private funds, in the spring of 1727. This house soon became a noted trading-station, for it proved a formidable rival to the French stations intended to supply the wants of the Indians on the borders of the Great Lakes. When Montcalm captured the place (Saturday, August 14, 1756), one of the defending structures was known on the frontier as Fort Rascal, because of the character of the work done by its builders.

every night; one of our men being weakened by his wounds, and rendered unable to keep pace with them, was killed and scalped on the road!—I was all this time almost naked, travelling through deep snow, and wading through rivers cold as ice!

After seven days' march, we arrived at Lake Ontario, where I eat some horse-flesh, which tasted very agreeably, for to the hungry man, as Solomon observes, every bitter thing is sweet. On the Friday before we arrived at the lake, the Indians killed a porcupine, which is in bigness equal to a large raccoon, with short legs, is covered with long hair, intermixed with sharp quills, which are their defence: It is indeed dangerous coming very near them, because they cast their quills[6] (which are like barbed irons or darts) at anything that opposeth them, which when they pierce, are not easy to be drawn out; for, though their points are sharp and smooth, they have a kind of beard, which makes them stick fast: However, the Indians threw it on a large fire, burnt off the hair and quills, roasted and eat of it, with whom I had a part. The French carried several of their wounded men all the way upon their backs, and (many of them wore no breeches in their travels in this cold season, they are strong, hardy men.) The Indians had three of their party wounded, which they likewise carried on their backs, I wish there was more of this hardness, so necessary for war, in our nation, which would open a more encouraging scene than appears at present! The prisoners were so divided, that but few could converse together on our march, and (which was still more disagreeable and distressing) an Indian, who had a large bunch of green scalps, taken off our men's heads, marched before me, and another with a sharp spear behind, to drive me after him; by which means, the scalps were very often close to my face, and as we marched, they frequently everyday gave the dead shout[7]

---

6. It is now known that porcupines do not cast or throw their quills, and are not able to do so, though commonly believed to do so, at Eastburn's time. Many a backwoodsman has eaten a porcupine. When young the flesh is as good as that of a possum, they say.
7. Schoolcraft writes *Sa-sa-kuon* to give an idea of the dead shout. It was the whoop by which the Indians announced, when approaching a village, their victory, and the number of scalps and prisoners taken.

which was repeated as many times, as there were captives and scalps taken! In the midst of this gloomy scene, when I considered, how many poor souls were hurried into a vast eternity, with doubts of their unfitness for such a change, it made me lament and expostulate in the manner following; O Sin what hast thou done! what desolation and ruin hast thou brought into this miserable world? What am I, that I should be thus spared! My afflictions are certainly far less than my sins deserve! Through the exceeding riches of divine goodness and grace, I was in this distressing situation supported and comforted, by these passages of sacred scripture, *viz.* That our light afflictions, which last but for a moment, shall work for us a far more exceeding and eternal weight of glory. And that, though no afflictions are for the present joyous, but grievous; yet nevertheless, they afterwards yield the peaceable fruits of righteousness, to them who are exercised thereby. And farther, that all Things shall work together for good, to them that love God; to them who are the called, according to his purpose. But to return.

I may, with justice and truth observe, that our enemies leave no stone unturned to compass our ruin; they pray, work, and travel to bring it about, and are unwearied in the pursuit; while many among us sleep in a storm, that has laid a good part of our country desolate, and threatens the whole with definition: O may the Almighty awake us, cause us to fee our danger, before it be too late, and grant us salvation! O that we may be of good courage, and play the man, for our people, and the cities of our God! But alas, I am obliged to turn my face towards cold Canada, among inveterate enemies, and innumerable dangers! O Lord, I pray thee, be my safeguard; thou hast already covered me in the hollow of thy hand; when death cast darts all around me, and many fell on every side, I beheld thy salvation! April 4th, several French battoes met us, and brought a large supply of provision; the sight of which caused great joy, for we were in great want; then a place was soon erected to celebrate Mass in, which being ended, we all went over the mouth of a river, where it empties itself into the east end of

Lake Ontario, a great part of our company set off on foot towards Oswegotchy;[8] while the rest were ordered into battoes, and carried towards the entrance of St Lawrence (where that river takes its beginning) but by reason of bad weather, wind, rain, and snow, whereby the waters of the lake were troubled, we were obliged to lie by, and haul our battoes on shore; here I lay on the cold shore two days. Tuesday set off, and entered the head of St. Lawrence, in the afternoon; came too late at night, made fires, but did not lie down to sleep; embarked long before day, and after some miles' progress down the river, we saw many fires on our right-hand, which were made by the men who left us, and went by land; with them we staid till day, and then again embarked in our battoes; the weather was very bad (it snowed fast all day) near night arrived at Oswegotchy; I was almost starved to death, but hoped to stay in this Indian town till warm weather; slept in an Indian wigwam, rose early in the morning (being Thursday) and soon to my grief discovered my disappointment! several of the prisoners had leave to tarry here, but I must go 200 miles farther downstream, to another Indian town; the morning being extremely cold, I applied to a French merchant (or trader) for some old rags of cloathing, for I was almost naked, but to no purpose!

About ten o'clock, was ordered into a battoe, on our way down the river, with eight or nine Indians, one of which was the man wounded in the skirmish before mentioned; at night we went on shore, the snow being much deeper than before, we cleared it away, and made a large fire; here, when the wounded Indian cast his eyes upon me, his old grudge revived, he took my blanket from

---

8. Oswegotchie. It was a settlement of Iroquois Indians who had been converted by Abbé Piquet, a French missionary. It was established in 1749 where Ogdensburg, New York, now stands, and it was intended for the promotion of French political and trade interests, as well as the propagation of religion. Piquet called it "La Presentation." In 1753 it contained a palisaded fort, "flanked with block houses; a chapel, a storehouse, a barn, a stable, ovens, a sawmill, broad fields of corn and beans, and three villages of Iroquois, containing in all forty-nine bark lodges each holding three or four families, and as time went on this number was increased."—Parkman. The fort was armed with five two-pounder cannon and garrisoned with a squad of French soldiers.

me, and commanded me to dance round the fire barefoot, and sing the *Prisoner's Song,* which I utterly refused; this surprised one of my fellow prisoners, who told me they would put me to death (for he understood what they said) he therefore tried to persuade me to comply, but I desired him to let me alone, and was through great mercy, enabled to reject: his importunity with abhorrence! The Indian also continued urging, saying, you shall dance and sing; but apprehending my compliance sinful, I determined to persist in declining it at all adventures, and to leave the issue to the divine disposal! The Indian perceiving his orders disobeyed, was fired with indignation, and endeavoured to push me into the fire, which I leapt over, and he being weak with his wounds, and not being assisted by any of his brethren, was obliged to desist: For this gracious interposure of providence, in preserving me both from sin and danger, I desire to bless God while I live!

Friday morning, was almost perished with cold. Saturday, proceeded on our way, and soon came in sight of the upper part of the inhabitants of Canada; here I was in great hopes of some relief, not knowing the manner of the Indians, who do not make many stops among the French, in their return from war, till they get home: However when they came near some rapid falls of water, one of my fellow prisoners, and several Indians, together with myself, were put on shore, to travel by land, which pleased me well, it being much warmer running on the snow, than lying still in the battoe; we past by several French houses, but stopt at none; the vessel going down a rapid stream, it required haste to keep pace with her, we eroded over a point of land, and found the battoe waiting for us, as near the shore as the ice would permit: Here we left St. Lawrence and turned up Conafadauga River[9] but it being frozen up, we hauled our battoe on shore, and each of us took our share of her loading on our backs, and marched towards Conafadauga,[10] an Indian town, which was

---

9. The river St. Lawrence, at Lake Ontario, takes its beginning through several islands, by which we are in no necessity of coming within sight of Frontenac, when we go down the river; it is smooth water from thence to Oswegotchy (or as it is called by the French *Legalet*) but from hence to Montreal, the water is more swift, with a number of rapid streams, though not dangerous (continued opposite)

our designed port, but could not reach it that night; Came to a French house, cold, weary, and hungry; here my old friend, the wounded Indian, again appeared, and related to the Frenchman, the affair of my refusing to dance, who immediately assisted the Indian to strip me of my flannel veil, before mentioned, which was my all: Now they were resolved to compel me to dance and sing! The Frenchman was as violent as the Indian, in promoting this imposition; but the women belonging to the house, feeing the rough usage I had, took pity on me, and rescued me out of their hands, till their heat was over, and prevailed with the Indian to excuse me from dancing; but he insisted that I must be shaved, and then he would let me alone (I had at that time a long beard, which the Indians hate) with this motion I readily complied, and then the Indian seemed content.

Sunday, April 11th, Set off towards Conafadauga, travelled about two hours, and then saw the town, over a great river, which was still frozen; the Indians stopped, and we were soon joined with a number of our own company, which we had not seen for several days: The prisoners, in number eight, were ordered to lay down our packs, and be painted; the wounded Indian painted me, and put a belt of wampum round my neck, instead of the rope which I had worn 400 miles. Then set off towards the town on the ice, which was four miles over; our heads were not allowed to

---

to pass through with small boats and bark canoes, provided the steer-men are careful, and acquainted with the places. In transporting provision and warlike stores up stream from Canada to Lake Ontario, there is a necessity of unloading battoes at several of the rapid streams, and hauling them empty through shoal water near the shore; and carrying the loading by land to where the water is more slack; though there be several of these places, yet the land carriage is not very far: The land on both sides the river, appears fertile a great part of the way from the lake to Montreal; but the nearer the latter the worse, more mirey and stony: The timber is white pine, ash, maple, beech, hickory, hemlock, spruce; and from the lake about 150 miles down, plenty of white oak, but none about Montreal of that kind.—R. E.

10. A mission settlement of Indians containing a village of Iroquois and another of Algonquins. It was called also the Lake of the Two Mountains mission. The site is "a point on the St. Lawrence, just at the [west] extremity of the island of Montreal, where the river widens into a kind of lake. Two slight eminences, which soon obtained the name of mountains, gave it its name. Near these the mission was begun in 1720."—*Shea's American Catholic Missions.*

be covered, lest our fine paint should be hid, the weather in the meantime very cold, like to freeze our ears; after we had advanced nearer to the town, the Indian women came out to meet us, and relieved their husbands of their packs. As soon as we landed at Conafadauga, a large body of Indians came and encompassed us round, and ordered the prisoners to dance and sing the *Prisoner's Song*, (which I was still enabled to decline) at the conclusion of which, the Indians gave a shout, and opened the ring to let us run, and then fell on us with their fists, and knocked several down; in the meantime, one ran before to direct us to an Indian house, which was open, and as soon as we got in, we were beat no more; my head was sore with beating, and pained me several days. The squaws were kind to us, gave us boiled corn and beans to eat, and fire to warm us, which was a great mercy, for I was both, cold and hungry: This town lies about thirty miles north-west from Montreal, I staid here till the ice was gone, which was about ten days, and then was sent to Cohnewago, in company with some Indians, who when they came within hearing, gave notice by their way of shouting, that they had a prisoner, on which the whole town rose to welcome me, which was the more distressing, as there was no other prisoner in their hands; when we came near shore, a stout Indian took hold of me, and hauled me into the water, which was knee-deep, and very cold: As soon as I got a-shore, the Indians gathered round me, and ordered me to dance and sing, now when I was stiff with cold and wet, and lying long in the canoe; here I only stamped to prepare for my race, and was encompassed with about 500 Indians, who danced and sung, and at last gave a shout, and opened the circle; about 150 young lads made ready to pelt me with dirt and gravel stones, and on my setting off gave me a stout volley, without my suffering great hurt; but an Indian seeing me run, met me, and held me fast, till the boys had stored themselves again with dirt and small stones, and let me run; but then I fared much worse than before, for a small stone among the mud hit my right-eye, and my head and face were so covered with dirt, that I could scarce see my way; but discovering a door of an Indian house standing open, I run in:

From this retreat I was soon hauled, in order to be pelted more; but the Indian women being more merciful interposed, took me into a house, brought me water to wash, and gave me boiled corn and beans to eat. The next day, I was brought to the centre of the town, and cried according to the Indian custom, in order to be sent to a family of Indians, 200 miles up stream, at Oswegotchy, and there to be adopted, and abused no more: To this end, I was delivered to three young men, who said I was their brother, and set forward on our way to the aforesaid town, with about twenty more Indians, but by reason of bad weather, we were obliged to encamp on a cold, stony shore, three days, and then proceeded on; called at Conafadauga, staid there about a week, in which time, I went and viewed four houses at a distance from the town, about a quarter of a mile from each other; in which, are represented in large paintwork, the sufferings of our Saviour, with design to draw the Indians to the Papist's religion; the work is curiously done: A little farther stand three houses near together, on the top of a high hill, which they call Mount Calvary[11] with three large crosses before them, which complete the whole representation : To all these houses, the priests and Indians repair, in performing their grand processions, which takes up much time.[12]

Set off on our journey for Oswegotchy, against a rapid stream, and being long in it, and our provision growing short, the Indians put to shore a little before night; my lot was to get wood, others were ordered to get fires, and some to hunt; our kettle was put

---

11. Abbé Piquet, who established the mission at Oswegatchie, erected this Calvary and way of the cross. It "is even now a pilgrimage worthy of attention."— Shea.
12. The pains the Papists take to propagate such a bloody and absurd religion as theirs, is truly amazing! This brings to my remembrance, the following discourse, I had with two French priests in my captivity; one of them asked me, if I was a Catholic; apprehending he meant the Romish religion, I answered no; he replied, no *Bon*. On my relating the above to a fellow prisoner, he said, I had answered wrong, because by the word Catholic he meant a Christian: Sometime after, I was again asked by the other priest, if I was a Catholic, I answered yes, but not a Roman Catholic; at which he smiled, and asked, if I was a Lutheran. I replied, no; he again inquired whether I was a Calvanist, I told him I was; to which he said, with warmth, no *Bon*! no *Bon*! which signifies, it is not good, it is not good. O! may not the zeal of Papists, in propagating superstition and idolatry, make Protestants ashamed of their lukewarmness, in promoting the religion of the Bible!—R. E.

over the fire with some pounded Indian corn, and after it had boiled about two hours, my oldest Indian brother, returned with a she beaver, big with young, which he soon cut to pieces, and threw into the kettle, together with the guts, and took the four young beavers, whole as they came out from the dam, and put them likewise into the kettle, and when all was well boiled, gave each one of us a large dishfull of the broth, of which we eat freely, and then part of the old beaver, the tail of which was divided equally among us, there being eight at our fire; the four young beavers were cut in the middle, and each of us got half of a beaver; I watched for an opportunity to hide my share (having satisfied myself before that tender dish came to hand) which if they had seen, would have much displeased them. The other Indians catched young musk-rats, run a stick through their bodies, and roasted, without being skinned or gutted, and so eat them. Next morning hastened on our journey, which continued several days, till we came near Oswegotchy, where we landed about three miles from the town, on the contrary side of the river; here I was to be adopted, my father and mother that I had never seen before were waiting, and ordered me into an Indian house, where we were directed to sit down silent for a considerable time, the Indians appeared very sad, and my mother began to cry, and continued crying aloud for sometime, and then dried up her tears, and received me for her son, and took me over the river to the Indian town; the next day I was ordered to go to Mass with them, but I refused once and again, yet they continued their importunity several days, saying it was good to go to Mass, but I still refused; and feeing they could not prevail with, me, they seemed much displeased with their new son.[13] I was then sent over the river, to be employed

---

13. When I was at Oswegotchy, the Indians took notice, that I frequently retired alone, and supposing I had some bad design, threatened if I did not desist, they would tomahawk me; but my fellow prisoner, who understood their language, told them it would be a pity to hurt me on that account, for I only went into a private place to pray, which was true; the Indians replied, if so, it was good; but being yet suspicious, took pains, by watching to find out how the case was, and when they satisfied themselves, seemed pleased! and did not offer to interrupt me any more, which was a great mercy; as the contrary would have in some degree, marred my converse with God. — R. E.

in hard labour, as a punishment for not going to Mass, and not allowed a sight of, or any conversation with my fellow prisoners; the old Indian man that I was ordered to work with, had a wife, and some children, he took me into the woods with him, and made signs that I must chop, giving me an axe, the Indian soon saw that I could handle the axe: Here I tried to reconcile myself to this employ, that they might have no occasion against me, except concerning the law of my God; the old man began to appear kind, and his wife gave me milk and bread when we came home, and when she got fish, gave me the gills to eat, out of real kindness; but perceiving I did not like them, gave me my own choice, and behaved lovingly! Here I saw that God could make friends of cruel enemies, as he once turned the heart of angry Esau into love and tenderness; when we had finished our fence, which had employed us about a week, I shewed the old squaw my shirt (having worn it from the time I was first taken prisoner, which was about seven weeks) all in rags, dirt, and lice; she said it was not good, and brought me a new one, with ruffled sleeves (saying that is good) which I thankfully accepted. The next day they carried me back to the Indian town, and admitted me to converse with my fellow prisoners, who told me we were all to be sent to Montreal, which accordingly came to pass.

Montreal, at our arrival here, we had our lodging first in the Jesuits Convent, where I saw a great number of priests, and people that came to confession; after some stay, we were ordered to attend, with the Indians, at a Grand Council, held before the head General Vaudriel;[14] we prisoners sat in our rank (surrounded with our fathers and brethren) but were asked no questions: the general had a number of officers to attend him in Council, where a noted Priest, called Picket,[15] sat at his right-

---

14. Pierre François de Rigaud, Marquis de Vaudreuil-Cavagnal. He was governor of Canada from the summer of 1755 till the French lost the country, 1759.
15. Abbé François Piquet. He was one of the most patriotic and zealous priests in French America. Though best known as the founder of Oswegatchie, his work at the Lake of the Two Mountains was notable in the annals of the Church. He was stationed at Fort Frontenac, at one time. When Montcalm captured Oswego, Piquet was present, and erected a huge cross to commemorate (continued overleaf)

hand, who understands the Indian tongue well, and does more hurt to the English, than any other of his order in Canada (his dwelling is at Oswegotchy). Here I was informed that some measures were concerted to destroy Oswego, which they had been long preparing to execute; we in our journey met many battoes going upstream, with provision and men for an attack on our frontiers, which confirmed the report: The Council adjourned to another day, and then broke up. My Indian father and mother took me with them to several of their old acquaintance, who were French, to shew them their lately adopted son; these persons had been concerned with my father and other Indians, in destroying many English families in their younger days; and (as one standing by who understood their language, said,) were boasting of their former murders! After some days the Council was again called, before which, several of the Oneida chiefs appeared, and offered some complaint against the French's attacking our carrying-place, it being their land; but the general laboured to make them easy, and gave them sundry presents of value, which they accepted:[16] After which, I knowing these

---

the French victory. He accompanied a number of raiding parties that invaded the British settlements. His energy was untiring. Though called vain and boastful, it is certain that he was ever ready to back his words with deeds.

16. The French in Canada, well knowing the great importance of having the Indians in their interest, to promote their ambitious and unjust designs, use a variety of methods with them, among which, the following one is excellent in itself, and well worthy of imitation, viz. They are exceeding careful to prevent spirituous liquors being sold to the Indians, and if any of the inhabitants are proved guilty of it, their temporal interest is quite broke, and corporal punishment inflicted on them; unless the general, on some particular occasion, orders his commissioners to deliver some to them. I may add, that knowing their number is small, compared with the British inhabitants on this continent, and must quickly fall into their hands, in case we united, and entered boldly into the heart of their country with a sufficient force; for that very reason, they choose to keep us continually on the defensive, by sending when occasion requires, large bodies of regulars, together with great numbers of Indians, upon long and tedious marches, that we may not come near their borders; and especially by employing the latter, constantly to waste and ravage our frontiers, by which we are murdered by inches, and beat without a battle! By what I could learn when I was among them, they do not fear our numbers, because of our unhappy divisions, which they deride, and from them, strongly expect to conquer us entirely! which may a gracious God, in mercy, prevent! — R. E.

Indians were acquainted with Captain Williams, at the carrying-place, sent a letter by them, to let my family and friends know I was yet alive, and longed for redemption; but it never came to hand. The treaty being ended, the general sent about ten gallons of red wine to the Indians, which they divided among us; after came the presents, consisting of coats, blankets, shirts, skins (to make Indian shoes) cloth (to make stockings) powder, lead, shot, and to each a bag of paint, for their own use, &c. After we prisoners had our share, my mother came to me with an interpreter, and told me I might stay in the town, at a place she had found for me, if I pleased (this was doubtless the consequence of my declining to obey her orders, in some instances that affected my conscience) this proposal I almost agreed to; but one of my fellow prisoners, with whom I had before some discourse, about making our escape from the Indian town, opposed the motion, and said, "pray do not stay, for if you do, we shall not be able to form a plan for our deliverance;" on which I told her I chose to go home with her, and soon set off by land in our way thither, to Lascheen,[17] distant from Montreal about nine miles, where we left our canoes, and then proceeded, without delay, on our journey; in which I saw, to my sorrow, great numbers of soldiers, and much provisions, in motion towards Lake Ontario.

After a painful and distressing journey, we arrived at Oswegotchy, where we likewise saw many battoes, with provision

---

17. La Chine was the name given by envious competitors to the frontier trading-post, established by La Salle, soon after his arrival (1666) in New France. It stood at the head of the rapids above and nine miles from Montreal. It was the most dangerous, and probably it was then the most profitable post in America. Having learned from Seneca Indians that a river heading in their country flowed to a great salt sea, far away to the south, La Salle supposed it emptied into the South Sea, and that he might, by following that route, reach China. With unsurpassed courage and enterprise he mortgaged his trading-post, though it was yielding him large profits, to raise funds for the exploration of this river. He succeeded in following it as far as the falls of the Ohio (Louisville, Kentucky), and then, because his men deserted him, he was obliged to return, mined, to Montreal. He had gone to find China; he returned to find the mortgage on his post at the rapids fore-closed. His old rivals, to deride him, began to call his lost post China La Chine and the name remains to this day, perpetuating the story of La Salle's first expedition into the wilds of America, and the ill nature of his competitors.

and soldiers, daily passing by in their way to Frontenac,[18] which greatly distressed me for Oswego! Hence I resolved, if possible, to give our people notice of their danger: To this end, I told two of my fellow prisoners, that it was not a time to sleep, and asked if they would go with me, to this they heartily agreed; but we had no provision, were closely eyed by the enemy, and could not lay up a stock out of our allowance: However, at this time, Mr. Picket (before mentioned) had concluded to dig a large trench round the town; I therefore went to a negro, the principal manager of this work (who could speak English, French, and Indian, well) and asked him, if he could get employ for two others, and myself, which he soon did; for which we were to have meat and wages. Here we had a prospect of procuring provision for our flight; this, I in some Time effected for myself, and then asked my brethren if they were ready, who replied they were not yet, but said, Ann Bowman, our fellow prisoner, had brought 130 dollars from Bull's Fort, and would give them all they had need of; I told them it was not safe to disclose such a secret to her, but they blamed me for my fears, and applied to her for provision, letting her know our intention, who immediately informed the priest of it; on which we were apprehended, the Indians apprised of our design, and a court called; by order of which, four of us were confined under a strong guard, in a room within the fort, for several days.

From hence, another and myself were sent to Cohnewago, under a strong guard of sixty Indians, to prevent my plotting any more against the French, and banish all hope of my escape! However, when we arrived at this place, it pleased that gracious God, who has the hearts of all creatures in his hand, to incline the captain of the guard, to shew me great kindness, in giving me liberty to walk or work where I pleased, within any small distance; on which I went to work with a French smith, for six

---

18. Frontenac was the name (called also Cataraqui) of the fort, trading-post, and settlement established (1673) by La Salle and Count de Frontenac, where Kingston, Ontario, now stands. It was the first of the chain of forts intended to extend from Montreal to New Orleans that La Salle planned to secure the interior of the continent to the French crown.

livres and five *souse* per week; which the captain let me have to myself, and farther favoured me with the privilege of lodging at his mother's house, an English woman (named Mary Harris,[19] taken captive when a child, from Dearfield, in New England) who told me she was my grandmother, and was kind; but the wages being small, and not sufficient to procure such cloathing as I was in want of, I proceeded no farther with the French Smith, but went to my Uncle Peter, and told him I wanted cloaths, and that it would be better to let me go to Montreal, and work there, where I could cloath myself better, than by staying with him, and that with out any charge to him, who after some reasoning consented.

Set off on my journey to Montreal, and on my entering the city met an English Smith, who took me to work with him; after some time, we fettled to work in a shop, opposite to the general's door, where we had the opportunity of feeing a great part of the forces of Canada (both soldiers and Indians) who were commonly brought there, before their going out to war; and likewise all prisoners, by which means we got intelligence how our people were preparing for defence; but no good news from Oswego, which made me fear, knowing that great numbers of French were gone against it, and hearing of but few to defend it. Prayers were put up in all the churches of Canada, and great processions made, in order to procure success to their arms, against poor Oswego; but our People knew little of their Danger, till it was too late: Certainly if more frequent and earnest application (both in private and public) was made to the God of battle, we might with greater probability, expect success would crown our military attempts! To my surprise, the dismal news came, that the French had taken one of the Oswego Forts; in a few hours, in confirmation of this, I saw the English standards (the melancholy trophy of victory) and the French rejoicing at

---

19. Mary Harris was one of a considerable number of captured New England children who learned to prefer the Indian way of living to that of civilized people. According to Parkman, a tributary of the Muskingum River, in Ohio, was named White Woman's Creek, in her honour.

our downfall, and mocking us poor prisoners, in our exile and extremity, which was no great argument either of humanity, or true greatness of mind; great joy appeared in all their faces, which they expressed by loud shouts, firing of cannon, and returning thanks in their churches; but our faces were covered with shame, and our hearts filled with grief! Soon after; I saw several of the officers brought in prisoners, in small parties, and the soldiers in the same manner, and confined within the walls, in a starving condition, in order to make them work, which some complied with, but others bravely refused; and last of all came the tradesmen, among whom was my son, who looking round saw his father, who he thought had long been dead; this joyful sight so affected him, that he wept!— nor could I, in seeing my son, remain unconcerned!—no; the tenderness of a father's bowels, upon so extraordinary an occasion, I am not able to express, and therefore must cover it with a veil of silence!—But he, with all my Philadelphia friends, being guarded by soldiers, with fixed bayonets, we could not come near each other, they were sent to the common pound; but I hastened to the interpreter, to try if I could get my child at liberty, which was soon effected! When we had the happiness of an interview, he gave me some information of the state of our family, and told me, as soon as the news were sent home, that I was killed, or taken, his mother was not allowed any more support from my wages, which grieved me much, and added to my other afflictions!

In the meantime, it gave me some pleasure, in this situation, to see an expression of equal duty and prudence in my son's conduct, who, though young in years (about seventeen) and in such a confused state of things, had taken care to bring, with much labour and fatigue, a large bundle of considerable value to me, it being cloathing, &c. which I was in great need of; he likewise saved a quantity of wampum, which we brought from New York, and afterwards sold here, for 150 *livres*. He travelled with me part of the journey towards Oswego, but not being so far on his way, as I was when taken, he did not then fall into the enemy's hands, but continued free till Oswego was taken, and was then remarkably delivered from the hands of the Indians, in the following manner, fifteen young lads were drafted out to be delivered to them (which from their known custom, it is reasonable to conclude, was to fill up the number they had lost in the battle[20]) among which he was one: This barbarous design, which is contrary to the laws of war, among all civilized nations, the French artfully concealed, under the pretext of sending them to work in the battoes; but my child taking notice, that all that were chosen were small lads, doubted their real intention was bad,

When the people taken at Oswego, were setting out on their way to Quebec, I made application for liberty to go with them; but the interpreter replied, that I was an Indian prisoner, and the general would not suffer it, till the Indians were satisfied; and as they lived two hundred miles from Montreal, it could not be done at that time: Finding that all arguments, farther on that head, would not avail, because I was not included in the capitulation; I told the interpreter, my son must go and leave me! in order to be ready at Quebec to go home, when the Oswego People went, which probably would be soon; he replied it would be better to keep him with me, for he might be a means to get me clear much sooner. The officers belonging to Oswego, would

---

20. In *Delafield's biography of Francis Lewis* (one of the prisoners captured at Oswego) is this paragraph (p. 20): "Montcalm allowed his Indian allies to select thirty prisoners as their share of the booty, and Lewis was one of the number. The Indians retreated northward. Toward the close of each day when they found a pleasant spot which invited them to rest and feast, they lit their fires and celebrated their victory by the sacrifice of a captive." and therefore slipt out of his rank and concealed himself, by which means, under God, he was preferred from a state of perpetual captivity; his place being filled up in his absence, the other unhappy youths were delivered up a sacrifice to the Indian enemy, to be instructed in Popish principles, and employed in murdering their countrymen; yea, perhaps, their fathers and brethren, O horrible! O lamentable! How can the French be guilty in cold blood, of such prodigious iniquity? Besides their insatiable thirst of Empire, doubtless the pardons they get from their Pope, and their priests, embolden them, which brings to my mind, what I saw when among them: On a Sabbath day, perceiving a great concourse of people at a chapel, built on the commons, at some distance from the city, I went to see what was the occasion, and found a kind of a fair, at which were sold cakes, wine, brandy, &c. I likewise saw many carts and chases attending, the chapel doors in the meantime open, numbers of people going in and out, and a board hanging over the door, on which was written, in large letters, Indulgence Plenary, or Full Pardon.

gladly have had me with them, but found it impracticable; this is an instance of kindness and condescension, for which I am obliged! Captain Bradley, gave me a good coat, vest, and shirt; and a young gentleman, who formerly lived in Philadelphia, gave four *pistoles* (his name is James Stone, he was doctor at Oswego). these generous expressions of kindness and humanity, I am under great obligations to remember with affectionate gratitude, and if ever it be in the compass of my power, to requite: This money, together with what my son brought, I was in hopes would go far towards procuring my release from my Indian masters; but seeing a number of prisoners in sore distress, among which were, the Captains Grant and Shepherd,[21] and about seven more in company, I thought it my duty to relieve them, and commit my release to the disposal of providence! Nor was this suffered to turn to my disadvantage in the issue, for my deliverance was brought about in due time, in another, and unexpected way. This company informed me of their intention to escape, accordingly I gave them all the help in my power, saw them clear of the town, on a Saturday evening, before the sentries were set at the gates, and advised them not to part from each other, and delivered to Captain Shepherd two pocket compasses; but they contrary to this counsel parted, and saw each other no more: By their separating, Captain Grant, and Serjeant Newel, were deprived of the benefit of a compass; the other part got safe to Fort William Henry, as I was informed by Serjeant Henry, who was brought in prisoner, being taken in a battle, when gallant, indefatigable Captain Rogers, made a brave stand, against more than twice his number! But I have not heard any account of Captain Grant! Was enabled, through much mercy, to continue communicating some relief to other prisoners, out of the wages I received for my labour, which was forty *livres* per month!

In the latter part of the winter, coal and iron were so scarce, that I was hard set to get any more work; I then offered to work

---

21. Shepard was picked up by a scouting party that was under the active Major Robert Rogers. They had gone down Lake George on skates to look after French stragglers and examine the French posts.

for my diet and lodging, rather than be thrust into a stinking dungeon, or sent among the Indians: The interpreter took some pains (which I thankfully acknowledge) but without success; however, as I offered to work without wages, a French man took me and my son in, upon these terms, till a better berth presented; here we staid one week, but heard of no other place, then he offered me and my son, thirty *livres* per month, to strike and blow the bellows, which I did for about two months, and then was discharged, and travelled about from place to place, having no fixed abode, and was obliged to lay out the small remains of my cash, in buying a little victuals, and took a hayloft for my lodging: I then made my case known to the kind interpreter, and requested him to consider of some means for my relief, who replied he would; in the meantime, as I was taking a walk in the city, I met an Indian prisoner, that belonged to the town where my father lived, who reported, that a great part of the Indians there, were just come, with a resolution to carry me back with them; and knowing him to be a very honest fellow, I believed the truth of it, and fled from the town to be concealed from the Indians; in the mean while, schemes were formed for an escape, and well prosecuted: The issue of which was fortunate. General Vaudriel, gave me and my son, liberty (under his hand) to go to Quebec, and work there at our pleasure, without confinement, as prisoners of war; by which means, I was freed from paying a ransom.

The Commissary, Monsieur Partwe, being about to set off for Quebec, my son informed me that I must come to town in the evening, a passage being provided for us; I waited till near dark, and then entered the town, with great care, to escape the Indians, who kept watch for me (and had done so for sometime) which made it very difficult and dangerous to move; however, as they had no knowledge of my son, he could watch their motions, without their suspicion (the providence of God is a great deep, this help was provided for my extremity, not only beyond my expectation, but contrary to my design.) In the morning, upon seeing an Indian set to watch for me, over against the house I was in, I quickly made my escape, through the back part of the house, over some high pickets, and out of the city, to the riverside, and fled!

A friend knowing my scheme for deliverance, kindly assisted me to conceal myself: The commissary had by this time got ready for his voyage, of which my son giving me notice, I immediately, with no lingering motion, repaired to the boat, was received on board, set off quite undiscovered, and saw the Indians no more! A very narrow and surprising escape, from a violent death! (For they had determined to kill me, in case I ever attempted to leave them) which lays me under the strongest obligations, to improve a life rescued from the jaws of so many deaths, to the honour of my gracious benefactor! But to return, the commissary, upon seeing the dismission I had from the general, treated us courteously![22]

Arrived at Quebec, May 1st, The Honourable Colonel Peter Schuyler[23] hearing of my coming there, kindly sent for me, and after enquiries about my welfare, &c. generously told me I should be supplied, and need not trouble myself for support! This public spirited gentleman, who is indeed an honour to his country, did in like manner, nobly relieve many other poor prisoners at Quebec! Here I had full liberty to walk where I pleased, and view the city, which is well situated for strength, but far from being impregnable.

---

22. Saw many houses and villages in our pass along the River St. Lawrence towards the Metropolis; and here it may be with justice observed, that the inhabitants of Canada in general, are principally (if not wholly) settled upon rivers, by reason that their back lands being flat and swampy, are therefore unfit to bear grain: Their wheat is sown in the spring of the year, because the winter is long, and would drown it; they seem to have no good notion of making meadow (so far as I had an opportunity of observing) their horned cattle are few and poor, their living in general mean, they eat but little flesh, nevertheless they are strong and hardy.

23. Colonel Peter Schuyler. He was the son of Arent Schuyler, and both were notable men in the British colonies. The colonel was in command of a New Jersey regiment at Oswego when the French captured the place. "While a prisoner in Canada he kept open house for the relief of his fellow sufferers, and gave large sums to the Indians for the redemption of captives; many of whom he afterwards, at his own expense, maintained while there, and provided for their return, trusting to their abilities and honour for repayment; and lost considerable that way, but seemed to think it money well bestowed." He lived at No. 1 Broadway, New York City, at one time.

Here, I hope, it will not be judged improper, to give a short hint of the French Governor's conduct; even in time of peace, he gives the Indians great encouragement to murder and captivate the poor inhabitants on our frontiers; an honest, good man, named William Ross, was taken prisoner twice in the time of peace; when he was first taken, he learned a little of the French tongue, was after some time redeemed, and got to his place of abode: Yet some years after, he, with two sons, was again taken, and brought to Quebec; the Governor seeing the poor man was lame, and one of his legs smaller than the other, reproved the Indians for not killing him, asking, what they brought a lame man there for, who could do nothing but eat; "you should", said he, "have brought his scalp!" However, another of his countrymen, more merciful than his excellency, knowing the poor prisoner to be a quiet, hard-working man, redeemed him from the Indians; and two other Frenchmen bought his two sons: Here they had been slaves more than three years, when I first arrived at Quebec; this account I had from Mr. Ross himself, who farther added, that the Governor gave the Indians presents, to encourage them to proceed, in that kind of work, which is a scandal to any civilized nation, and what many pagans would abhor! Here also, I saw one Mr. Johnson, who was taken in a time of peace, with his wife, and three small children (his wife was big with child of a fourth, and delivered on the road to Canada, which she called captive[24]) all which, had been prisoners between three and four years, several young men, and his wife's sister, were likewise taken captive with them, and made slaves!

Our cartel being ready, I obtained liberty to go to England in her; we set sail the 23rd of July, 1757, in the morning, and discharged our pilot about 4 o'clock in the afternoon; after which, we neither cast anchor or lead, till we got clear of the

---

24. Parkman refers to the daughter of John Smead and wife, as a child that was named "Captivity" under similar circumstances. The Smeads were captured when Fort Massachusetts was destroyed (1746). The child was born while they travelled through the woods. The Indians made a litter of poles and deerskins, placed mother and child on it, covered them with a bearskin, and then carried them on their way to the settlement in Canada.

great River St. Lawrence, from which, I conclude, the navigation is much safer than the French have reported; in twenty-eight days we arrived at Plymouth, which occasioned great joy, for we were ragged, lousy, sick, and in a manner, starved; and many of the prisoners, who in all were about 300 in number, were sick of the smallpox: My son and self, having each a blanket coat (which we bought in Canada to keep us warm) and now expecting relief, gave them to two poor sick men, almost naked! But as we were not allowed to go on shore, but removed to a King's ship, and sent to Portsmouth, where we were still confined on board, near two weeks, and then removed to the *Mermaid*,[25] to be sent to Boston; we now repented our well meant, though rash charity, in giving our coats away, as we were not to get any more, all application to the captain for any kind of covering being in vain; our joy was turned into sorrow, at the prospect of coming on a cold coast, in the beginning of winter, almost naked, which was not a little increased, by a near view of our Mother Country, the soil and comforts of which, we were not suffered to touch or taste.)[26]

---

25. According to *Allen's Battles of the British Navy* the *Mermaid* was a 28-gun frigate. During our war of the Revolution the *Mermaid* fell in with the fleet under Count D'Estaing, as it was sailing up the American coast to attack General Howe, who was then (1778) in Philadelphia. The fleet went in chase of the *Mermaid*, and drove her ashore on Cape Henlopen, but were thereby so much delayed in what was already an overlong passage, that Howe, and such few ships as were at Philadelphia, got clear of the Delaware.

26. On board the *Mermaid* man of war, being in a distressed condition, and hearing little from the mouths of many of my countrymen, but oaths and curses (which much increased my affliction) and finding it difficult to get a retired place, I crept down into the hold among the water casks, to cry to God; here the Lord was graciously pleased to meet with me, and give me a sense of his fatherly love and care; here he enabled me (blessed be his name for ever) to look back and view how he had led me, and guarded me with a watchful eye and strong arm, and what pains he had taken to wean me from an over-love of time things, and make me content that he should choose for me: Here I was enabled to fee his great goodness in all my disappointments, and that afflictions were not evidences of God's wrath, but the contrary, to all that honestly endeavour to seek him with faith and love; here I could say, God is worthy to be served, loved, and obeyed, though it be attended with many miseries in this world! What I have here mentioned, so far as I know my heart, is neither to exalt myself, or offend any one upon earth, but to glorify God, for his goodness and faithfulness to the meanest of his servants, and to encourage others to trust in him!

September the 6th, set sail for Boston, with a fleet in convoy, at which we arrived on the seventh of November, in the evening; it being dark, and we strangers, and poor, it was difficult to get a lodging (I had no shoes, and but pieces of stockings, and the weather in the meantime very cold) we were indeed directed to a tavern, but found cold entertainment there, the master of the house feeing a ragged and lousy company, turned us out to wander in the dark; he was suspicious of us, and feared we came from Halifax, where the smallpox then was, and told us, he was ordered not to receive such as came from thence: We soon met a young man, who said he could find a lodging for us, but still detained us by asking many questions; on which I told him we were in no condition to answer, till we came to a proper place, which he quickly found, where we were used well; but as we were lousy, could not expect beds. The next morning, we made application for cloathing; Mr. Erwing, son-in-law to the late General Shirley,[27] gave us relief, not only in respect of apparel, but also three dollars per man, to bear our charges to Newport: When I put on fresh cloaths, I was seized with a cold fit, which was followed by a high fever, and in that condition obliged to travel on foot, as far as providence, in our way to Rhode Island (our money not being sufficient to hire any carriage, and find us what was needful for support:) In this journey, I was exceedingly distressed! Our comforts in this life, are often allayed with miseries, which are doubtless great mercies when suitably improved; at Newport, met with Captain Gibbs, and agreed with him for our passage to New York, where we arrived, November

---

27. William Shirley was Governor of Massachusetts when this war began. After the conference with Braddock in Virginia Shirley was placed in command of the expedition that was to reduce Niagara. At Braddock's death he became commander-in-chief of the British forces in America, and he held that position at the time Eastburn was captured. It was by his orders that Fort Bull was filled with supplies, though but poorly garrisoned to resist a French invasion. He was an earnest, energetic, and capable civil officer, but was most unfortunate in this war, for his military enterprises failed, and he lost two sons in the army. Franklin in his autobiography says of him: "Tho Shirley was not a bred soldier, he was sensible and sagacious in himself, and attentive to good advice from others, capable of forming judicious plans, and quick and active in carrying them into execution."

21st, met with many friends, who expressed much satisfaction at our return, and treated us kindly, particularly Messrs. Livingston, and Waldron.

November 26th, 1757. Arrived at Philadelphia, to the great joy of all my friends, and particularly of my poor afflicted wife and family, who thought they should never see me again, till we met beyond the grave; being returned, sick and weak in body, and empty-handed, not having anything for my family's and my own support, several humane and generous persons, of different denominations, in this city (without any application of mine, directly or indirectly) have freely given seasonable relief; for which, may God grant them blessings in this world, and in the world to come everlasting life, for Christ's sake!

Now, God, in his great mercy, hath granted me a temporal salvation, and what is a thousand times better, he hath given me with it, a soul-satisfying evidence of an eternal in the world to come!

And now, what shall I render to the Lord for all his benefits, alas I am nonplussed! O that saints and angels might praise thee, for I am not worthy to take thy name into my mouth any more! Yet notwithstanding, thou art pleased to accept poor endeavours, because Jesus Christ has opened the door, whereby we may come boldly to the throne of thy Grace, praised be the Lord God Jehovah, by men and angels, throughout all eternity!

But to hasten to the conclusion, suffer me with humility and sorrow to observe, that our enemies seem to make a better use of a bad religion, than we of a good one; they rise up long before day in winter, and go through the snow in the coldest seasons, to perform their devotions in the churches; which when over, they return to be ready for their work as soon as daylight appears: The Indians are as zealous in religion, as the French, they oblige their children to pray morning and evening, particularly at Conafadauga; are punctual in performing their stated acts of devotion themselves, are still and peaceable in their own families, and among each other as neighbours!

When I compared our manner of living with theirs, it made me fear that the righteous and jealous God (who is wont to make judgement begin at his own house first) was about to deliver us into their hands, to be severely punished for our departure from him; how long has he waited for our return, O that we may therefore turn to him, before his anger break out into a flame, and there be no remedy!

Our case appears to me indeed very gloomy! notwithstanding our enemies are inconsiderable in number, compared with us; yet they are united as one man, while we may be justly compared to a house divided against itself, and therefore cannot stand long, in our present situation.

May Almighty God, graciously incline us to look to him for deliverance, to repent of our sins, reform our lives, and unite in the vigorous and manly use of all proper means to this end.

The Journal of Rufus Putnam
—Provincial Infantry

Biographical Sketch of Rufus Putnam

Rufus Putnam was born in Sutton, Massachusetts, April 9, 1738. His father died in 1745 and he was sent to live with Mr. Jonathan Fuller, his maternal grandfather, at Danvers where he was taught to read. His mother married Captain Sadler of Upton in 1747 and young Rufus returned to her. Captain Sadler was uneducated himself and denied the boy all opportunities for instruction. At the age of sixteen he was apprenticed to Daniel Matthews, of Brookfield, a millwright. While with him he managed to obtain a fair knowledge of arithmetic, geometry and history. In March, 1757, he enlisted as a private soldier in a company raised by Captain Ebenezer Learned for service against the French and Indians. He again enlisted in each succeeding year until 1761, serving in 1759 as orderly sergeant and in 1760 as ensign. The story of these campaigns is told in the journal following this sketch. In April, 1761, he married Miss Elizabeth Ayres of Brookfield, and settled on a small farm of fifty acres in New Brain tree, which he had purchased with money saved from his pay and bounty. His wife died in childbirth in November of that year. In 1765 he married Miss Persis Rice of Westborough and moved to a small farm in the north parish of Brookfield. His family remained here until 1780 when he moved them to the town of Rutland, where he had purchased a large confiscated estate.

At the close of his service in the French war, he devoted his spare time for several years to the study of surveying, in which he became so proficient that he soon found constant employment. In 1773 he went with Colonel Israel Putnam, Captain Roger Enos and Mr. Thaddeus Lyman to examine lands in Florida which the king, through the efforts of General Phineas Lyman, had promised to grant to the colonial officers and soldiers who had served in the Provincial regiments in the French war. To facilitate his work Mr, Putnam was appointed deputy surveyor of that province by the governor of Florida. The party sailed up the Mississippi river to the mouth of the Yazoo, up the Yazoo to Haines bluff and explored the land back to Big Black river, down that stream to its mouth and along the banks of the Mississippi below. So favourable was their report, upon their return in the fall, that several hundred families from New England emigrated early in 1774 to settle on the lands. Many others were deterred, probably the Putnams among them, by the critical state of public affairs and a rumour that the king had refused to issue a patent[1] for the lands.

At the outbreak of the revolution in 1775, Mr. Putnam was commissioned lieutenant-colonel of the Massachusetts regiment commanded by Colonel David Brewer. He planned and superintended the construction of the line of defence of the continental army at Roxbury. General Washington was so pleased with these works that he detailed him as acting chief engineer of the army.

On the 11th of August, 1776, he was appointed by Congress, chief engineer of the army with the rank of colonel. Preferring field service with troops he resigned in December to accept the command of the fifth Massachusetts regiment. With it he greatly distinguished himself in the campaign against Burgoyne as well as in the subsequent operations of the army. In January, 1783, he was appointed brigadier general. Throughout the war he possessed to a marked degree the confidence of General Washington.

Early in 1783, General Putnam became much interested in a plan, proposed by Colonel Timothy Pickering, for establishing a settlement and creating a new State west of the Ohio river.

---

1. A patent for twenty thousand acres in what is now Claiborne county, Mississippi, was issued to Thaddeus Lyman, Feb. 2, 1775.

In June of that year he forwarded to the president of Congress, through General Washington who strongly recommended it, a petition signed by 288 officers of the Continental line asking that their bounty lands be located in that part of what is now the state of Ohio, east of the Scioto river and that an additional amount be sold to them for public securities. Congress took no action on this petition. Virginia claimed the entire territory north-west of the Ohio river by right of the conquest of George Rogers Clark. Her claim had been ceded to the United States upon condition that the territory be divided into ten states, that the expense of its conquest be repaid, and that a tract of land be set apart for bounties to her officers and soldiers. These terms were opposed by Maryland and New Jersey who flatly disputed Virginia's claim. The cession was finally accepted by Congress, substantially upon the original conditions, in March, 1784. An ordinance for the government of the territory, drawn by Thomas Jefferson, was adopted a month later. An ordinance providing a method for survey and sale of the lands, after much discussion, was passed in May, 1785. Indian troubles on the frontier prevented the surveyors from commencing their work until the spring of 1786.

During these years General Putnam had resumed his occupation as a civil engineer. He was chosen by Congress one of the surveyors of territory under the ordinance of 1785, but owing to a previous engagement with the State of Massachusetts was unable to accept at once and secured the temporary appointment of General Benjamin Tupper in his place. In the fall of 1785 General Tupper visited Pittsburgh. The glowing accounts he received while there, from all sources, of the fertility of the lands along the Ohio, determined him to move to the Western territory as soon as possible. He returned to Massachusetts about the first of January, 1786.

On the 10th of January, Generals Putnam and Tupper after a full conference, united in a call for a meeting of all who wished to become adventurers in the Ohio country to be held in Boston, March first, 1786. The result of this meeting was the formation of the Ohio company with a capital of one million of dollars in public securities, divided into one thousand shares of one thousand dollars each, to be expended in the purchase of lands in the North-western territory. The plan of sale adopted by Congress was so unsatisfactory, that after a lapse of a year but one-fourth of the shares had been subscribed. In March, 1787, General Putnam, General S. H. Parsons and Reverend Manasseh Cutler, were chosen directors and empowered to treat with Congress for the purchase of a tract of land on a different basis. Doctor Cutler visited Congress, then in session in New York, in July, 1787, and succeeded in making a contract for the purchase of one and a half million acres of land in a compact body, including a large part of the vallies of the Muskingum and Big Hockhocking rivers, on terms far more favourable than provided in the ordinances of 1785. A new ordinance for the government of the territory, famous in history as the ordinance of 1787, was passed at the same time. Some of its provisions were framed by Doctor Cutler to accord with the wishes and interests of the Ohio company. The remaining shares in the company were quickly taken. In November, 1787, General Putnam, who was then serving as a member of the Massachusetts General Court from the town of Rutland, was made superintendent of the company. He conducted the first party of emigrants and on the 7th of April, 1788, landed with them at the mouth of the Muskingum river, where now is the city of Marietta and commenced the first organized settlement of the North-western territory. General Putnam continued to be the most active and influential member of the Ohio company until the final settlement of its affairs in 1796.

In March, 1790, he was appointed by President Washington one of the judges of the United States Court in the North-western territory. He removed his family, his wife eight children and two grand children, to Marietta this year. He was also made superintendent of the affairs in the west of the Scioto company, but resigned before the close of the year. In 1792, while attending a meeting of the Ohio company in Philadelphia, he was commissioned brigadier general in the army to rank from the date of his original appointment in 1783. The directors of the Ohio company, seconded by Vice-president John Adams, endeavoured to secure his assignment to command the forces operating against the Indians vice St. Clair. The choice for a time seemed to be between Generals Putnam and Lincoln. The objection to Putnam was the fact that his rank during the revolutionary war was not as high as that of others whose friends were supporting them for this command. General Anthony Wayne was finally chosen.

In the fall of 1792, General Putnam concluded a treaty at Vincennes with eight of the Wabash Indian tribes. In February, 1793, he resigned his commission in the army. In January, 1791, the Indians surprised the station of the Ohio company at Big Bottom killing or capturing its inmates. The settlements of the company were almost entirely without aid from the government. General Putnam organized the inhabitants for their own protection. The entire force that could be mustered was but two hundred and fifty men, divided between the stations at Marietta, Belpre and Waterford. Many war parties were sent to attack these posts but so perfect were the defences he planned and so completely were the garrisons covered by the company of rangers he organized, that during the remainder of the war, no hostile force was able to approach within striking distance without detection and no serious losses were suffered by the colonists.

In 1796, General Putnam resigned as judge to accept the appointment, tendered him by President Washington, of surveyor general of the United States. He was removed from this office for political reasons in 1803, by President Jefferson. In 1802, he was elected one of the delegates from Washington county to the convention which formed the first constitution of Ohio. He was chosen by the territorial legislature one of the first trustees of the Ohio University at Athens in 1801. The election of Jefferson to the presidency and the triumph of his followers in the new state of Ohio, ended the public life of General Putnam, who to the end of his days remained a staunch Federalist.

In 1798, he was the prime mover in establishing in Marietta the first academy of learning; in 1807, he planned and superintended the building of the church still used by the Congregational Society there; in 1812, he organized there the first Bible Society west of the mountains; in 1817, the first Sunday school and he was the largest subscriber to the funds of each.

He died in 1824, in his eighty-seventh year. His wife died in 1820. Five children, two sons and three daughters, survived them. Their descendants are widely scattered through the west and are among its leading and influential citizens.

About the year 1812, General Putnam wrote for his children a narrative of the leading events of his life. This, with the original of the journal which follows and other manuscripts, embracing an extensive correspondence with Washington, Pickering, Trumbull, Wolcott, Fisher Ames and others of the prominent men of his time, is deposited in the library of the college at Marietta, Ohio. A number of extracts from these memoirs appear in the notes. They show his matured opinion of the men and events mentioned in the journal.

E. C. Dawes

Putnam's Journal 1757

Rufus Putnam's journal, For the year A. D. 1757, who belonged to the Militia Company in Brookfield, under the command of Captain Nathaniel Woolcut, and enlisted into His Majesty's Service, in a Provincial Regiment of Foot of whom Joseph Fry, Esq., is Colonel and in the Company of Captain Ebenezer Learned.[1] To serve one year from the second day of February, 1757, and no longer. Colonel Fry's[2] regiment consisted of 1800 men, and they were in seventeen companies. Captain Chevers, Saltinson,[3] Burk,[4] Kerver,[5] Hartwell, Thaxter, Taplee,[6] Davis,[7] Indecut, Ingersol, Aberthonate,[8] Walldo, Learned, Ball, Nelson, West, Baly.

---

1. Ebenezer Learned, born Framingham, Mass., 1728; died Oxford, Mass., 1801. Captain in French war 1757. Marched to Cambridge with 3rd Mass, regiment day after battle of Lexington. April 2nd, 1777, appointed brigadier general by Congress. Commanded brigade at battle of Still water, Sept. 19th, 1777. Was at Valley Forge in winter of 1777 and 1778. Retired from the army, March 24th, 1778.—Drakes Dictionary American Biography.
2. Joseph Frye, born in Andover, Mass., 1709; died Fryeburg, Maine, Jan. 8th, 1794, justice of peace and member Mass. General Court. Served as ensign in Male's Mass. Regiment at taking of Louisburg in 1745. Colonel of Mass. Regiment in 1757. Appointed major general by state of Massachusetts, 1775. Brigadier general by Congress in 1776. Resigned on account of ill health, April 23rd, 1776.—*Drake's Dictionary American Biography.*
3. Richard Saltonstall, was born at Haverhill, Mass., April 5th, 1732. He graduated at Harvard College, 1751. In 1754 he was colonel of militia. In 1757 he was captain in Colonel Frye's provincial regiment and was with the troops surrendered at Fort William Henry. In 1760 he was colonel of a provincial regiment. At the close of the war he was appointed high sheriff of Essex county. He was an ardent royalist and in 1774 settled in England, The king granted him a pension, although he refused to enter the army. He died at Kensington, England, in 1785.—See *Chase's History of Haverhill.*
4. Captain John Burk "at the surrender of Fort William (continued overleaf)

March ye 15, 1757. Then enlisted myself into his majesty's service.

March 25. Then passed muster at Deacon James Woods in New Brantry, before Colonel Timothy Ruggles, Esq.,[9] of Hardwick.

April ye 12 and 13. Drawed our arms and clothing at Worster. The same day I went to Sutton to my brothers.

April 15. Returned from Sutton to Brookfield.

April 29. Captain Learned's company mustered together at Brookfield in order to march.

April 30. Marched to Kingston.

May ye 1. Marched from Kingston to Springfield.

May 2. It being very windy all the fore part of the day, so that we could not cross the river until just night. After we crossed the river we marched about five miles.

Henry was seized and stripped of his clothes, but escaped."—Trumbull's Indian Wars.
5. Kerver. Probably Captain Jonathan Carver, the famous traveller; he was with Frye's regiment in this campaign.
6. There was a Captain Jno. Taplin from Sutton.
7. Captain Davis of Brimfield, Mass., was tarred and feathered at Union, Connecticut, in 1774 for his obnoxious acts and sentiments.—Sabine's Loyalists
8. "Captain Arbuthnot, who was in the fort (William Henry) at the time of its surrender, hailed from Marlborough."—Hudson's History Marlborough.
9. Timothy Ruggles, born Rochester, Mass., Oct. 11th, 1711; died at Wilmot, Nova Scotia, August 4th, 1795. Graduated Harvard University, 1732. Practised law at Sandwich and Hardwick. Member Mass, legislature, 1736. Colonel of a Mass. Provincial regiment, 1755, 1756 and 1757. Brigadier general in 1759 and 1760. Chief justice Mass , from 1762 till 1775. Speaker of assembly 1762-3. Delegate to Stamp Act Congress at New York in 1765. Adhered to the royal cause during the revolution. Left Boston when it was evacuated by the British, and accompanied the army to Long Island, where he organized a battalion of loyal militia. His estate was confiscated by Mass, in 1779. He settled in Nova Scotia. He was a successful lawyer, a scholar of note, and a brave and capable soldier. Drake's Dictionary of American Biography.

May 3. Marched to Glasgow.

May 4. Marched through the Green Woods[10] to No. 1.

May 5. Marched to Lovejoys about ten miles beyond Sheffield.

May 6. Marched into Kinderhook, where we were lodged in two barns.

May 7. Drawed stores for one week which were very mean and scanty, and we had not yet drawed anything to cook in, which made it very difficult for us.

May ye 10. By reason of other companies coming into town, our company was obliged to move about one mile and a-half all into one barn.

May 12. Lieutenant Moore of Worster came to see us from Albany, and several other rangers with him.

May 17. We had orders to march to Scocook. During our stay at this place Captain Learned went to prayer with his Company morning and evening and on the Sabbaths read in a sermon book.

May 18. Marched this day to Greenbush, where we lodged in Colonel Ranelow's barn.

May 19. Every man had nine rounds delivered to him which was the first ammunition that we drawed after we marched to Albany Flats, and the same day we drawed our tents, kettles, bowls, platters, spoons. This night we pitched our tents and lodged in them.

---

10. Green Woods. The forest between the Connecticut and Hudson rivers. "In 1736 a committee of the General Court of Massachusetts recommended the laying out a range of townships between the Merrimack and the Connecticut and on each side the last named river. These townships were numbered 1 to 9. Of these Number 4 was afterwards called Charleston in honour of Admiral Sir Charles Knowles." *Collections of the New Hampshire Historical Society*, N. 102, 103, 113.

May 20. This morning, sun about an hour high, one of our company was shot through the hip with a single ball. The ball is cut out, and the man is likely to do well. His name is Jedediah Winslow.

May 21. Marched from the flats to Scocook this town is on the Hoosack river and is about three miles from Stillwater. Has been a settled town by the Dutch, but its inhabitants are all drawn in, for fear of the enemy. There were two other companies came into this town this night, *viz*: Davis and Indecuts.

May 24. There came three companies more into town viz: Ingersol, Thaxter, Baly, the companies all belonged to Massachusetts Regiments'.

May 26. About nine o'clock Captain Indecut's Company and Captain Learned's marched back three miles to the mills and opposite to the halfway house, and the other companies marched to Stillwater, and we found that our companies with Captain Burk's, which we found there, were left there to mend up the fences at Scocook, in order to cut hay for the king's baggage horses.

May 27. Captain Learned, Lieutenant Walker with seventy men went to Scocook to work.

May 30. Captain Learned finished the fences at Scocook and turned out the horses and it was judged by all that there was 1,500 acres within fence, all of the best of mowing. After which we returned back to the landing, where we found that Jedediah Winslow who was shot, down at the flats, was come up, and was able to stand upon crutches.

June 3. Colonel Fry came up to this place.

June 4. Colonel Fry went up to Stillwater with a guard of thirty men.

June 8. Received orders to march.

June 9. Marched to Stillwater where there were ten companies belonging to our regiment

June 11. Colonel Fry with thirteen companies marched to Saratoga where the rest of our regiment lay.

June 13. Two hundred and fifty Hampshire men came to Saratoga.

June 14. Colonel Fry marched his regiment toward Fort Edward,[11] but we could not reach the fort this night but encamped in the old field opposite to the Brick-kilns.

June 15. Crossed the river and pitched our tents.

June 16. Captain Putnam[12] came in from Ticonderoga and had taken a prisoner.

---

11. "Fort Edward stood on the easterly bank of the Hudson or North river about sixty-six miles above Albany. The river washed one side of its wall. Its form was somewhat irregular, having two bastions and half bastions. The walls were high and thick, composed of hewed timber and earth. A broad rampart with casement or bomb-proof. A deep ditch with a draw-bridge. A covered way, glacis, etc. I have been particular in this description; because in 1777 there was by no means so great an appearance of there having been a fortification there as we find in the ancient works at Marietta and other parts of the Ohio country.—*Mss. Memoirs.*

12. Israel Putnam. He is often confounded with Rufus Putnam. He was a cousin of Rufus Putnam's father. Israel Putnam was born in West Salem, Massachusetts, January 7th, 1718. In 1755, he raised and commanded a company for the French war and greatly distinguished himself by his courage. He was promoted to major in 1757; to lieutenant colonel in 1759; and colonel in 1764. He commanded a Connecticut regiment in the expedition against Havana and was with Bradstreet in his campaign against the western Indians. After the (continued overleaf)

June 17. Our regiment was drawn up and viewed by Major Fletcher and afterwards had the Articles of War read to us.

June 18. This day two of our Bay forces, were buried which was the first that was buried out of our regiment This day likewise there went a party of men part of the way down to Saratoga and there encamped.

June 19. About break of day those men arose and began to march toward Saratoga, but they had not marched far, before they were fired upon by the enemy. They shot one man through the body so that he died the next day. Another man was slightly wounded in the head. Both these were regulars. The rest of the men all came in well. This day there were orders for every man should fire his piece, except they were newly loaded.

June 20. I went on guard.

June 21. There came a scout of men in who had been out under Captain Ingersol, they went out the 19 instant. The scout consisted of about eighty men.

June 22. The Mohawks brought in a prisoner from Ticonderoga.

---

expiration of his term of service, he was several times elected to civil office in Connecticut. In 1773, he went with Rufus Putnam, Thaddeus Lyman, Roger Enos and others to examine lands in Florida, that were to be granted to the colonial officers and soldiers who had served in the French war. He returned the following year and resumed his occupation as a farmer. On hearing of the battle of Lexington in 1775, he unhitched his horse from the plow and rode to the scene of action. He returned, recruited a regiment and marched to Cambridge. He was commissioned brigadier general by Connecticut April 26th, 1775; major general by the continental congress June 19th, 1775.

In command of the American forces at Bunker Hill he displayed the same reckless gallantry that made him famous in the French war. He commanded in New York after the evacuation of Boston by the British; was engaged in the battle of Long Island, commanded at Philadelphia and on the New Jersey front in the winter of 1776 and 1777; located the fort at West Point in 1777.

June 23. Captain Flecher of the 35th Regiment with about thirty regulars, twenty Royal Americans and Captain Saltinson with ninety-two Bay men besides officers mustered down to Saratoga in order for to guard up General Webb, and arrived there about four o'clock in the afternoon, and at our arrival we did expect to find General Webb,[13] but he was not come.

June 24. This day about 11 o'clock General Webb came to the fort and in the afternoon we returned back to Fort Edward.

June 25. This day I went on command at Saratoga to guard teams, and when we came there we (found) a great number of regulars and twelve field pieces.

June 26. We returned to Fort Edward and the regulars with the artillery also went up as far as the river but they did not go over this night.

June 27. There were two men whipped twenty lashes apiece, and they were the first that were whipped in our regiment

---

13. Lieutenant General Daniel Webb, entered the army as ensign of the Coldstream Guards, 29th May, 1745, but resigned in February, 1747, and joined, it is supposed some other regiment. He succeeded Colonel Dunbar in the command of the 48th foot, on the 11th November, 1755, and arrived at New York from England, 7th June, 1756, with the rank of brigadier general, to relieve General Shirley. In succeeding to the regiment of Colonel Dunbar, he seems to have inherited also his disposition to take to flight, on the least appearance of danger; for being dispatched in 1756 with a considerable force to the relief of Oswego, as soon as he got to the carrying place, now Rome, Oneida county, N.Y., he became so alarmed on hearing of the fall of the fort he was sent to relieve, that he filled Wood Creek with trees to prevent the approach of the enemy. One would think that this would prevent his being again put in any position of responsibility, but no, the next year he shamefully abandoned Colonel Munroe at Fort William Henry, though at the head of 4000 men. He was ordered home in consequence, but was protected in some inexplicable way. from censure. On the 25th June, 1759, he was promoted to be major general; in June, 1761, became lieutenant general; in December, 1766, was appointed colonel of the 8th or King's Regiment of Foot; on the 20th October, 1772, colonel of the 14th Dragoons, and died in October or November, 1771.—Documents relating to Colonial History, New York, volume 10, p. 574.

June 28. Thirteen Frenchmen that broke goal at York and were going up toward Crown Point, by being lost came into this fort. This night I went on the picket guard.

June 29. There were orders that a true list of what officers and soldiers were willing to go a scouting and be freed from other duty, should be given in

July 1. This day there came in two of Captain Putnam's men and brought in news that Captain Putnam fired upon three or four hundred French and Indians on South Bay, but when they got to shore they were too hard for him and he wanted help. General Lyman with about 400 men went out for his relief. I was on the picket guard so that I could not go. About four hours after Captain Putnam came in, who said that when he fired on the Indians it was about three o'clock at night, and being bright moonlight and the enemy came up the bay quietly, and they lying undiscovered till they fired on them, and they poured in their buck shot so thick that they cut off a great part of their boats before they could land. The enemy tried to land against him but could not easily do it, he fired so thick upon them; at length the enemy got to shore below him in spite of their fire. The Indians wounded three of his men and he sent of a party to help them away. After the Indians got on shore he was forced to retreat, for he judged that there was three or four hundred of the enemy; and he had but sixty-eight men when he fired on them on the bay. On Captain Putnam's return home, there was another scout met him and carelessly fired on him and wounded one of his men, so that he died the night after.[14] This day was also two scalps brought in by the Mohawks.

July 2. I went on a guard to escort teams to the lake.

---

14. *Humphrey's Life of Israel Putnam* gives an account of this action, not materially different from this; though it is made to occur after the surrender of Fort William Henry.
Watson's History of Essex Co. N.Y., also speaks of this action as occurring in 1758.

July 3. We returned to Fort Edward with four French regulars who deserted from Ticonderoga. An ensign also who was taken last year came in from Canada.

July 4. General Lyman[15] came in with all the men that went out with him; but they found that two of those wounded men of Captain Putnam's were carried off, and the third they found barbecued at a most doleful rate, for they found him with his nails all pulled out, his lips cut off down to his chin and up to his nose, and his jaws lay bare; his scalp was taken off, his breast cut open, his heart pulled out and his bullet pouch put in the room of it; his left hand clenched round his gall, a Tomahawk left in his bowels and a dart struck through him; the little finger of his left hand cut off and the little toe of his left foot cut off.

July 5. Six companies of rangers were appointed out of all the provincials; these were to do ranging duty and no other. Out of our regiment was Captain West and Captain Learned, Out of Connecticut was Captain Putnam and Captain Sefford, and out of York forces Captain Meginiss, out of Rhode Island Captain Wall. There were fifty-two men of Captain Learned's original company enlisted with him, also there went his first lieutenant, and ensign, one sergeant and two corporals.

---

15. Major General Phineas Lyman was born at Durham, Connecticut, about 1716; was graduated in 1738 at Yale College, in which he was afterwards a tutor three years; and settled as a lawyer in Suffield. He sustained various public offices. In 1755, he was appointed major general and commander-in-chief of the Connecticut forces, and built Fort Lyman now called Fort Edward, New York. In 1758 he served under Abercrombie. He was at the capture of Crown Point by Amherst, and at the surrender of Montreal. In 1762, he commanded the provincial troops in the expedition against Havana. In 1763 he went to England, as the agent of his brother officers, to to receive their prize money; also as agent of a company called the "Military Adventurers," to solicit a grant of land on the Mississippi, and wasted eleven years of his life. Being deluded for years by idle promises, his mind sunk down to imbecility. At last his wife, who was a sister of Dr. Dwight's father, sent his second son to England to solicit his return in 1774. A tract of 20,000 acres was granted to the petitioners February 2, 1775. After his return he embarked with his eldest son, for the Mississippi, and both died soon after their arrival at West Florida, in 1775.—*Dwight's Travels,* 1, 305; 31, 361.

July 6. In the afternoon the rangers were mustered together and there fell to Captain Learned, the men that went out of Captain Kerver's, Captain A. Hartwell, Captain Burk's, Captain Taplees' companies; and the rest of our regiment went under Captain West. This night we had twenty-four rounds delivered to us with what we had before.

July 8. This morning, Lieutenant Colings, who joined our company, went out a scout for six days, with twenty-two men. Our orders were to go and lie on the mountains West of South Bay and lie there three days. We marched about ten miles and then encamped.

July 9. We marched on in the path that the French Army came in the first. We marched about ten miles and then Lieutenant Colings concluded that we were got so near the South Bay that it was not safe to go on the road any further, and he sent three of us off, to see which was the best way to come on the mountain to view the bay. And we were gone so long that they concluded the enemy had taken us, and so they marched off carrying off all our provisions and blankets. When we returned, we hunted for to track off, but could not, for we found they went upon the mountains. We fired a gun to see if they would answer us, but they did not, though afterwards they told us they heard us. This night we encamped as well, but the gnats and mosquitoes were a great trouble to us, having no blankets; and I had nothing but a shirt and Indian stockings, and no man can tell what an affliction those little animals were.

July 10. This morning we fired two guns but had no answer. We hunted till about noon, but could not find them. About noon we were on the mountains west of South Bay, and, after hunting till about one o clock and then not finding them, we set off for Fort Edward and arrived the same night within about eight miles of it.

July 11. This morning about ten o clock we arrived at Fort Edward, and now for three days I had not eaten any food, but what grew wild in the woods.

July 12. Came in Lieutenant Colings and the rest of the scout that went out with me to South Bay.

July 15. Captain Learned went out a scout for eight days with eighty men. Orders given out that if any man was found playing cards, he should receive 500 lashes.

July 16. A sick man was sent in from Captain Learned's scout. This day there was one of Captain Taplee's men a playing ball and immediately dropped down dead.

July 19. Captain Nelson, with about one hundred and fifty men, went down to work on the roads between Saratoga and Fort Edward.

July 21. This day here was a soldier belonging to the Second Battalion of Royal Americans, shot for desertion. This day also came in a scout of men that went out under Lieutenant Dormit, and they said they were fired upon near South Bay and Lieutenant Dormit was killed. This day also came in Captain Learned who went out the fifteen day.

July 23. This morning about eight o'clock in the morning about 400 Indians fired on our workmen within eighty rods of the fort. Captain Learned's company being the first on the ground, for they were the nearest, and they were smartly engaged some time before any other help could get there. Captain Putnam and his company was the next though they had to come from the island. The fight continued about one hour and then the enemy retreated. We recovered some packs and some guns; but no prisoners, nor scalps. The enemy killed eleven men, and one is missing; two more died the night after. In the afternoon,

Captain Learned, Captain Putnam and Captain West pursued them with about 250 men, and we made great discovery of their dead and wounded, but recovered none. We marched about ten miles and then encamped.[16]

July 24. Returned home safely.

July 25. General Webb went up to the lake.

July 26. There was a man shot off his gun accidentally, and shot a man in the next tent through the body; who never spoke more words than these: I am a dead man; the Lord have mercy on me.

July 27. This day our men growing very unwilling to go a scouting without some consideration for it, they made their complaint to the captain and he made application to Major Fletcher, the commanding officer of the fort who came out and spoke to us on behalf of the general and told us if we would still stand as rangers, we should (have) three dollars per month allowed us, extraordinary; and half a pint of rum when we scouted. The rum we got sometimes; but the money we never see.

July 28, The rangers shot at marks by order of Major Fletcher.

July 29. Captain West came in of his scout, who had been to South Bay and buried Lieutenant Dormit; whom they found with his head and arms cut off and his body cut to pieces.

---

16. This fight is spoken of in Humphrey's life of Israel Putnam, as having occurred after the surrender of Fort William Henry. Humphrey says that Israel Putnam was stationed "on an island adjacent to the fort." At sound of the firing he plunged into the river at the head of his men and hurried to the rescue. As he passed the fort, General Lyman ordered him to halt. He disobeyed the order, and with the assistance of the men he brought, the troops engaged; who were nearly overpowered, rallied and repulsed the enemy. General Lyman feared that the firing was the prelude to a general attack, and that the whole party would be lost. Humphrey says nothing of Captain Learned; but says the working party were protected by Captain Little with fifty British regulars.

July 30. General Webb came down from the lake.

July 31. This day the whole army was set at a minute's warning.

August 1. This day Colonel Fry's regiment ordered to march to the lake tomorrow.

August 2. Colonel Fry marched his regiment to the lake, except two companies of rangers and a great number of invalids. Part of the 2nd Battalion of Royal Americans, and the Independent Regiment marched with them and eight field pieces.

August 3. This morning, I being out on the morning scout with Captain Learned, sun about a quarter of an hour high, we heard the cannons fired at Fort William Henry, and before we got in, we heard fifteen cannons fired and a great many small arms. When we came into Fort Edward we found that Captain Putnam had sent off three men for spies.

August 4. There came in an express from Fort William and brought news that there was near 12000 French landed against Fort William.

August 5. There came another express from Fort William and brought news that for the first two days, the French fired no cannon, and that they had killed but few men; and that the men were in good spirits and of good courage.

August 6. This day there came another express from the lake and brought news that the French flung no bombs as yet. Further they brought news that Lieutenant Jonson was out on a scout when the siege first began and that he came through the French Army into our breastwork without losing one man. He also brought news that there was but about 300 men in the fort; the rest were in the breastwork on the hill, or the old encampment; and that the enemy had not hurt the fort in any shape.

August 9. Mr. Crofford, Chaplain to our regiment. Preached from *1 Samuel 14 : 6.* In the afternoon there came in another express from the lake and brought news that the French flung their bombs into the fort, but they killed but few men.

August 8. There came no express from the lake.

August 9. There came another express from the lake and brought news that the fort was well last night at nine o'clock. Last night also we saw the signals that were flung up for signals of distress at Fort William Henry. The post also said that they had split most of their cannon, and that they must be obliged to give up the fort, except they had relief from this fort. This express arrived in about ten o'clock, and before he came in, the cannon ceased, but we knew not the meaning of it. Just at night there came in a Frenchman that belonged to Captain Thaxter, and he said that the French flag was hoisted in Fort William Henry at eight o clock this morning; and as soon as he saw it, he jumped over the breastwork and escaped.

August 10. This day the enemy fell on our people, contrary to the articles of capitulation.[17]

August 11. This day several of the officers belonging to our regiment came and among them all there was but one that had not lost the most of his clothes, and all his regimental rigging. This night came in Colonel Fry.

August 12. This day the most of the men that came in from the lake were sent off.

August 13. Colonel Fry went off from this fort.

---

17. In his manuscript memoirs General Putnam, in speaking of the surrender of Fort William Henry, says that the general opinion in the army at that time was that General Webb was a coward, and that he could and should have made an effort to relieve the fort. There was much excitement in regard to his conduct in neglecting to bury the dead who had been butchered by the Indians or to search among them if by chance any might be living.

August 14. Just at night there came a flag of truce from the lake to warn a guard to come and receive the prisoners that were left.

August 15. General Webb sent a guard to receive the prisoners, at the halfway brook; where they went and returned home to the fort the same day.

August 16. In the afternoon Lieutenant Walker with about twenty men, went out after a man that was wounded on the road; and about two miles from Fort Edward we lit of an Englishman, who was taken at Oswego last year, and became waiter to a French officer down to the siege of Fort William Henry and had now made his escape from them. And he gave us intelligence that the army which came to the siege of Fort William Henry marched from Quebec the last day of April, and that the army besides Indians (consisted of) 15000 (perhaps these figures are 18000) regulars and Canadians. We found the man and carried him into Fort Edward the same night.

August 17. There came in one of our regiment who had been in the woods ever since the 9th day.

August 19. Came in one of the regulars who had been out in the woods ever since Fort William Henry was taken.

August 20. Captain Learned was carried into the hospital sick with the smallpox.

August 21. This day Captain Putnam went for eleven days' scout. This day came in Lieutenant Coone who was taken last June at Scocook Landing (and) another who was taken thirteen months ago, at (Hoosack). They came from Montreal twenty days ago.

August 24. This day came in George Robins of Petersham, who was taken the 17th of last April, twenty miles from No. 4 fort. There were three more men that came in with him. The name of the Indian Town he lived in was Caughneeawaukee. He brought news that the French hired 200 savages to fight for them, and that they would bite pieces out of their arms and shoulders, as they travelled along, and suck their blood; and that they would when they killed them, cut out their breast bone and suck their blood up with it; and further he said that the French could not command them; but that they would kill horses, sheep and cattle, and that they killed one Frenchman to eat, and when they came through the town, the squaws pulled the prisoners into the houses for fear of those horrible Towevans for so they call them.

August 26. Peter Thair of our company, who had deserted, was brought back and put under the regular guard.

August 30. Captain Putnam came in who had been out twelve days' scout up to Ticonderoga, and had left a negro sick in the woods and two Indians to look after him.

September ye 1. Came in two men from the French that were taken some years ago. This day Lieutenant Walker, with forty men, went out after the negro that Captain Putnam left in the woods. We took six days' provisions and marched this day about twenty miles.

Sept. 2. After encamping we marched on our way about five miles, and then met the two Indians that were left with the negro, and they said that as one of them was some way off boiling some cocolatt (?) and he said that he saw an Indian come up a sharp ridge and look down upon him; then the Indian stepped back and a Frenchman looked over the ridge. He said he made as if he did not see him; but went directly off and told his mate which made his escape with him and left the negro. After we found these men, we returned some part of the way, and then encamped.

Sept. 3. We came to Fort Edward. This day Peter Thair was set at liberty.

Sept. 4. Two high Dutchmen came in from Ticondaroga who deserted from there six days ago. In the afternoon came in two Frenchmen. The sun about an hour high, John Weeks of Captain Learned's company, was out a frying some beef and immediately dropped down dead.

Sept. 5. This morning there was two of the Royal Americans shot for their deserting, and was taken up near the lake. A Connecticut man whipped 500 lashes for enlisting into York forces. And this evening three Yorkers whipped 600 lashes apiece and were to receive the remainder of a thousand; which lashes they received for deserting. Eight prisoners came in from the French, that were taken at Fort William Henry.

Sept. 6. This day there went out three scouts, twenty men on a scout. One was to go to East Bay; the second, toward the South Bay; the third toward the East side of Lake George. These scouts went out for six days.

Sept. 14. Twenty of Captain Learned's company was drafted into Captain West's and the rest were sent on to the island to do camp duty, Lieutenant Walker also tarried with those that went into Captain West's company.

Sept. 16. Ensign Manton of Captain West Company, went out with twenty men with two days' provisions, in order to go and see what discovery we could make at the lake. We marched up to the halfway brook and then encamped.

Sept. 17. Ten of our party was sent into Fort Edward and the rest of us marched on toward the lake and on our march we met with a Hampshire man that had made his escape from Ticonderoga. We went up to the lake, but discovered nothing but the ruins of that famous fort and the bodies of those men that the enemy so barbarously murdered on the 10 of August. We loaded ourselves with choice turnips and then returned to Fort Edward. At our return we found that Captain Learned was come out of the smallpox hospital which we were all very glad to see.

Sept. 19. Two Frenchmen that belonged to our regiment and was taken at Fort William came in from Ticonderoga.

Sept. 20. Major Rogers[18] came up with his rangers who had been down to Halifax all the summer with my Lord Louden.

Sept. 27. Captain Learned had a furlough to New England for the recovery of his health.

October ye 2. A Frenchman taken between this fort and the lake by some Connecticut men was brought in. This day I went out a scout for three days with Sergeant Martin Sephorance[19]

---

18. Robert Rogers, born Dumbarton, N. H., about 1730; died in England about 1800. During the French war, he commanded with great credit to himself, a battalion of rangers who rendered excellent service. This battalion was the model from which Rufus Putnam organized the company of rangers which so effectively protected the Ohio Company settlements during the Indian war, 1791 to 1795. In 1760 Major Rogers with 200 men took possession of Detroit. In 1766 he was appointed by the king, governor of Michilimacinac. He was accused of plotting to sell the post to the French and was sent in irons to Montreal tried by court martial and acquitted; but deprived of his office. Visited England in 1769, was imprisoned for debt; when released he returned to America and, shortly after the out break of the revolution, was arrested by General Washington as a spy. Released upon parole, he violated it, joined the British Army, was commissioned colonel and placed in command of the Queens Ranger's. He saw but little service, and about 1778, returned to England. In 1778, was proscribed and banished by the State of New Hampshire. In 1765, he published a journal of the French war, which was republished in 1769, with an account of Bouquet's expedition against the Ohio Indians. He also published *The Tragedy of Ponteack*. His diary of the siege of Detroit was published in 1860.

19. Probably Sergeant Martin Severance. Surgeon Thomas Williams in a letter to his wife Aug. 25th, 1756, acknowledges receipt of one from her by hand of Sergeant Severance who had been on a scout.— See *Dawson's Historical Magazine* April, 1870.

of Major Roger's company. In our scout we discovered nothing remarkable. We steered our course up the great river.

Oct. 4. We returned home to Fort Edward. The same day came in Lieutenant McCurda[20] from the Narrows and brought in a French prisoner which he had taken at the Narrows.

Oct. 8. Our ranging company broke up and we were ordered into the regiment to do camp duty.

Oct. 10. This day there was one of Colonel Ottaway's regiment that was taken at Fort William Henry came into this fort and brought news that there was a flag of truce come to the halfway brook, with six prisoners, and that they sent him to inform the general and to desire him to send a guard to come and receive them. The same day went a guard to receive them.

Oct. 11. I went on the main guard; and the guard that was sent for the prisoners came with them.

Oct. 14. Went on command to Saratoga.

Oct. 15. Returned home to Fort Edward.

Oct. 17. I went to work on the fort.

Oct. 18. I went on the main guard.

Oct. 20. Two Royal Americans hanged for theft and desertions.

Oct. 24. There was a man found dead about sixty rods from the Brick-Kilns.

---

20. Lieutenant McCurdy of Haverhill was an officer in Captain Richard Rogers' company of Major Robert Rogers' battalion of rangers.

Monday Oct. 25. There was another man found dead at the Brick-Kilns. This man was shot through the body with two balls. These men were both butchers, and went out after their sheep, on Sunday. There were three went out, and the other is not found yet.

Oct. 30. The snow fell two inches deep.

Nov. ye 7. This day we launched a scow fifty feet long and fifteen feet wide. This day His Excellency, The Right Honourable Earl of Louden[21] and Chief General of North America, came to Fort Edward.

Nov 9. The carpenters were all dismissed from the king's work and the fort was finished.

Nov. 10. This morning they fired a round of cannon in the fort as a sign of finishing. This day my Lord Louden went off for Albany. This day our regiment was ordered to march from this fort into the Half Moon. We marched about four miles.

Nov. 11. We marched about five miles below Saratoga and then encamped.

Nov. 12. Marched down to Stillwater.

Nov. 14. We marched down to Halfmoon.

Nov. 17. We keep this day as Thanksgiving day for we heard that it was so in our province.

---

21. Lord Loudoun. He is thus described in official documents: "His Excellency, John, Earl of Loudoun, Lord Machline and Tairanfeen, etc., etc., etc., one of the sixteen peers of Scotland, governor and captain general of Virginia and vice admiral of the same, colonel of the 13th Regiment of Foot, colonel-in-chief of the Royal American Regiment, major general and commander-in-chief of all his majesty's forces raised or to be raised in North America." Had command in America from August, 1756 till March, 1758.

Nov. 18. This day 360 of us were drafted to stay, and the rest sent home. We were drafted into four companies under Captain Kerver, Captain Nelson, Captain Cain, Lieutenant Brown. Captain Kerver's company winter at Halfmoon; Nelson's at Sopas; Cairn's at Schenectady; Brown's into which Lieutenant Walker (went) with Captain Learned's Company, to winter at Stillwater.

Nov. 26. Lieutenant Brown marched our company to Stillwater. But I and four more were left to work as carpenters at the Halfmoon. This day I went to work.

Dec. ye 15. Five Frenchmen brought down that were taken by Major Rogers' men.

Dec. 22. We were ordered down to Albany to receive our pay.

Dec. 23. Received our pay.

Dec. 24. Returned home to Halfmoon.

Dec. 29. Returned to Stillwater, with the rest of the carpenters, to our company.

Jan. ye 1, 1758. This day being the first day of the year and the first day of the week, we kept it with joy, and wished for Candlemas.

Jan. ye 5. Captain Learned came up to his company, at the coming of whom we rejoiced greatly.

Feb. 1. This day I went on command to Saratoga, to guard cattle.

Feb. 2. This day we returned home to Stillwater, and now the day was come that we wished for, and the most happy Candlemas that ever I see. Quick after our return we were all ordered into the fort, when Captain Skean[22] read a part of a letter to us, that Major General Abercrombie sent to him, the contents of which was this. You are hereby required to persuade the Massachusetts (men) that are under your care to tarry a few days longer, till I shall hear from their government, to know what the government intends to do with them. To these orders, there was answer made by some of our company, that they looked upon him to be a good soldier, that tarried till his time was out; and that the province had no business to detain us any longer; neither would we be detained any longer by any power that they could raise. He told us that if any man had been duly enlisted into His Majesty's service and should leave the same, without a regular discharge, he should suffer death. We told him we did not value that, for according to our enlistment, neither they nor the province could hold us any longer, and that we did not break the Court Act by going off.

---

22. Philip Skene was a native of Halyards in Fifeshire, Scotland, and was a descendant of Sir William Wallace. He entered the army in 1739 and was with the expedition against Portabello; in 1741 was at the capture of Carthegena; in 1745 was in the battle of Fontenoy, and was at Culloden in the following year. In 1747 he was present at the battle of Laffeldt. He came to America in 1756. In 1757 he was made commander of a company in the 27th or Enniskillen regiment. He was in the unsuccessful attack on Ticonderoga, 1758. In the campaign of 1759 he was appointed by Sir Jeffry Amherst brigade major. In October of that year he was left in charge of Crown Point and encouraged by Amherst, projected a settlement at the head of Lake Champlain and established some thirty families there. In 1762 he was with the expedition against Martinique, Havana, and distinguished himself at the storming of Moro Castle. He returned to America in 1763 and renewed his efforts to build up the settlement at Lake Champlain. In 1765 after a visit to England he obtained from the king a grant of a township of land including the settlement he had founded and which he called Skenesborough. His regiment having been ordered to Ireland he exchanged into the 10th Foot in 1768 to remain in America. In 1769 he left the army and settled at Skenesborough (now Whitehall). He erected here forges for smelting iron and large saw mills. At the outbreak of the revolution he was arrested by a band of Connecticut volunteers and with his family taken to Hartford. He was finally exchanged in 1776. He sailed for England immediately but returned with Burgoyne and was taken prisoner with his army. In 1779 his property was confiscated by the legislature of New York. After the war he came to America and made an unsuccessful effort to recover his property. He returned to England and died at Addersey Lodge near Stoke Goldington, Bucks in 1810. —*See Colonial History New York Documents.* (continued opposite)

Feb. 3. About three o clock in the morning we marched for Stillwater, in all seventy persons with about three days' provisions, in order to go Hoosack where we expected to arrive in two days. We all marched on snow shoes and the foremost man sunk in half leg deep; about the tenth man had good travelling. We marched about eighteen miles this day and then encamped. This night it was a very bad snow storm.

Feb 4. We marched up the river to Dutch Hoosack when we missed our way and travelled on the river called Loonstock (?) River, which we learn since comes down within about ten miles west of Hoosack Fort. In our march in this river this day Captain Learned[23] killed two turkeys. We travelled on this river till night, not mistrusting that we were wrong, and yet wondered that we did not arrive at Hoosack; but had no mistrust that we were on the wrong river and therefore ate plentifully of our provisions, and of the turkeys.

Feb 5. Set out early in the morning with the expectation to get into Hoosack Fort before noon, but missed all our expectations, for we did not see it this night. And now we were altogether of the mind that we were lost; but yet were resolved to be certain before we turned our course. We killed another turkey this day which we spared for necessity. This night our provisions was chiefly gone. We encamped this night with sad hearts and the countenance of every man showed he was perplexed in mind, in consideration that the turkey was the chief of the provision that we had. The weather exceeding cold and stormy and the snow at least five feet deep. And John Kelly, of our company, fell into the river this day when he lost one of his snowshoes, by reason of which he suffered very much. But yet we had some hopes that we should see Hoosack in the morning.

---

23. In his *Memoirs* General Putnam censures Captain Learned very severely for his conduct in leaving his post with his men before they were regularly discharged. He also says that Captain Learned was never afterward able "to obtain a commission during that war." The history of the town of Sutton says that Captain Learned served long and suffered much and returned with a commission of major.

Feb. 6. We marched up this stream till about noon and then we came to where the stream parted; the stream yesterday and today steered about north and there was a branch came into it that came from the east. When we came to this place we found that we were lost, but yet for our satisfaction the captain followed up the north stream about four miles till we found we were on the wrong stream and then turned back and came to the parting of the streams; when the captain called all the men together, to know what they would do. There was in number seventy men. The substance of what the captain said was this: That it evidently appeared that we were on the wrong stream; and that we were at least, thirty miles north of Hoosack; and as for provisions, we had but little, but said he don't be discouraged; for, my life on it said he, if the men hold out to travel four or five days if I don't bring you to see the inhabitants of New England. But said he, if any man has a mind to go back to Stillwater, he may in welcome; for my part said he, I will die in the woods before I will go back. They all cried out, that they would die with him. So after refreshing ourselves a little we marched off a South East Point and travelled up several mountains, and about sundown we came upon the top of a very large mountain, which seemed to be the height of land, and now we were satisfied whereabouts we were. We judged ourselves to be thirty miles north-east of Hoosack. The weather was exceeding cold, and the snow five feet deep and the provisions very short.

Feb. 1. This morning thirty of us made a good breakfast of a small poor turkey without salt or bread; and now our provision was gone. In about five miles from where we lodged, we came upon a small stream descending toward the south-east, at the seeing of which we were all very much rejoiced; there seemed to be a smiling countenance on all the company, to think that we were got on the borders of New England. And on our way down this stream, there were several small streams come into it, so that it got to be a large river. This night we camped but felt exceeding faint for want of victuals, but yet our courage held out. At present courage was the only thing we had to support us, except it was beech buds and some high swamp cranberries.

Feb. 8. This day we had exceeding bad travelling all day, and the river turned contrary to our expectations; so that we had but little hopes of getting into any post these some days. It was now exceeding stormy weather and heavy travelling, only on the river when the ice would bear; and had we not had some relief by that means, we had all perished in the woods. About sundown we came to camp and being exceeding faint, living without victuals some days and we having a large dog with us we killed him and divided him among seventy men, giving every man his equal share. None can tell what a sweet morsel this dog's guts and feet were but those that eat them as I did the feet and the riddings of the guts.

Feb. 9. This day we had better travelling on the river and it seemed to steer the way we wanted, and about noon we came to where some trees were cut for shingles, and at night we came to where one of our men knew the ground, and told the captain we were within three miles of Hawk's Fort, on the Charlemont; notwithstanding the captain would not go on because a great part of the men had froze their feet, and were at least two miles behind. But we went to camping, and the captain and James Call, who knew the ground went down the river about a mile till the captain was satisfied the man knew as much as he pretended, and then sent him on, and ordered him to have a breakfast prepared in the morning; after which the captain returned back to us by which time those lame men came up, and as the captain came up to us, we were all very zealous to hear what news? But we soon learned by the captain's countenance, before he got within some rods of us and as the captain come up to us, he said. Eat what you you have to eat this night; for the promised land is just by. Some were for going on this night, but the captain told them; No, by no means, for it would hazard the lives of a great many. The news that the captain brought raised the spirits of all the men, so that those whose countenance looked sad, were brought to a very smiling complexion.

Feb. 10. This morning we set out on our march, and about one mile from where we camped, we saw three men a-coming up the river which we were glad to see, and when they come to us, we found that one of them was the man we sent on the night before and he brought out some bread and meat boiled; which we reed, very kindly, and about ten o clock we came into Hawk's Fort on Charlemont, where we refreshed ourselves until about noon; after which we marched to Rice's Fort about one mile, where twenty of us stayed, all which were lame by reason of their feet being froze on our march except Samuel Dexter.[24] Lemuel Cobb, and myself. Through all this march I brought Ichabod Dexter's pack, because he froze his feet before we. set out from Stillwater, and I tarried to help him along further.[25]

Feb. 11. The twenty of us that were left behind marched down to Galon's Fort about six mile.

Feb. 12. Marched to Deerfield.

Feb. 13. Marched to Hadley.

Feb. 14. Marched to Greenwich.

Feb. 15. Home to Brookfield.

---

24. Samuel Dexter and Ichabod Dexter were from Hardwick, both commissioned officers in revolutionary war, both were engaged in Shay's rebellion, 1786, and were pardoned.—See *Paige's Hist. Hardwick.*
25. See letter in Appendix.

Putnam's Journal 1758

Rufus Putman's Journal for the Second Campaign which he undertook, being in the year 1758.

April 10, 1758. Then enlisted myself into a Provincial Regiment of whom Timothy Haggles Esq. is Colonel, and in Captain Joseph Whitcomb's Company.

April 14. Passed muster at Hardwick before Colonel Ruggles.

April 15. Returned to Sutton where I now made my home; but I went into the service this year for the town of Hardwick.

May 20. Received orders to meet the company at Brookfield on the 23—23rd. Met the company at Brookfield.

May 25. Marched from Brookfield.

May 27. Arrived at Northampton, where we were billeted out till further orders.

June 3. Marched from Northampton in order for Pantoosuck. This day marched about ten miles, and this night there were some of Captain Nixon's [1] men a falling some trees, to build

---

1. Captain John Nixon was born at Framingham, Mass., March 4th, 1725. He was at the siege of Louisburg in 1745. He served as captain during the French war and was esteemed a valiant soldier. He was made colonel of a Massachusetts regiment at the outbreak of the revolution and brigadier general in the (continued overleaf)

their camps, fell a tree onto some men as they were in another camp, and wounded three of them. One of the men that was wounded, his life is despaired of.

June 6. We arrived at Pantoosuck and drew stores of bread and marched about six miles to the other fort; from thence about one mile and then camped.

June 8. Arrived at Greenbush, where we heard that General Abercrombie[2] marched his troops from Albany yesterday.

June 9. Marched to Albany Flats.

June ye 12. A return was made of all the carpenters in Colonel Ruggle's regiment and all, being about eighty, were sent off under the command of Lieutenant Pool; in order to go to Fort Miller, marched this day to Halfmoon.

June 13. Marched to Stillwater and from thence by water to Saratoga.

June 14. Marched to Fort Miller.

June 15. Went to work at Fort Miller.

June 16. Thirty of us marched to Fort Edward, under the command of Lieutenant Hall.

---

continental line in August, 1776. Resigned on account of ill health in 1780. Died March 24th, 1815.—Lossing's Field Book of the Revolution.
2. James Abercrombie, born in Scotland, 1706; died deputy governor of Stirling Castle, April 28th, 1781; colonel in British army, 1746; major general, 1756; lieutenant general, 1759; general, 1772. Had chief command of royal forces in America from 1756 until 1759, except during the stay of Lord Loudon. Was superceded by Amherst, Sept. 30th, 1758. Displayed very little capacity in command of troops. The disaster of Ticonderoga in 1758 was generally attributed to his incompetence. He was a member of parliament after his return to England in 1759 and supported the acts, the passage of which resulted in the revolt of the colonies.—Drake.

June 17. Went to work on the island at the King's Hospitals and worked there till June 21.

June 21. Received ten days' provisions and marched to Halfway Brook.

June 22. Marched to the lake and was there employed in building two picket forts, in building floating batteries, and in fixing the boats. June 18 was the first that any forces came to the lake.

June 26. General Abercrombie came to the lake. Forces came on now very fast.

June 28. Colonel Ruggle's regiment came to the lake. Every thing here seems to carry the face of war on it. Ammunitions, provisions and artillery &c loading continually into the bateaux in order for Ticonderoga.

July ye 1. Camp at Lake George. The orders of this day; Parole, Hartford; Brigadier General for the day, tomorrow Lord How; Colonel for the day tomorrow, Colonel Donaldson; Field Officer of the picket this night, Major Eyre; [3] for the Provincials, Major Hunt; Brigadier Major Moneypenny.[4] The Provincial troops to be victualled to the sixth of July inclu-

---

3. William Eyre was promoted to be major in the 44th Foot, 7th January, 1756; in which year he built Fort William Henry, at the head of Lake George; in January, 1758, was commissioned engineer in ordinary, and on the 17th July following was advanced to the rank of lieutenant colonel in the army, and next of the 55th regiment; in July, 1759, during Amherst's campaign, he was appointed chief engineer to the army, and soon after laid out the ground for a new fort at Ticonderoga. In October, 1759, he became lieutenant colonel of his old regiment, the 44th ; accompanied Amherst from Oswego to Montreal in 1760, and remained in America until 1764, in the fall of which year he was unfortunately drowned, in the prime of his life, on his passage to Ireland.— *New York Colonial History*, vol.10, p. 729.
4. Alexander Moneypenny, appointed captain Aug. 29, 1756, assigned to 55th Foot in Feb., 1757 and sailed to America in the expedition with Lord Loudon. He was one of the brigade majors in this and the succeeding (continued overleaf)

sive when they next receive. Any soldier found gaming to be immediately confined, and they will receive 300 lashes. The Provost to go his rounds every day. He is to see that the camp be kept clean, and all filth buried; he is to apply to the nearest regiment for men for that purpose; and to report all extraordinary. The regiment to give a return of their sick to be sent to Fort Edward at four o clock this afternoon. Advance to apply to the quarter master general. for carriages; the commanding officer of each regiment to be answerable that they have no more battoes than what is allowed them in the orders; what they have over to be immediately returned. The regiments to report to the brigadier major as soon as the battoes are finished, and ready to load. They are then to dismiss the Corkers with a non-commissioned officer to Colonel Bradstreet. The Regulars and Provincials to give in their return immediately to the brigadier-major of what ammunition is wanting to complete every man with thirty-six rounds per man. A guard of one subaltern and twenty privates to mount immediately at the artillery boats. Captain Ord[5] will give the officer his directions. The battoes' men (to) make no fire between their tents and the lake where the artillery boats lie. Captain Shepherds Company to fire pieces this afternoon, between 3 and 5 o'clock; the regiments may try their rifles at the same time.

July 2. The orders given yesterday were complied with.

---

campaign. Was Major 27th Foot in 1760; Lieutenant Colonel 56th in 1762. Died or resigned his commission in 1776.
5. Thomas Ord was appointed captain in the royal artillery on 1st March, 1746. He was an excellent officer, and stood high in the Duke of Cumberland"s esteem, by whom he was selected to command the artillery in the expedition under Braddock. Landing in Newfoundland, he hastened to New York, and arrived at Philadelphia, 7th June, 1755, whence he proceeded for the seat of war accompanied by thirteen non-commissioned officers (*Sargent's Expedition of Braddock*, 364). In 1759 he was major and accompanied Amherst in the expedition up the lakes, after which he was promoted to be lieutenant colonel on the 21st November, same year. On the 1st January, 1771, he became colonel commandant of the 4th battalion of the royal artillery serving in America, and died in 1777. Colonel Ord received a grant of 500

July 3. Every man ordered to be ready to embark on the 5th at the drums beating and to boil all our provisions before we set out; which were taken until the ninth day.

July 4. All preparations (made) for embarking tomorrow. All ordered to put our heaviest baggage on board this night.

July 5. According to the orders heretofore given, the whole army embarked for Ticonderoga, under the command of Major General Abercrombie[6] and there were in all twenty-four regiments; but in them but 17000 according to the account that we had from the adjutant general. The embarkation was completed by seven o clock in the morning and all rowed to a place called Sabbath Day Point, when we arrived about dark, and all went on shore and refreshed ourselves. After which we set out and rowed all night.

July 6. And in the morning we arrived to a place within about four miles of the French advance guard.[7] When we came in sight of the enemy at the advance guard, (they) were wonderfully surprised to see so many men a-coming in battoes, and immediately fled so that we had no chance at them there. Colonel Dotey and the battoe men went in the front in whale boats, and landed first; but were soon seconded by troops of all sorts. Colonel Ruggles' regiment landed the nearest of any to the enemy, and in fair sight of their encampment. At this place Major Rogers killed one Frenchman and that was all. The enemy left a considerable of valuable baggage, which our men plundered.

---

6. In his memoirs General Putnam says of the officers in command: "General Abercrombie was an old man and frequently called 'Granny.' Lord Howe was the idol of the army; in him they placed the utmost confidence. General Gage was a man who never acquired a high reputation, and the furious Bradstreet was hated by all the army."
7. "The French guard ran at our appearance. Major Roger's rangers came up with part of the French guard, killed seven of them, lost two of our men. In the afternoon engaged the French, took 180 of them prisoners and killed 110 more. Lord Howe was killed in the battle and about sixty of our men a-missing." Journal of an officer (name unknown) in Colonel Preble's regiment.—Dawson's Historical Magazine, August, 1871.

Part of our people had a smart skirmish with the enemy, down the lake, in which skirmish we lost but few men, but among them a brave and bold commander, that worthy man, my Lord Howe,[8] who is lamented by us all, and whose death calls for our revenge. There were a great many of the enemy killed that day, and one hundred and odd taken prisoners.

July 7. The chief of the army march down to the sawmills, and some field pieces. Our chief employ was in fixing for an engagement the next day. Nothing at ail appeared of any discouragement, but everything seemed to carry success with it. This night General Johnson[9] came down with his Indians[10] to us.[11]

---

8. George Augustus Howe, Lord Viscount, was born in 1724. He was commissioned colonel of the Royal American or 60th regiment, in 1757 and ordered to America. In September, 1757, he was appointed colonel of the 55th Foot and brigadier general in America. The failure of the expedition against Ticonderoga was by many attributed to his death. Rogers Journal (page 103) gives this account of it. "My Lord Howe, with a detachment from his front, had broke the enemy and hemmed them in on every side; but advancing himself with great eagerness and intrepidity upon them, was unfortunately shot and died immediately." A foot note, same page, adds: "This noble and brave officer, being universally beloved by both officers and soldiers of the army, his fall was not only most sincerely lamented, but seemed to produce an almost general consternation and languor through the army."
"The greatness of mind, inimitable activity and masterly skill in military command of this truly great officer (Lord Howe) was known, was felt by the whole army, and his death was as sensibly felt." Sermon on "Total reduction of Canada" Reverend Eli Forbes, Brookfield, Mass.
The date of Lord Howe's death is sometimes incorrectly given July 5th. He was with the battalion of rangers commanded by Israel Putnam when killed.
9. Sir William Johnson, Baronet, born in Ireland about 1714. At the age of twenty came to America to oversee the estate of his uncle, Sir Peter Warren. He settled in Mohawk, among the Indians, acquired their language and soon obtained a remark able influence over them. In the French war, 1755-65 he was major general of the New York militia and brought into service for the English, one thousand Indians. He died in 1774.
10. "By sunrise next morning (July 8th) Sir William Johnson joined the army with four hundred and fifty Indians."—Rogers Journal, p. 103.
11. Humphrey's life of Israel Putnam says that on the morning of July 7th, Major Rogers was sent to reconnoitre the field where Lord Howe was killed "and bring off the wounded prisoners; but, finding the wounded unable to help themselves, in order to save trouble, he dispatched every one of them to the world of spirits."

July 8. All preparations for marching down to engage the enemy at the breastwork which we found was chiefly finished. About 11 o'clock our men marched down to the battle. There were also some field pieces went down the river toward the fort, on floating batteries which our men builded below the falls. How far these field pieces went, I am not able to say. Colonel Lyman's and Colonel Ruggles' regiments were left at the mills as a rearguard, and to build a breastwork in, or for defence if the enemy attacked us in the rear. There was a party of Colonel Ruggles' regiment sent down under the command of Lieutenant Williams, to carry powder and about 3 o'clock Colonel Lyman's regiment was called off to the battle. About sun an hour high, there was another party sent down to carry powder, under the command of Ensign Brown, among whom I was. When I came to the army they were retreated into a breastwork that Colonel Williams'[12] men had builded. I was very much amazed to see so many of our men killed and wounded. The path all the

---

12. William Williams, born in Western Mass, 1711; graduated at Harvard College, 1729; studied medicine, but soon abandoned the practice and established himself as a merchant in Boston. Failed in business in 1740; was commissioned ensign and took part in the unsuccessful expedition against St. Augustine. With the same rank in the following year he was in the expedition against Carthagena led by Admiral Vernon. He returned to Massachusetts in 1743, and in 1744 received a commission in Stoddard's regiment of Hampshire militia and was detailed to construct the line of forts between the Connecticut and Hudson rivers. While this work was in progress he was promoted major. In 1745 he was commissioned lieutenant colonel of the 8th Massachusetts regiment and sailed for Cape Breton June 23d. Louisburg capitulated before his arrival, but the regiment garrisoned the place till the spring of 1746. In 1747 Colonel Williams was detached as quartermaster and continued in that capacity till the close of the war in 1748. He settled in Pontoosuck (now Pittsfield) in 1753 and there built Fort Anson for protection against the Indians. In 1755 he was appointed captain in the regiment commanded by Sir William Pepperell. He served with the rank of captain three campaigns; further promotion being prevented by a personal difficulty with Sir Wm. Johnson. In 1758 he was commissioned colonel by Governor Pownal and commanded a regiment in the campaign against Ticonderoga. With this campaign, his military career ended. In 1759 he was chosen "Proprietor's clerk" of the town of Pontoosuck and continued many years in that office. He was representative to the General Court in 1762, 1764, 1769, 1770. In 1774 he was chief justice of the Common Pleas and judge of the Probate for Berkshire. He was slow to join in the revolt of the colonies, but after the revolution was fairly under way became an ardent patriot. In 1779 he was chosen (continued overleaf)

way was full of wounded men. I was much amazed to see the floating batteries rowing back, the meaning of which, I could not tell. I came to the regiment where I found them employed as before. The most of the troops retreated into the breast (-work) which we had builded. After proper guards were posted, we were ordered to refresh our selves, which we accordingly did, and then camped. About midnight we were all mustered and ordered to march—where; we knew not; but concluded we were a-going to take post on the hill east of Ticonderoga ; but it proved otherwise, for we marched directly to the advance guard where our battoes lay.[13]

July 9. About nine o'clock in the morning we all went on board our battoes and set out for the place where Fort William Henry stood, and arrived about sundown.

During our stay at the lake, after our return from Fort Ticonderoga we were employed in almost every thing, in the building of breastworks and moving of our encampment from one place to another had hardly time to pitch in one place before we were ordered to remove and pitch in another; and no body, to see us, would be able to tell what we were about.

July 20. Near the Halfway Brook, was killed by a party of Indians, Captain Samuel Dakin of Sudborough, Captain Lawrence of Groton, Captain Johns of Wilmington, Lieutenant

---

delegate to the Massachusetts Constitutional Convention and took an active part in its deliberations. He died in 1785. Major Stoddard summed up his married life thus: "He married, first Miriam Taylor for good sense, and got it; secondly, Miss Wells for love and beauty and had it; thirdly, Aunt Hannah Dickerson and got horribly cheated."—See Smith's History of Pittsfield.

13. Speaking of this campaign in his Mss. Memoirs, General Putnam says: "I have heard that some men should say they loved to fight as well as to eat. I never had any such feelings. So far as I am able to judge of myself, it was pride and a wish to excel, or, at least, to come behind none, which influenced me, at that period of my life, to be among the foremost on all occasions that offered." He also criticises the assault as follows: "When I subsequently became acquainted with the strength of the works and the mode of attack, I considered it the most injudicious and wanton sacrifice of men that ever came within my knowledge or reading."

Curtis of Sudbury, Lieutenant Godfrey of Billerica, Ensign Davis of Andover, two sergeants, one corporal and ten men, and five missing.

July 22. Colonel Haggles' regiment marched to Fort Edward.

July 23. Marched down about four miles and then encamped and went to mending the roads.

July 25. Two hundred of the Light Infantry marched down by our encampment to Stillwater.

July 28. Marched down within about three miles of Saratoga to a place called Lord Howe's Encampment. Received news that yesterday there was a party of Indians fell on some teams that were going from Fort Edward to Halfway Brook, where they killed twenty-five men and thirty-eight teams.

August ye 7. This day moved our camp three miles below Saratoga.

Do 12. Moved three miles down the river.

Do 17. Marched down to the Halfmoon, and there went to our old post, of mending the road.

Do 27. Being Sabbath Day, we were very unexpectedly, allowed to rest; and it was the only Sabbath that we were allowed to rest since we came from home.[14]

Do 28. Moved our camp up the river about five miles to Halfway house.

---

14. The journal of an officer of Colonel Preble's regiment, this day, reads: "I did not work this day. Went to meeting. Mr. Cleveland preached two sermons from 146th Psalm, 5 verse." He had previously complained of being compelled to work Sundays.

September ye 5. Moved our camp up the river to Captain Samson's, which was about three miles.

Do 14. Captain Cox[15] marched his company to Lowden's Ferry, joined by Captain Billings and six carpenters, to work on the roads from thence to Albany.

Do 20. Captain Read's company with the rest of the carpenters marched up to the Great Fly, about five miles above Stillwater.

Do 25. The regiment marched down to Halfmoon to mend the roads from thence to Albany. Captain Whitcomb's company tarried behind to repair the roads that we had mended before.

Do 29. Our company marched to Lowden's Ferry, where we went to work as usual.

October ye 4th. His Excellency General Amherst[16] went up by our camp to the lake.

Do 8. We joined our regiment at the Halfmoon and marched from thence to the Great Fly above Stillwater.

---

15. Captain Ebenezer Cox of Wrentham. He commanded a company in each of the campaigns of 1758, 1759, 1760 and 1761. In 1762 removed to Hardwick and commanded a company mainly from Hardwick in that year. He had probably served previous to 1758, for his tombstone declares that he: In six campaigns intrepid trod ye field, Nor to ye Gallic power would ever yield. He died March 2nd, 1768, aged 42.—See Paige's History Hardwick.

16. Jeffrey Amherst, baron, born Kent, England, Jan. 21), 1717; died Aug. 3rd, 1797. Entered British army as ensign at the age of fourteen. Was at Fontenoy as aide to Lord Ligonier. Appointed major general in 1756. Appointed commander-in chief of the royal forces in America, Sept. 30th, 1758, vice Abercrombie. Governor of Virginia, 1763; of Guernsey in 1771; commander-in-chief of British army, 1778 to 1795, field marshal, 1796. He was "a sagacious, humane and experienced commander."—See Drake's Dictionary American Biography.

Do 13. Captain Robeson,[17] with a detachment of subalterns, five sergeants, fifteen corporals, eighty-eight privates, marched up to the first camp we made below Fort Edward, when we came from Lake George where we went to repairing the roads as usual.

Do 14. The Indians killed and took three men at Saratoga and another was drowned as he was endeavouring to swim over the river. A party of men marched with us, consisting of fifty, to Saratoga Meadows for the same purpose.

Do 16. A great number of invalids was sent home from the lake, and this day marched by our camp.

Do 18. Colonel Bradstreet's[18] battoe men marched down by our camp to carry provisions up the Mohawk River to the German Flats.

October 24. This day Colonel Preble,[19] Colonel Nichols and Colonel Wm. Williams' regiments marched down by our camp, in order for home.

---

17. This is probably Captain Samuel Robinson of Hardwick, who commanded a company in each of the campaigns of 1755, 1758, 1759 and was also in the service in some capacity in 1757. —See *Paige's History Hardwick*.
18. Colonel John Bradstreet, born 1711; died in New York City, Sept. 25th, 1774. Was lieutenant colonel of Maine regiment, in the expedition against Louisburg in 1745; lieutenant governor, St. Johns, Newfoundland, 1746; Captain in 60th Regiment British Army, March, 1749; lieutenant colonel and deputy quartermaster general Dec., 1757; colonel in Feb., 1762. Commanded expedition against western Indians in 1764. He attained marked distinction as an officer; but his violent temper made him as much feared by his friends as hated by his enemies.
19. Jedediah Preble, born Wells, Maine, 1707, died Portland, Maine, March 11th, 1784. Early in life was a sailor; appointed captain in Waldo's regiment, 1746; lieutenant colonel, 1755; Colonel, March 13th, 1758; brigadier general, March 12th, 1759. Was twelve years' member of the legislature. Massachusetts commissioned him major general at the outbreak of the revolution; but he declined on account of his age. Judge of Common Pleas in 1778. Member state senate in 1780. The journal of a captain in Colonel Preble's regiment for the campaign of 1758 is published in *Dawson's Historical Magazine*, Aug., 1871.—See *Drake's Dictionary American Biography*.

Do 26. Colonel Partridge's regiment marched home.

Do 27. Our detachment marched down and joined their regiment at the Great Fly. General Abercrombie went down to Stillwater this night.

Do 28. Our regiment marched down to Albany where we arrived the 29th and drawed stores for our march home and crossed the river at Green Bush.

Do 30. Marched down to Kinderhook.

Do 31. Marched to Lovejoy's, about twenty miles.

November ye 1. Marched to No.1- eighteen miles.

Do 2. Marched through the Green Woods to Glasgow eighteen miles.

Do 3. From Glasgow to Springfield twenty miles.

Do 4th. Marched to Ware River to Landlord Scotts.

Do 5. Marched about eight miles; where we tarried all day, because of the rains.

Do 6. Marched to Brookfield. Tarried at Brookfield until the 8th then marched to Sutton to Mr. Trasks'.

Do 9th. Arrived at brother Amos Putnam's.

Putnam's Journal 1759.

April 2nd. Then enlisted I, myself, into ye Provincial Service for the 3rd Campaign at Sutton.[1]

April 9. Passed muster at Worcester, I was put under the command of Samuel Clark Paine[2] Captain and was ordered to appear at Worcester the 12th Instant.

Do 12. Appeared at Worcester and was ordered to appear there the 13th.

Do 13. Appeared at Worcester and was ordered to appear there the 16th.

Do 16. Appeared at Worcester and received orders that we should all be billeted out; but obtained the favour to return home and stand at a minutes warning.

Do 21. Being at Worcester, I obtained leave to billet with Captain Paige's men at Brookfield.

May 3. Captain Paige[3] marched for Springfield and ordered

---
1. He enlisted as a substitute for Moses Leland, who had been drafted. For this enlistment he received fourteen pounds, thirteen shillings, Massachusetts currency, or $45.50. —Hildreth's Lives of the Pioneers.
2. Samuel Clark Paine of Worcester, died in December, 1759.
3. Captain Paige appointed Putnam orderly sergeant, he was in the 1st battalion of Ruggles' regiment, commanded by Lieutenant Colonel Ingersoll.

me to Hardwick to fetch the brigade baggage to Brookfield and to wait till the teams came up from Worcester.

Do 11. Marched to Captain Days in Springfield with the baggage cart.

Do 12. Marched to Captain White's in Springfield and passed muster before Captain Wheelock.

Do 14. Passed muster before Lieutenant. Small[4] of the Highland Regiment, also the 11th Company that marched from Worcester came to town.

Do 15. Drawed stores for eight days, and marched to Westfield.

Do 16. Marched to Glasgow.

May 17. Marched into the Green Woods, with our teams and baggage and arrived within about four miles and half of Chaddock. This night it rained exceeding hard which made it very tedious lodging.

Do 18. Marched to Sheffield where our teams were dismissed.

Do 19. We had a recruit of other teams, soon loaded our baggage again, and we marched to Lovejoys.

Do 20. Marched to Kinderhook.

---

4. Jno. Small was born in Scotland in 1726. Died at Guernsey in 1796. Served in America during the French and Indian war, as lieutenant in 42nd Highlanders. Served in the West Indies in 1762. June 14th, 1775, appointed major of a company of Highlanders raised in Nova Scotia for service in the English army during the American revolution. At Bunker Hill General Israel Putnam saved Major Small's life by throwing up the muskets of the men who were about to shoot him. Major Small was promoted to lieutenant colonel in 1780, colonel 1790, major general 1794, lieutenant governor of Guernsey in 1793.

Do 21. Marched to Greenbush, where we unloaded our carts, and put our stores into Captain Dows' barn.

May 22. Crossed the river and camped on Albany hill

Do 23. Drawed our tents and pitched them.

Do 24. A weekly return made of the men on this side the river were all mustered before a major of the regulars. The other companies that belonged to each battalion, under the command of Brigadier General Ruggles, came over the river and encamped. This night at roll calling we had the Articles of War read to us.

May 25. The other companies that came in belonging to Colonel Ruggles were mustered and the battalions were properly encamped. Sergeant Lackey of Captain Baldwin's Company, was taken up by the regulars as a deserter from their troops at Halifax.

Do 29. This day Samuel Harris of the Rhode Island Regiment was shot for desertion. David Rogers, of the same regiment condemned to be shot, for the same crime, was pardoned. This day a detachment from all the Provincial troops marched up the Mohawk River in order to battoe up that river. The detachment consisted of captains eight; subalterns fifteen; sergeants twenty-one; rank and file 554. This day the following detachment from Connecticut, Massachusetts, New Jersey troops for to carry battoes to Halfmoon loaded with provisions; captains two; subalterns ten; sergeant ten; rank and file 250.

May 30. The following detachment from the Massachusetts, Connecticut, New Jersey troops for Halfmoon tomorrow morning to take up provision. Captains two; subalterns eight; sergeant eight; rank and file, 200. The Rhode Island Regiment this day marched for Fort Edward.

June ye 1. Marched this day from Albany in order for Fort Edward, or rather embarked in bateaux and arrived this night at Halfmoon. We had in all eighty bateaux; twenty barrels in each bateaux.

Do 2. Set up the river as far as the Halfway house where we encamped.

Do 3. We set our boats as far as Captain Samsons' where we unloaded our boats and took our boats up the falls to Stillwater, where we loaded our bateaux again and lodged about half a mile above the Fort.

June 4. Proceeded with our boats as far as Saratoga falls where we unloaded our boats and the provisions were taken up in wagons, as far as Lord Howes' encampment, about three miles.

Do 5. Loaded our boats again, and proceeded up the river as far as Fort Miller, where we unloaded our provisions, drew our boats out of the river, loaded them on carriages, carried them by the falls, put them in the water, loaded our provisions again and proceeded as far as Fort Edward the same day, where we arrived about sundown with the boat that I was in. There arrived but about thirty boats this night.

Do 6. Lay at Fort Edward, and the boats that were left behind came up.

Do 7. The ground for our encampment was marked out; but it was exceeding rainy, for which reason it could not be cleared.

June 8. Our people were all set to work to clear the ground for our encampment, and we moved our tents and pitched them.

Do 10. Although the encampment was cleared; yet our men were still on fatigue; some cutting off stumps, and all manner of duty going forward. Cannons bringing out of the fort and mounting on carriages.

Do 13. A detachment of 400 men of the Provincials ordered to join the Royal Highlanders tomorrow morning, and march with them under the command of Colonel Grant[5] to Halfway Brook. A detachment of 200 of our regiment and 100 of the Jerseys, were ordered to relieve the garrison in the fort. This day the Reverend Eli Forbes[6] came up as chaplain to our regiment.

June 15. This day the bateaux (with) shot, shells, wadding and such kind of loading was sent off to the Halfway Brook in abundance.

June 17. Received orders to strike our tents at two o'clock this afternoon and march to Halfway Brook; but, it being exceeding rainy, we received orders to the contrary. About 9 o'clock this morning we received orders to strike our tents at reveille beating in the morning, and marched to Halfway Brook.

Do 18. The first battalion of Colonel Ruggles marched to Halfway Brook under the command of Colonel Ingersol.

Do 19. This morning every man in camp was ordered on fatigue, there was not one man excused.

---

5. Francis Grant, Lieutenant Colonel 42nd Highlanders. He served in America from 1756 to 1762, was promoted colonel, 1762, major general in 1770, lieutenant general in 1777. Died in 1782.

6. Eli Forbes was born in Westborough, Mass., Oct., 1726. He entered Harvard college in 1744. In 1745 he served as a private soldier in a short campaign against the French and Indians. He returned to his studies in the following year and graduated in 1751. He was ordained minister at Brookfield in 1752. In 1758 and again in 1759, he served as chaplain in the provincial regiment commanded by Colonel Timothy Ruggles. In 1762 he established a Christian church among the Oneida Indians. In March, 1776, having been unjustly accused of toryism, he was dismissed from the church at Brookfield. In June of the same year, he was installed pastor of the church at Gloucester where he remained until his death in 1804. Harvard college conferred the degree of doctor of divinity upon him, 1804. He was one of the early subscribers to the Ohio company but relinquished his share.

On the 17th there was a flag of truce came into Fort Edward, and this day they were sent back again to Ticonderoga.

July 1st. From the time that we came to this place till now, nothing remarkable ; but bateaux, cannon and all kind of stores carrying up, forces marching daily to the lake and duty exceeding hard,

July 2. We received news that the Indians this day killed nine men and took five at Lake George.

July 4th. The artillery was carried from Fort Edward to Lake George and was guarded by Colonel Willard's regiment of the Massachusetts. There was carried up 1062 barrels of powder. Colonel Montgomery's regiment marched up as a guard for the artillery.

Do 7. We had the news that Captain Jacobs[7] was cut off by the enemy.

Do 12. We had news that Major Rogers had had an engagement with the enemy, but the circumstances of it we have not yet heard.

Do 13. We hear that Major Rogers had one man killed and another wounded in his skirmish but what damage he has done to the enemy we can not tell.

Do 14. We marched to the lake and at our arrival we found all the preparations possible for moving forward.

Do 18. All that marched into camp yesterday, were ordered out and fired three rounds by platoons.

---

7. Jacobs was a captain of a company of Indians in Rogers' battalion. He was a Mohegan. His Indian name was Nawnawapateoonks.

Do 21. This morning at three o'clock we struck our tents through the whole army. About 7 o'clock the whole army embarked and sailed for Ticonderoga. This night we arrived within about four miles of the landing place.

July 22. The army landed this morning about 6 o'clock. The artillery landed about 10 o'clock on the same wharf that the French Army put theirs off board in the year 1757. The reddow[8] sailed in the front of the column which accounted twenty-two 4-pounders and six 6-pounders and a number of swivels. We landed without any molestation from the enemy. We never so much as see or heard one of them, till Major Rogers with some rangers marched down to the mills, where he found about thirty of them carelessly a-picking of herbs or some such thing. He fired upon them, killed one and wounded another, which he took (and) took another unhurt. The first column, part of them with Colonel Ruggles (marched) to a point of land south-west of the fort. The other part, *viz*: Major Rogers Grenadiers and Light Infantry marched on to the hills between the mills and the breastwork, and kept a guard advanced. Ye 2nd column marched and lay to cover the roads from the landing to the mills in order to keep the communication clear. Ye 3rd column; part marched and lay on the road for the same purpose, and the other part *viz*: the Jersey regiment and Ruggles' first battalion, were ordered to clear the trees that the French had fell in the road to prevent our coming; and also to repair such places as wanted. Ye 4th column marched down to the mills and part lay there and part joined Major Rogers. The first battalion of Colonel Ruggles, after clearing the roads, marched back to the landing and from thence, after refreshing themselves, marched down to the mills and went to digging the road part of the way from the mill

---

8. Radeau; a raft made to carry artillery. This one was probably one of those built under the superintendence of the officer of Colonel Preble's regiment, whose journal has been quoted from in these notes. He describes them Oct 20th, 58: "This day we launched two raddows. The first is the following dimensions: 50 feet long, 19 feet wide and 6 feet deep; 2nd 30 feet long 7 feet wide and 3½ feet deep."

to the fort, as far as our advance guard lay; in doing of which, some French and Indians came down within about fifty rods, and fired on us, but did no hurt.[9] But we were ordered not to pay them so much regard as to fire at them, except when they came nearer. Four field pieces were this night drawed up as far as our advanced posts. The first battalion of Colonel Ruggles this night marched back and lay on the road.

July 23. Our people took possession of the French breastworks and went to intrenching. The first battalion of Colonel Ruggles this day marched and took possession of a hill, northwest of the mills; and had four field pieces delivered to us, and soon had a strong breastwork builded for our defence as this post was very much exposed provided the enemy had any succour come to them. The enemy this day kept a continual fire of cannon and mortars at our people in the trenches, but did little hurt. This night there was a fire on some of the regular troops, in which there was an officer killed, and twelve men wounded.

July 24. This day Colonel Townshend[10] was killed by a cannon ball. The French continued their fire on our people but did but little hurt.

Do 25. The enemy's fire increased, but did no considerable damage; neither were they much regarded by our people, who were very diligent in opening the trenches. One hundred and sixty horses arrived this day, by which means the artillery and stores were forwarded with great dispatch.

July 26. This day Captain Willard by the general's orders went to building a sawmill in the same place the French mill, we

---

9. "The enemy kept out a scouting party with a body of Canadians and Indians, which killed several of our men and galled us prodigiously."—*Rogers' Journal,* p. 126.
10. Colonel Roger Townsend was Lord Amherst's adjutant general. A foot note to page 128, *Rogers' Journal,* says: "The brave and worthy Colonel Townshend was killed by a cannon ball from the enemy, whose fall was much lamented by the general."

burnt last year, stood; in which service I was employed as master. The enemy's fire this day was vastly heavy. This day a party of Indians came to our post and killed and scalped James Wallis of Captain Fletcher's Company in the first battalion. This night the platforms of the batteries were laid.

July 27. This morning about one o clock, or before, the enemy set fire to their magazine of powder blew up their fort and run away by the light of the same. Also nineteen Frenchmen deserted to our men.[11]

July 28. The Indians came from Crown Point and killed an ensign of the rangers.

Aug. 4. The army embarked for Crown Point and on their arrival there found it evacuated. I, being ordered to build the mills at this place, and tarrying on that business, am not able to give any further account of the army. During my stay at this place, which was till the first of December, I was very hardly fatigued, having the whole care of the work upon me. The business I performed faithfully in hopes of having a handsome reward; but was cheated of the whole except the wages of common men.

December 1st. Set out from the sawmills with Colonel Miller and Captain Foote and some other men in order for Fort George. Colonel Miller had two horses and a chair; therefore for our safer passage, we took bateaux and lashed them together. We had a small matter of provision and some liquor, the weather was calm and pleasant, and a great prospect of a quick passage. When we set out we had some wind ; but about sundown, we came within about a mile of Sabbath Day Point and the wind failed; wherefore in the evening we altered our opinion of pass-

---

11. Rogers says under date July 26th: "About nine o'clock (at night) when I had got about halfway from the place where I had embarked, the enemy who had undermined their fort, sprung their mine, which blew up with a loud explosion; the enemy being all ready to embark on board their boats and make a retreat."

ing the lake that night, and concluded to go ashore, make a fire, and there stay till morning unless the wind favoured. But before morning we found to our sorrow, that the wind was changed into the north-westward, that we could not prosecute our design without endangering our lives.

December 2nd. Wherefore in the morning we hauled on shore on the Point; (for before we were on an island) builded a fire, and there tarried until the 4th day; in which time we suffered some for want of victuals, but much more by reason of the cold, for it never was colder in my remembrance. We found on the Point a piece of pork, that was left by some people as they passed there and we had some meal or flour which we made dumplings of and boiled them with the pork, on which Colonel Miller, with the rest of us, fed very heartily.

Dec. 4th. The wind had been so high ever since we came on shore, that it was impossible for us to pass forward; but this day was a fine calm ; therefore we pushed forward very early and arrived at Fort George about sun down; having suffered very much by reason of the cold and for want of provisions. We pushed forward this night at far as Fort Edward.

Dec. 5th. Travelled to the Fly to Landlord Brown's.

Do 6th. Came down to Halfmoon.

Do 7th. Came down as far as Green Bush to the widow Lumese's.

Do 8. Travelled as far as the mills.

Do 9. By reason of the rain, I travelled no farther than Jordenears (Gardiniers?)

Do 10. Travelled as far as Sheffield.

Do 11, Tarried at Sheffield with Captain Doolittle.

Do 12. Took charge of a horse and pack of deer skins and beaver, for Captain Doolittle and marched to No. 1.

Do 13. Marched through the Green Woods and arrived at Blanford.

Do 14. Travelled to Springfield, leaving part of my pack of leather at Westfield.

Do 15. Rode to Brimfield to Samuel Shaw's.

Do 16. Arrived home to brother Daniel Mathew's at Brookfield.

Putnam's Journal 1760

After my arrival home I removed my quarters to Deacon Wm Witts' at New Brantree, and there tarried till some time in March, when unexpected to me, I received bearing orders from the Governor; in order to recruit for his Majesty's Service; and according to the method practised that year, received a commission[1] bearing date ye 11 of March 1760 ; under Colonel Abijah Willard[2] in Captain Thos. Beamans[3] Company. And being detained to recruit longer than I expected, I did not march with my company.

---

1. This commission is among the Putnam manuscripts in the library of Marietta College.
2. Abijah Willard was the son of Colonel Samuel Willard of Lancaster, Worcester county, Massachusetts, where he was born in the year 1722. He served in the army at the taking of Cape Breton, and rose to the rank of captain in the above campaign. Having recovered from his wound he commanded one of the Massachusetts regiments in the campaign of 1759, under Amherst, and in 1760 entered Montreal, by way of the lakes, with the army under the command of Brigadier General Haviland. In 1774, he was appointed a mandamus counsellor, in consequence of which he became very unpopular. While at Union, Connecticut, he was seized and held through the night in confinement, and next day found himself obliged to sign a declaration that he would not act, asking, at the same time forgiveness for having taken the oath of office On the morning of the 19th of April, 1775, he mounted his horse and was proceeding to Beverly, where he had a farm, to superintend the spring work. While on his way the uprising of the country led him to fear for his personal safety, and he turned his horse's head towards Boston, where he proposed to remain only a few days. He was caught by Gage's proclamation in a trap, and was too far compromised to return amongst his old neighbours. He subsequently accompanied the royal army to Halifax. Though offered a commission by General Howe, he refused, saying "he should never fight against his country." He was afterwards commissary to the British troops at New York, and in 1778 was proscribed, and his property confiscated. In July, 1783, he was one of the fifty-five petitioners, in the city of New York, to General Carleton for lands in Nova Scotia He settled (continued opposite)

June 2nd 1760. Began my march for the fourth campaign, and marched to Springfield, which was about thirty miles.

June 3. Tarried in Springfield because the muster master was not in town.

Do 4. Rode from Springfield to Blanford, and falling in company with Captain Howe, we agreed to travel together, till we joined our companies. He having a horse, I purchased part of him, put my pack on with his and our servants, and we travelled through the Green Woods, to Landlord Chaddock's.

Do 6. It rained very hard this day, so that we tarried there all day.

Do 7. Travelled to Garret Burgins at Sheffield.

Do 8. Sunday Travelled from Sheffield to Kinderhook to Mr. Van Buren's.

Do 9. Travelled to Fitches, an English tavern between Kinderhook and Green Bush.

Do 10. Travelled to Albany and lodged at Mr. Williams .

Do 11. Travelled to Md. Schuyler's at the Flats.

Do 12. Travelled to Stillwater.

Do 13. Travelled to Fort Miller, to Major Hawks' camp, where I lodged.

---

in New Brunswick and called the town Lancaster, after his native place in Massachusetts. He was a member of the Provincial Council and died at Lancaster, N. B., in May, 1789, aged 67 years. His estate in Massachusetts was redeemed by his family.
3. Captain Thomas Beaman adhered to the royal cause during the revolution.

June 14. Tarried with Major Hawks, and Captain Howe went forward.

Do 15. Sunday. Set out the morning and travelled to Fort George, where Captain Howe found his company and I lodged with him this night.

Do 16. Intended to cross the lake with Captain Jackson. Lighting of some of Captain Beaman's Company, that were, come over for stores, and were to return this day tarried for them; and about three o'clock set out in a bateau and arrived at Long Island about seven miles down the lake.

Do 17. Arrived at the sawmills near Ticonderoga.

Do 18. Arrived at Ticonderoga and joined Captain Thos. Beaman's Company, which was stationed for the present, at Ticonderoga, under the command of Colonel Miller. This detachment consisted of four companies.

June 20. Went on fatigue this day; also received news that the French had sent in about 150 of our English prisoners, who were received by Major Rogers at his post near Nut Island and the French sent back.

Do 22. Removed our camp to the landing place and Colonel Miller to the sawmills, leaving two companies at Ticonderoga. We were here employed in all kinds of duty, which was very fatiguing.

June 27. At night when sleeping I dreamed that I was at a wedding in Brookfield; but whose it was I could not tell, and when that was over, I was about to be married myself; but when I was dressed, I was one half in women's clothes, at which I was very much troubled. I also about this time dreamed that I was at Esquire Ayres' house in Brookfield, and that there was a cup of drink given me and that there was no person in the room but his daughter Betsey, to whom I drank. But she immediately passed out of the room, looking with a strange countenance, and I was left alone, very much damped in my spirits, to think that she, with whom I had been so well acquainted, and from whom I had never had the frown, should not take the cup and drink with me.[4]

August 10. From the 27th of June to this nothing material, but everything carrying on the campaign. And this day the army embarked, and sailed toward Saint Johns.

Do 16. Colonel Haverland[5] landed with the army of regulars and Provincials under his command at Isle Deaux.

Do 28. The enemy evacuated Isle Deaux.

Sept. 8th. Montreal capitulated to General Amherst.

Do 17. The Provincials that went down under the command of Colonel Haviland returned to Crown Point.

Oct. 14. General Amherst arrived at Crown Point.

Do 28. He passed our post.

Nov. 10. I went to Crown Point.

Do 23. Returned to the landing.

Do 18. Received orders to march to No 4.

---

4. Rufus Putnam married Elizabeth (Betsey) Ayres at Brookfield, Mass., April, 1761. She died within the year.
5. William Haviland, Lieutenant Colonel of the 27th or Inniskillen Regiment. He served with distinction in the campaign in America from 1757 to 1762, commanded a brigade in the siege of Savannah in August, 1762; was made colonel in 1767, lieutenant general in 1772, general in 1783 and died in 1788.

Do 19. Marched to Ticonderoga where we were detained on account of not having our bread baked.

November 20. Having crossed the lake by cutting the ice away; about half after 11 o'clock we began our march for No. 4 and come to camp about sundown, having marched about ten miles.

Do 21. Marched as soon as light in the morning, but being very much hindered by the sick men the Rhode Islands left behind, we marched but about twelve miles and then camped.

Do 22. Having marched about two miles this morning, we found a man of Captain Herrick's Company, dead, that had been left by Captain Howe as they told us; and found by Captain Paige. He left two men to take care of him, and they leaving him, he was left alone; and being in a fit, he fell into the fire and burnt himself so that his ribs lay bare; then having suffered much by reason of the cold for some days till Colonel Thomas came along, who left two of Captain Herrick's Company to take care of him; and he had not been dead eight minutes when we came up. From thence we marched about twelve miles and lodged.

November 23, 1760. Marched about two miles and breakfasted. About ten o clock we crossed Otter Creek, and from there we marched about eight miles and camped.

Do 24. Marched by a little after daybreak, and about 10 o'clock breakfasted. Yesterday afternoon we sent forward a man sick with the smallpox. Marched this night within about twenty miles of No. 4, where was an old encampment, and there lodged.

Do 25. Marched to No. 4.

Do 26. Marched to Westmoreland.

Do 27. To Keene.

Do 28. To Winchester.

Do 29. To Landlord Paige's at Petersham.

Do 30. To Solomon Matthews' at the south part of Petersham.

December 1st. Arrived home at Daniel Matthews' at New Braintree.
And now, soon after my return home, I concluded not to go into the service any more, not from any dislike to the service of my King and country, or any misfortunes in the service, for, through the goodness of divine providence, I was always prospered in some measure, and had my health entirely the whole four years that I have been out. And, although I underwent many hardships and difficulties; yet, by the good hand of my God upon me, I was enabled to bear up under them all.

(Remainder of the page torn off in the original journal.)

Appendix

Boston
21st of Feb., 1810.
Rufus Putnam, Esq.

Dear Sir: I expect this letter will be handed to you by Mr. Oliver Putnam, a very respectable merchant of this town, and whom I would recommend to your notice and particular attention. Any civilities shewn him will be thankfully acknowledged by me. Mr. Putnam, having mentioned to me, a few days since that he proposed setting out in a day or two on a visit to your part of the country, I mentioned to him my acquaintance with you, and that I wished to write you by him. For I presumed it would not be unpleasant to you to hear from an old friend, who had been your messmate during the campaign of 1757, and who had waded through the deep snow on the banks of the Hoosick river, and over the lofty mountains of that name, in the cold month of February, 1758, and reduced to the sad necessity of eating dog. Friendships formed on such trying occasions are not easily obliterated, and, I assure you that I still feel a lively friendship for you, and have often thought of writing you; but, no direct opportunity offering, have hitherto neglected it. You are the only one of my old comrades that I know of who is living. There may be others yet alive but I do not know where they dwell. I observed last summer in the newspapers, the insertion of the death of Samuel Wiswal. I expect you remember his leaving us at Fort Edward, soon after the taking of Fort William Henry.

I noticed in the public prints, a few years since, that T. Jefferson had honoured you, by removing you from an office bestowed upon you by the great and virtuous Washington, the real Father of his Country. Your removal from office is full evidence of your adherence to the principles of the good old Washington school, of which I avow myself to be a true disciple ; and the numerous removals of honest, capable men from office, and, in many instances, the vacancies so made by T. Jefferson filled again by him with d—d rascals, has excited my warmest indignation.

I consider that heaven, in its wrath, for the sins of our nation, permitted him to preside over our nation I did hope that his successor was fully convinced of the mad, weak and foolish measures of his immediate predecessor, and that he would administer the Government with impartiality; but I find myself disappointed, and that we are still to bear French insults and that Great Britain is to be treated with every possible insult, to provoke her to commence hostilities against us, and we thus compelled to go to war with her, and to form an alliance with the tyrant and scourge of Europe, which I pray heaven to avert.

You will see that this letter is dated at Boston. I came here about a month since, on a visit to my son and daughter, who live here; they being all the children I have. My daughter is married and her husband and my son are doing business together as merchants under the firm of Richards and Jones. My wife is still living, but has not enjoyed very good health for some years past, I have generally, enjoyed very good health, but now feel the infirmities of old age. I entered my 72nd year the 8th instant. I believe your age is not much different from mine. I came on from Machias to Boston by land, and expect to return again the same way, the fore part of next month. If you have any Federal Newspapers edited with you, the spirited resolutions passed by our legislature in their present session, will undoubtedly be published in them and you will read them with much satisfaction; they manifest the true spirit of 75. If you find it convenient to write to me. I assure you that it will be very acceptable to

Your old friend and Humble Servant,
Stephen Jones

Orderly Book and Journal of Major John Hawks on the Ticonderoga-Crown Point Campaign

Note

The manuscript *Orderly Book and Journal* of Major John Hawks came into the possession of Reverend Dr. George B. Spalding in 1865, while he was pastor of the North, now Park Congregational Church, Hartford, Conn. It is now the property of the Vermont Historical Society. The material which it contains relates to military operations which took place in the Province of New York in the successful campaign of General Jeffrey Amherst against Ticonderoga and Crown Point, in 1759. The Society of Colonial Wars of the State of New York has put this very valuable manuscript into this type-written form with the expectation that it will sometime be published.

The original book is now (1901), one hundred and forty-two years old. The paper is of standard English manufacture, of stoutest linen, stamped with the Coat of Arms of England. The writing is a fine specimen of the ancient clear penmanship. The writer, John Hawks, was born in Deerfield, Mass., December 5, 1707. He was among the bravest defenders of Fort Massachusetts in 1746. In 1754 he was commissioned as Lieutenant by Governor Shirley, and had charge of the Colrain Forts. He commanded a company in the Army of General Abercrombie at Fort Ticonderoga in 1758, and as Major with General Amherst the following year. He served as Lieutenant-Colonel in the successful Canadian campaign which closed the war. He died at Deerfield, Mass., June, 1784.

The "Orders" in his book from June 18, 1759 to July 13, 1759, were issued at Half Way Brook, about seven miles from

Fort Edward on the military road to Lake George. The troops at Half Way Brook formed a separate camp. They made up the First Battalion under the command of Brigadier-General Timothy Ruggles of Massachusetts.

The daily order appears at the head of each paragraph, and in case of the issue of a second order on any day it was headed as After Order.

The manuscript of this *Orderly Book and Journal* was in 1842 (nearly sixty years ago) in the hands of General Epaphras Hoyt, who held many civil and military offices in Massachusetts, and was an historian of distinction. General Hoyt made many explanatory notes on the text of the Orderly Book, which appear in full in this copy, greatly increasing its value.

George Burley Spalding
Syracuse, N.Y.
June 17, 1901

Introduction

In many respects this diary of Major John Hawks, which the Society of Colonial Wars in the State of New York has under taken to print, is remarkable in displaying the discipline that prevailed in the Provincial armies during the middle of the eighteenth century, and the general conduct of those armies. Although on sight, there would appear to be considerable matter that is extraneous, on deliberation it has been deemed advisable to print the diary as it is— making, of course, correction of errors that necessarily attend the transcription of original records.

These records are valuable to the historian and interesting to the layman. The original spelling has not been molested, except in instances where flagrant eccentricity might bewilder the mind not acquainted with it.

The military orders are conspicuous for the latitude allowed to subordinates. The militia chafed under the rigidity of the rules of war and the severe restrictions of camp life. Discipline offered no inducement to their independent souls. Ordinary infringements under the code encountered a punishment involving five hundred and even a thousand lashes of the cat-o-nine tails; the penalty of death was synonymous with desertion.

Particular stress was laid upon marksmanship. The gun of that day, seldom trustworthy in aim or velocity, was the long-barrelled weapon, the ammunition was not the fixed ammunition of today; the paper cartridge and ball were carried in cartouche boxes, the powder generally in a horn which was often carved in an ornate manner in token of the campaigns the owner participated in. The commanding officers were not always confident of the aim of the rank and file, for one officer is on record as declaring there were men who "never fired a gun off," at a time when modern civilization believed the average man was thoroughly proficient in handling firearms. Scalping of women and children was interdicted, with a warning of reprisal should the enemy transgress this merciful obligation.

The range of country covered during Jeffrey Amherst's memorable campaign is the most picturesque, topographically and historically, in the State of New York. History fairly bubbles at almost every foot from Albany to Crown Point. All the English-speaking armies that operated in upper New York during Colonial and Revolutionary days with the exception of the boastful Burgoyne's—were assembled, organized and began their campaigns at Albany. This venerable town was the general supply store of all the armies that operated to the north of it, from campaign to campaign. It has entertained and at times been the headquarters of the most distinguished English, Continental and American general officers who served in the American wars: General William Shirley; Sir William Johnson who owned a house there; General Abercrombie; Jeffrey Amherst; Philip Schuyler whose entertainments were the most lavish of the period; Thomas Gage who commanded the British forces at Boston at the outbreak of the Revolutionary War; Colonel William Eyre, the friend of Washington and of Braddock; Colonel William Haviland, subsequently the distinguished British General; John Stark; John Bradstreet; Israel Putnam; Charles Lee; David Wooster; the brothers Clinton—George afterward first Governor of New York, and James, later on in command of the northern department but better known as the father of DeWitt Clinton, the much-beloved Lord Howe who was killed at Ticonderoga and whose remains were escorted to Albany by Peter Schuyler and found a final resting place under the tower of the present St. Peter's Church at State and Chapel Streets. Many of the officers above mentioned, subsequently achieved distinction in the American Revolution.

French presumptuousness generated the disastrous tribulations that eventually culminated in the surrender of a French empire in America to England. Not satisfied with encroaching upon English territory at Crown Point, where they erected Fort Fredrich—the first of her insolent aggressions—the French authorities continued this offensive policy in other places and on other lines, until English patience gave way to English wrath and for thirty years the war raged with the destruction of the French regime in America.

Jeffrey Amherst never has been accorded full credit for masterful handling of military operations in America. Without exception he was the ablest general England ever sent to this country. Up to the time of Amherst's victory at Louisburg, the English arms had met reverse after reverse. It is true Sir William Johnson had defeated the gallant Dieskau at Lake George, but the fruit of that victory rotted on the ground because of Sir William's inactivity, of his over-caution and his lack of the instinct of a fighting soldier. John Forbes had been successful at Fort Duquesne, but Duquesne was a bloodless victory because of the abandonment of the post by the enemy. But Amherst's victory at Louisburg was the biggest nail driven into the French coffin in America.

The advantages gained by the French can be traced to two causes: incompetency of English generals and the contempt of the English for their adversaries. Braddock had been annihilated in Pennsylvania, Shirley balked at Niagara, Abercrombie discomfited at Ticonderoga and Colonel Monro massacred at Fort William Henry. Surely not a creditable record for a nation as powerful as the British, after three years of fighting?

The campaign of 1758 was laid on lines similar to that of 1755—three objectives. In 1755 the general plan contemplated the capture of Fort Duquesne by Braddock; of Fort Niagara by Shirley and of Ticonderoga and Crown Point by Sir William Johnson. The English scored one success and two failures. In 1758, England's greatest War Minister, William Pitt, with the determination of crushing the power of France in one campaign, organized the largest army America ever had seen, fifty thousand troops, of whom twenty thousand were Provincials.

The three objectives were Louisburg, which was assigned to Amherst; Fort Duquesne to General Forbes, Ticonderoga and Crown Point to General Abercrombie. In this campaign the British gained two victories and suffered one defeat. Louisburg succumbed to Amherst's brilliant generalship and Forbes encountered no especial obstacle in accomplishing the task, generally regarded as difficult, given to him. History has been unsparing in its denunciation of Abercrombie for permitting Montclam's four thousand, not only to check the advance of the English fifteen thousand but literally to put them to flight in "the extremist fright and consternation" from Lake Champlain to Lake George.

Amherst at Louisburg heard of the disaster to Abercrombie. Exercising the power vested in him as Commander in chief of his Majesty's forces in America and without waiting for orders, he assembled four regiments of the line and a battalion of Royal Americans, and sailed immediately for Boston. He landed at the Long Wharf in September. Delaying just long enough to replenish supplies, he marched his force through the woods to Albany. Here the troops were given a brief rest before the advance to Lake George was ordered. Unfortunately the season was too far advanced for hostile operations in that northern climate. In November, Abercrombie, relieved of command, returned to England.

In March, 1759, Amherst at Albany, began to assemble his army, the seventh England had organized for the conquest of Canada. The New England troops, Massachusetts, Connecticut and Rhode Island, gathered at Springfield. The first entry in the Hawk's diary is "Worcester, May 9th 1759." The second "Springfield, May 15th 1759." The next "Albany, 25th May, 1759." Six days later the Rhode Island regiment, under orders, with six days' provisions started for Fort Edward. At the same time a detail of two hundred men were directed to load battoes, which had been built at Albany, and proceed to Half Moon. On the thirty-first all the guards of the Royal Highlanders were relieved by Connecticut troops and the remainder of the command was ordered to be ready to move at a moment's notice.

June 7th the army was encamped at Fort Edward, the troops having marched over the old state road, which Sir William Johnson had put in excellent repair three years before, the supplies having been transported up the Hudson River in battoes. Here the troops were regaled with spruce beer, and discipline was tightened. The lines for the encampment were established, firing at marks was practised and details were selected to work on the roads. Careful attention was given to firearms. Indiscriminate firing was prohibited, arms were ordered to be kept clean and in good order, damaged cartridges turned in to the proper officer and commissary supplies provided for seven days. Arrangements were also made with the contractors for interchanging food where quantities were disproportionate or not sufficient or on the choice of a regiment preferring different proportions.

June 18th the troops were advanced to Half Way Brook, four miles, midway between Fort Edward and Lake George. Discipline here becomes more alert and severe. Special orders are given the guards and the pickets; officers to be extra vigilant on their outposts, to permit only two men to lie down at a time and to make their rounds very regularly; no man on any account to stray beyond the line of sentries, severe punishment to accompany any infraction. At the same time the morals of the men were not overlooked. Card-playing in camp was forbidden, an hour a day for exercise prescribed, profanity barred, and whoever is found guilty of disobeying the injunction against making noise in camp after tattoo, "will be took as a despiser of the martial law"!

June 20, Amherst issued orders for the main force to march to Lake George, where he arrived the following day "and encamped on its woody banks" an "intolerably hot day" "bringing unendurable discomfort to men and animals." During the four weeks following Amherst was a very busy man. His total force aggregated 11,133 of whom 5,279 were Colonial troops.

July 21st he "took the field" and passed down the lake, selecting for his camp the spot where Abercrombie disembarked the year before. The pressure on Quebec had forced the French commander to weaken the supports at Ticonderoga. When Amherst appeared the garrison consisted of scarcely twenty-three hundred men. Bourlemaque, the French commander, perceived at a glance the hopelessness of resistance and speedily made plans for withdrawing the main body of his force. Leaving Hebecourt with four hundred troops to mask the movement and with instructions to blow up the works as soon as the English batteries were established, he struck out through the wilderness for Crown Point and Canada. For two days the faithful little band of Frenchmen who had been left as a forlorn hope taught the British who trespassed within the zone of their gun fire several varieties of the strenuous life.

Amherst resolutely pushed forward his approaches, and had established his batteries within six hundred yards of the fort on the night of the 26th, when Hebecourt decided the hour had arrived to carry out Bourlemaque's orders. He loaded and pointed every gun, charged several mines, and lighted a fuse that connected with the overstocked powder magazine. The roar that followed was heard for miles. Flying, flaming and blazing embers and wreckage hurled through the air, set tiny fires to buildings that had escaped the general havoc.

At daylight the French flag on the fort was hauled down and the English flag was run to the staff head. The flames were extinguished. The fort itself was not seriously injured.

The diary supplies interesting information regarding the conduct of the troops before and after the fall of Ticonderoga, of the expedition of Major Robert Rogers to Crown Point and of the grave preparations of the army "under orders for marching for the reduction of all Canada."

August 4th, Amherst, arrived at Crown Point to find Bourlemaque had blown up the works. Acting under instructions from Pitt, he outlined the mammoth fortress upon which the English expended ten millions of dollars, which never was completed, and which to day is the most picturesque ruins in New York and one of the most beautiful in the country.

Hugh Hastings

Major John Hawks Orderly Book & Journal

July 26, 1759

About of two o'clock at night the French Blew up Fort Ty-anterogue after we besieged it four days.[1,2]

Regimental Orders
Worcester, May 9th, 1759

That all the troops that belong to General Ruggles' regiment that have passed muster by the regular muster master to get themselves ready to march tomorrow morning by sunrise.

The captains are to make a victualling return immediately to the adjutant to have all things ready to march early tomorrow morning. The captain will apply to Colonel John Chandler for carriages for their men. Captain Baldwin and Reed and Cox has two carriages for their three companies. Captain Nixon Willard and Williams has two carriages and Captain Whiting one and Captain Pain one and Captain Furnace one

---

1. The manuscript "Orderly Book" opens with an announcement of the destruction of Fort Ticonderoga. It was written by Major Hawks on the cover of the book under date of July 26, 1759. I therefore give this entry, and the note thereon by General Hoyt, the first place.
George B. Spalding.
2. Orderly Book for the campaign of 1759 and 1760, on the upper Hudson, Lake George and Champlain. Many of the orders are dated at Halfway Brook near Glens Falls, where small forts were kept up in 1758 and 1759, and some of the ruins may still be seen (in 1841). In 1760 the major rose to the rank of Lieutenant Colonel, and he saw much active military service both in the war of 1744 and that of 1755.—E. Hoyt.

and Captain Maynard one and Captain Butterfield one and it is expected that the commanding officers of every company comply with these orders.

Regimental Orders
Springfield, May 15, 1759

Let every man take out his provisions one days allowance. The rest with all his baggage to be sent to the river immediately in order to be conveyed by carts and that five men with one sergeant one corporal out of every company be paraded at the Black Horse forthwith in order to march as guards for the carts, By order of General Ruggles.

P. S. That Lieutenant Thomas Farington march ahead of the guard.

Albany, May 25, 1759
Parole, Glasgow

Rhode Island Regiment, to be ready to march at the least notice. Surgeon McCalm of the Royal to attend the hospital at Fort Edward and Mr. Bray mate of the hospital to do duty with the Royal as a surgeon. The Massachusetts troops be furnish out twenty-five teamsters and they are to be sent immediately to Colonel Bradstreet, a working party of hundred men with two subalterns, two sergeants, two corporals.

Albany, May 26, 1759
Parole, Guernsey

The Provincial regiment to be very exact when they send any man to the King's Hospital that they may have proper certificates of their names, regiment and company signed by an officer of the Company specifying the regiment they belong to; As wagons now are wanted for the service of the troops all sutlers, merchants etc. are to have paper to follow the army. They are for the future to make use of all carts in the same manners as regimental sutlers. Orders have been sent to the different post to stop all wagons. Officers shall pay for all horses they press when their duty requires it. Those of the regiments are to apply to the major brigade, the Artillery to their own commanding officer the engineer to the chief engineer.

The hospital to the director of the hospital for the payment; each account are to be laid before the commander-in-chief to allow the same if reasonable; Officers not to neglect to leave proper certificates to the drawers of wagons employed to carry baggage for the troops. Mentioning the time they have been employed to carry baggage for the troops; Complaint have been made for their omission.

The general court martial of which Colonel Grant is president to meet again tomorrow morning at eight o'clock; Baggage forage money to be paid to the several regiments immediately.

As the Provincials arrive the commanding officers are to apply to Mr. Lake for provision that he may be enabled when the whole of each regiment is arrived to proportion the delivery of provisions that they may all receive it to the same day; An officer and twenty-nine men of the Royal Highland Regiment with a week's provision to be sent to the widow McGenness' house to protect the settlement, two subalterns, two sergeants, two corporal and 100 private men of Colonel Ruggles' regiment for the fatigue, officers excepted; he will go his rounds and visit all guards and out post to see that the whole are alert and properly placed. And inform the colonel, who relieves him of the several guards and posts and time that he visited them.

Divine service to be performed every Sunday at the head of the regiment. A general court martial to set tomorrow morning at eight o'clock to try such prisoners as are in the private guard, all evidences are to attend president, Colonel Montgomery and Meerces; two from the Masa. and one from the Rhode Islanders members Lieutenant George Burton of the Royal Deputy Judge Advocate to whom the members names dates of commissions and the evidences names are to be sent at six o'clock this afternoon.

A marquee to be pitched on the centre of the lines where the court martial will assemble and a sergeant and twelve men of Montgomery's regiment to serve as a guard whilst the court martial is a letting; The Royal Highlanders and Montgomery's regiment to send as many men this afternoon at four o'clock as necessary to clear the ground. They will receives axes on applying to the store keeper in the fort: which they will return when they will have finished that work. The sergeant guards on the battoes to be reduced to a corporal and six men. As by the order of the 7th it was said that spruce beer would be brewed for the army it is not thereby intended to hinder any of our people from brewing spruce beer; All sutlers are at liberty to brew as much as they will; The general guards, magazines, artillery provost, battoes to be relieved every eighteen hours.

FORT EDWARD, MONDAY JUNE 11TH, 1759
PAROLE, NORFOLK

Colonel of this day, Colonel Grant; for tomorrow Colonel Schayler; Field Officer for the piquet, Major Campbell; tomorrow Lieutenant Colonel Hunt.

Each regiment will make a path to their front for their piquet to advance to in case of any alarm in the night. And that the regiment should be ordered out. No regiment is on any account whatsoever to fire a shot from their lines. The piquet will be ordered out and they will be supported.

Spruce beer is to be brewed for the health and convenience of the troops which will be served at prime cost; five quarts of meloses will be put into every barrel of spruce beer. Each gallon will cost near three coppers. The quarter masters of regiments regular and Provincial is to give notice this evening to Colonel Robinson of the quantity each corps is desirous to receive for which they must give receipt and pay the money before the regiment marches; each regiment to send a man acquainted with brewing or that is best able to assist the brewery tomorrow morning at six o'clock at the reveille. On the left of Montgomery those men are to remain and to be paid at the rate of 1s. 6d. per day a sergeant of the regulars and one of the Provincial to superintend the brewery who will be paid at 1s. 6d. per day. Spruce beer will be delivered to the regiment on Thursday night or Friday morning;

Tomorrow morning one subaltern, one sergeant, three corporals and thirty-two men to mount a guard on the island. He will detach a corporal and six men to take care of the battoes and a corporal and six men to take care of the whale boats.

To parade tomorrow morning at six o'clock two sergeants, two corporals and twenty four privates to parade for the town guard.

Albany, May 28, 1759
Parole, Mastrick

The Connecticut, Massachusetts and New Jersey troops are to send each a quarter master to Mr. Furniss, Controller of ordinances, at four clock this afternoon; They will receive arms for their several detachments ordered this day to march. Tomorrow morning they will receive also nine rounds of ammunition and the Rhode Island regiment sent as above will receive nine rounds of ammunition. Each man for this detachment Money Penny; The following detachment to be made from the Provincial troops. They are to take proper men for the battoe service, to find *viz*:

	Captain	Lieutenant	Sergeant	Per
The Connecticut	2	7	10	240
The Massachusetts	1	4	4	140
New Jersey	1	3	4	140
Rhode Island	1	2	0	54

This detachment is to parade tomorrow morning at five o'clock on the road on the right of the Rhode Islanders and wait till Brigadier-Major Moneypenny sees them march of; They are to take their arms proportion of camp necessaries and as many days provisions as they have received; Three wagons will be allowed for the Connecticut forces, two for the Massachusetts troops, two for the Jerseys, one for the Rhode Island troops to carry their tents; On sending to Mr. Coventry, a D.Q.M.G. This detachment perhaps stay out some months will be paid as per order of the 23 of May. This detachment tomorrow to go to Schenacety. An officer of each corp. will go forward when the detachment marches and to apply to Captain McClean of

Schenacety who has orders to mark out the ground for their encampment. The commanding officer will report to the commissary of provisions at Schenacety to what time they are provided. And will afterwards receive provisions from the stores. The Connecticut forces will remain at Schenacety and the commanding officer of each corps will receive particular orders when to march from thence; All the Provincial troops are to provide themselves immediately with everything they will have occasion for that they may be ready to march at the least notice.

AFTER ORDERS
CONCERNING THE MELANCHOLY DEATH
OF SAMUEL HARRIS &C.

The general court martial of which Colonel Grant was president is dissolved: The general has approved of the following sentences of the general court martial; John Haron soldier in Captain Bartlet's Company in the Rhode Island regiment is to receive one thousand lashes with a cat of nine tails; James Conolly, soldier in Captain Russel's Company in the seventeenth regiment is to receive one thousand lashes with a cat of nine tails; William Carrege, soldier in Captain Wealls' Company of the second battalion of the Royal Regiment of Foot accused of being accessory to the death of John McLeland soldier in said Company, is found not guilty of wilful murder and is requited. David Rogers, Corporal in Captain Ross's Company in the Rhode Island regiment is found guilty of desertion laid to his charge and is to suffer death. Samuel Harris, soldier in the Rhode Island regiment is found guilty of desertion laid to his charge and is to suffer death. Peter McMartin, soldier in Colonel Montgomery's regiment found guilty of mutiny that is laid to his charge and is to suffer death:

The Royal Highland Regiment Massachusetts, New Jerseys, Connecticut, Rhode Island troops to be out tomorrow morning at five o'clock leaving of proper guards for the care of the camp and to march immediately to the ground that will be marked out for them by the quarter master of the Royal Highland Regiment at six this evening, for which purpose a quarter master of each of the Provincials will attend; The troops are to be drawn up, the Royal Highlanders on the right, Massachusetts on the left, Connecticut on the left of the Royal Highlanders, New Jerseys on the right of the Massachusetts, Rhode Islanders on the centre. The detachment ordered this day for Schenacety is not to march till the execution is over and is to be drawn up on the left of the Massachusetts troops. They will afterwards march when Brigade Major Monypenny will direct them a platoon of the Rhode Island regiment to be drawn in the front of that regiment to be loaded with ball ready for the execution. The provote guard to march the two prisoners, David Rogers and Samuel Harris at six o'clock tomorrow morning from the prison to the right of the line and in the front of the centre where the execution is to be. A chaplain is to attend on the prisoners. Colonel Grant, colonel of the day tomorrow; Brigadier General Gage to command the whole.

Albany, May 29, 1759

Regimental orders for the first battalion of Colonel Ruggles' regiment: that a return from each company be made of what arms and acquirements are wanting to complete the battalion; likewise that a victualling return be made immediately that the places of cooking be on the side of the hill and no where else excepting officers, that the men attend every night at the beating of the retreat, and that an officer from each company likewise attend the same time; and it is further ordered that no non-commissioned officer or soldier lodge out of the camp after roll calling on whatsoever pretence. Per order of Joseph Ingels, Lieutenant Colonel

Albany Wednesday May 30th, 1759
Parole, Albany

The Rhode Island Regiment to march tomorrow morning for Fort Edward. They will strike their tents tomorrow morning at 5 o'clock. Their baggage is to go by water. They will apply to

Colonel Bradstreet for battoes for that purpose. They will likewise take up twenty battoes loaded with provisions which they are to load this evening. The regiments to be completed with six days provisions. A detachment of 200 men are to take battoes this after noon at four o'clock which they will load tomorrow morning at five o'clock and proceed with them to Half Moon, where they will deliver them to the commanding officer and then return to Albany in scows if any there.

For this detachment	Captain	Lieutenant	Sergeant	Privates
New Jerseys	1	4	4	100
Massachusetts	1	2	2	50
Connecticut	0	2	2	50
First Battalion	1	1	1	22

Albany, May 31st, 1759

Regimental Orders: For the first battalion of Colonel Ruggles' regiment that the captain or commanding officers of companies see that all the balls fit the men's guns so that they may run down their barrels and to have everything ready to march tomorrow morning by five o'clock. those that have not cartouche boxes must break their cartridges and put their powder into horns It is further expected that all their arms are clean and in good order. An officer from each company to see it done as soon as may be. The commanding officer of companies to give in returns of their effective men that is able to march to the adjutant immediately. Per order of Joseph Ingersoll, Lieutenant Colonel

A regimental court martial to be held at nine o'clock for the trial of John Williams and Henry McNeal and Elias Peter kow Dowick: for these Captain Nixon, president, Lieutenant Warrington, Lieutenant Cabourn, Lieutenant David Joy and Ensign Adam Wheeler, members.

Camp Albany, May 31st
Parole, Somerset

All the guards of the Royal Highland regiment to be relieved at four o'clock this afternoon by the Connecticut troops. They are to march tomorrow at five o'clock where they will take the Artillery under their care and escort to send to Fort Edward one wagon for a company, one for the commanding officer, and one for the staff officers and to be allowed to the regiment to take six days provisions with them. The women to be allowed four pence per day in lieu of provision which will be paid on applying to Lieutenant Coventry, D.Q.M.G. The Massachusetts troops are to take up eighty battoes this afternoon at three o'clock and load them with provisions, reserving six for their tents and baggage which they will load at five o'clock and proceed to Fort Edward. They are to take nine days' provisions with them. Colonel Ruggles will leave careful officers here to bring up those men that he doth expect to join them.

Major Orde to put the Artillery and stores into scows this evening which are to proceed to Half Moon tomorrow morning and to be escorted to Fort Edward as above; The regiments of Colonel Lyman and Fitch and Schayler to be ready to march on the first notice. Colonel Lyman and Fitch to leave proper officers here to bring the men which are left behind. Each officer commanding a company to remove their sick, who are unable to march, into the King's Hospital taking great care that the general orders are observed with respect to leaving certificates. A commissioned officer in each battoe to take care that no damage be done or disorder committed; a sergeant corporal and twelve privates Over the battoes this night; the tents to be struck and removed on board the battoes tomorrow morning at sunrise; the sergeant commanding the guard, to reserve six battoes for the tents and officers baggage. A daily return to be made of the state of the men's arms. Per order of Timothy Ruggles, B. G.

CAMP AT FORT EDWARD, JUNE 7TH, 1759
PAROLE, RICHELIEU

The regiment are not to change their encampment until the ground is quite dry; The regiments on their arriving here are all to give in a return to what time they have received provision that the particular time for the delivery to each corps may be hereafter regulated. It have been reported by the commissaries that waste has been made as the daily allowance for each man is fully sufficient if any have drawn for and expended more than the allowance they must make it good in the having overplus deducted in the allowance they are hereafter to receive. The regiments are to take for their effective. Only the commanding officers are to certify their number of their respective company on the issuing the provisions and the officers commanding the regiments to examine and see the whole is just.

Spruce beer will soon be brewed for the army. It is hoped sufficient for the whole and will cost men but a very moderate price.

Fort Edward, June 8th, 1759
Parole, Falmouth

Field officer for the piquet this day Lieutenant Colonel Salterson, for tomorrow Lieutenant Colonel Ingersoll. The field officer will go his round as usual and deputy adjutant general before orderly time one subaltern and thirty men for the general guard.

No man to go beyond the sentinel in line of block houses upon any account whatsoever except when sent out with a covering party. One sergeant and twelve men to mount guard at each of the provision sheds. One subaltern and thirty men as a guard over the battoes. The regiments to change their encampment at 1 o'clock.

Camp Fort Edward, June 9, 1759
Parole, Plymouth

Field officer for the piquet this night, Lieutenant Colonel Ingersoll for tomorrow Major Graham:

The detachment in garrison in the fort to encamp at five o'clock this afternoon on the left of the Light Infantry of the Royal Highland Regiment which is the ground the Royal regiment will encamp on. All sutlers who have paper and are not attached to regiment are to be encamped together on the ground. The deputy quartermaster general will mark out for them at 10 o'clock this day which ground is to be the centre of the line of the army and the market to be kept there for felling whatsoever the sutlers may have for the army.

The provote guard shall encamp there to keep good orders; the lights are not to be suffered at night and none of the soldiers are to be permitted to stay there after retreat beating; the sutlers are to encamp on this ground at four o'clock this day and none to be permitted to remain on the glacis of the fort: the Light Infantry of the Royal Highland Regiment is to practise firing of balls tomorrow morning at six of the o'clock near the Royal block house on the other side of the river. The camp not to be alarmed, the subalterns guards on the battoes to be taken of. And two guards to be posted in lieu there of a sergeant and fifteen men on this side the river and a sergeant and fifteen men on the island. It is a standing order that no dropping are fired; whensoever there are any fire locks which can not be drawn a report is to be made thereof that they may be collected together and fired of when the camp is advertised of it that this may be no unnecessary alarm. The Indians to be particular with these orders which if they disobey they shall be severely punished.

After Orders for the 9th of June, 1759

The Royal two subs, and seventy men of the Royal Highland Regiment to furnish six captains, twelve subalterns and 600 men.

This detachment to take battoes tomorrow morning at day break. The Royal will take ten battoes and the Royal Highlanders two hundred, and sixty of the two hundred men with arms to serve as a covering. The Massachusetts will take as many as they can man; Major Rogers will furnish forty rangers to serve as a covering party. The whole to take provisions for tomorrow with them. They are to proceed to Colonel Havilands who will order the battoes to be immediately loaded that the whole party may return to Fort Edward without loss of time. For this duty, Lieutenant Colonel Saltenstole and Major Hawks.

Camp Fort Edward, June 10th, 1759
Parole, Jersey

Field officer for the piquet, Major Graham; for tomorrow Major Connelly; Colonel of the day, tomorrow Colonel Grant.

All reports from the field officers of the piquet and extraordinaries that may happen in camp are to be made to the colonel of the day. All guards are to turn out to the colonel of the day only general. This guard to be relieved every 48 hours, the whole to take their tents and provisions with them and the guards on the Island to come of; orderly times at 10 o'clock in the morning and the adjutant to attend at six in the evening for whatever after orders there may be; The general guards tomorrow, Colonel Montgomery, the piquet and out-guards to load with running balls that there may be no waste of ammunition.

After Orders for the 11th of June

One field officer, six captains, twelve subalterns, eighteen sergeants 600 rank and file to be paraded immediately after the reveilles beating tomorrow morn to march to repair the roads. They may go in their wast coat but must carry their provisions with them. One half must carry their arms and the other half, spades and shovels. Major Graham, Field Officer: the Massachusetts must find one captain three subalterns four sergeants and 150 rank and file.

Camp at Fort Edward June 12th, 1759
Parole, Pitt

Colonel of the day Colonel Schayler, for tomorrow Colonel Ruggles; Field Officer of the piquet, Major Hawks and tomorrow Major Ruggles. The Royals, Prideaux, and Royal Artillery to receive provisions tomorrow for six days which will be to the 18th inclusive; the Royal and Royal Artillery at six o'clock predeux at the Royal block house to be relieved tomorrow by the lines of the one joining the brigade on the west side by one sergeant one corporal and twelve men of the Royal.

The one joining the east end of the parade by one subaltern

two sergeant two corporal and twenty-four men of the Massachusetts. The sergeant will be strictly observant of the orders that they receive from those they relieve and such as are wrote up in each block house they must take care to keep their block houses swept clean and they are to be answerable for the tools they have received, *viz*: axes, pickaxes, spades and shovels and water buckets to each of the block houses, which they will deliver over to the officer who relieves him. those guards to be relieved daily. Predeaux to be relieved to camp at the least notice: The several companies of Colonel Ruggles' regiment to be immediately completed with sergeants and corporals and all the watch coats that are dispersed in the several companies to be immediately paraded.

General After Orders, for the 12th of June 1759

It is the general orders that no scouting party or others in the army under his command shall whatsoever opportunity they may have scalp any women or children belonging to the enemy. They are to bring them away if they can, if not they are to leave them unhurt and we are determined if the enemy mould murder or scalp any women or children who are subject to the King of England, he will be revenged by the death of two of the enemies whenever he hast occasion for every woman or child so murdered by the enemy.

Camp at Fort Edward Wednesday June 13th 1759
Parole, Lewisburgh

Colonel of the day tomorrow Colonel Badcak. Field Officer for the piquet tomorrow Lieutenant Colonel Hunt.

The Royal Highland regiment to strike their tents at the reveille beating and to be joined by a detachment of the Provincials commanded by a field officer and the detachment to consist of 500 men rank and file. For this duty Lieutenant Colonel Pearson two six pounder with an officer and twelve men of the Royal Artillery and ammunition in proportion to march with said detachment. Captain Stark with his company of Rangers will join the detachment from the Four Mile post and the companies of Indians will be likewise ordered to join them. Colonel Grant will receive further orders from the general.

A wagon to each company and one for the Staff Officers and five for the 500 Provincials will be allowed to carry their baggage. The officers of the Provincials that command this detachment will send immediately to complete their men with thirty-six rounds of ammunition, and to be carefully examined and if any cartridges be damaged and if their horns will not hold it they are to take what their horns will hold. The arms likewise must be looked over and put in good order.

The Royal Highlanders posted in the block houses as by order of yesterday to be relieved by Prideaux's regiment immediately. The Provincial troops are to complete their provisions to the 19th inclusive. The grand parade is on the right of the Grenadiers. Ordinary guards to parade at 7 o'clock. Adjutant of the day tomorrow of the Royal General Guards, Massachusetts, one subaltern, one sergeant, one corporal and one drummer and twenty-nine private men.

CAMP AT FORT EDWARD, THURSDAY 14TH JUNE 1759
PAROLE, LANCASTER

Colonel of the day tomorrow, Colonel Montgomery. Field officer for the piquet, Lieutenant Colonel Saltentoll.

The general court martial of which Colonel Montgomery was president is dissolved and the general has been pleased to approve of the following sentences: Andrew Gates, soldier in Colonel Montgomery's regiment is to receive 1000 lashes with a cat of nine tails; John Elsworth, of the Rhode Island regiment is to receive 500 lashes with a cat of nine tails. Thos. Smith, of Captain Crookshanks Independent Company is to receive 100 lashes with a cat of nine tails. John Joaslen, Reuben Brown, Ephriam Knight to receive 500 lashes apiece. Thos. Smith, of the Independent Company is to receive his punishment in the following manner: this day to be marched by the provost guard to the right of the line and is to receive no lashes at the head of each of the following Corps: Predeaux Grenadiers and Light Infantry Montgomery and Jersey regiment

Simon Fitch and Rhode Island regiment first and 2nd Battalions of the Massachusetts Grenadiers and Light Infantry is supposed one corps, a mate of the hospital to attend the punishment. The Grenadiers and Light Infantry to be in the Waitcoats and legions. The Royal Highlanders and Predeaux Light Infantry and Montgomery's Grenadiers and Light Infantry on the hill on the right of the block house in the front of the Massachusetts. The eldest captain of both parties will receive their orders from the general at or before two o'clock. Spruce beer will be delivered to the Regiments tomorrow morning. Predeaux at six in the morning, the Grenadiers and Light Infantry half hour after, Montgomery at 7 o'clock, the Royal Artillery half hour after, and the Jersey regiment at eight o'clock, Connecticut half an hour after, the Rhode Islanders at 9 o'clock, the Massachusetts half an hour after; The quartermaster or an officer of each of the corps will attend on Lieutenant Colonel Robinson at six o'clock this evening at the brewery to fix the quantity that each is to receive.

After Orders for Thursday, June 14th, 1759

The quartermaster and captain, colourmen of Brigadier Predeaux Regiment to be ready when Lieutenant Colonel Robinson calls for them; the Grenadiers and Light Infantry to be ready to change their encampments when ordered.

Camp Fort Edward, Friday June 15th, 1759
Parole, Sussex

Colonel of the day tomorrow; Field officer of the piquet today Lieutenant Colonel Ingersoll.

The Light Infantry and Grenadiers to change their camp this after noon at two o'clock to take their ground in the front of the block house on the hill as Lieutenant Colonel Robinson has marked out; a wagon to each company will be allowed to each company to carry their tents at two o'clock this afternoon to march in half an hour after to the Halfway Brook where the officers commanding the regiment.

Such orders as he will receive from Colonel Grant. Ten wagons will be allowed to carry the tents of the companies and one for Lieutenant Colonel Eyre and another for the staff officers.

A general court martial to set this day at 12 o'clock for the trial of a deserter of Colonel Fitch's regiment at the president's tent. president Colonel Schayler, Major Campbell, Major Hawks two captains of the Royal, two of Montgomery's, one of the Royal Artillery, two of the Massachusetts, and three of the Connecticut troops members. Lieutenant George Barten of the Royal Deputy Judge Advocate. All the evidences are to attend.

Continuation of the Orders June 15th, 1759

Predeaux regiment having been countermanded to march tomorrow morning, they will strike their tents at reveilles beating and march in half an hour after; the commanding officer is to take under his escort the battoes or wagons loaded with artillery he will proceed with the same to Halfway Brook and follow such further orders as he shall receive from Colonel Grant.

It having been further reported to the general that some of the wagons have been to much loaded, the general would have no greater weights put into the wagons than Colonel Bradstreet directs.

The general court martial of which Colonel Schayler was president is dissolved the general approves of the sentence of the court martial for the trial of John Williams of Colonel Fitch's regiment and that he is to suffer death for the desertion proved against him. The piquet of the line to assemble tomorrow at six o'clock for the execution of the above prisoner. The commanding officer of each piquet will march his piquet to the right of Colonel Fitch's regiment where the field officer of the piquet will take the command of the said. piquet and obey such orders as he shall receive of the colonel of the day. Colonel Fitch's regiment to be under arms at six o'clock. A platoon to be loaded with ball and formed at the front of the regiment for the above execution. A chaplain to attend on the prisoner. Adjutant of the day, of Montgomery's Regiment General Guards N. Jerseys.

Fort Edward Saturday June 16th, 1759

Regimental orders for the first battalion the commanding officers of companies will not allow the soldiers who are for any guards to march on the parade without first examining of them and see them clean and their arms clean and in good order as they must answer for the neglect of this duty, if neglected; the battalion to turn out on the front of the camp at after six this evening. Except those on duty it is expected that the commissioned officers do not wear Scotch bonnets but wear something that they may be distinguished as officers. Per order of Joseph Ingersoll, Lieutenant Colonel

General Orders Fort Edward, June 16th, 1759
Parole, Boston

Colonel of the day tomorrow, Colonel Lyman. Field officer of the piquet this night, Lieutenant Colonel Ingersoll; for tomorrow Major Campbell, Colonel Whiting's regiment

Other regiments of the Provincials as they arrive must immediately put their arms in thorough good order, their cartridges must be examined into and if any are damaged must be new made to complete their number of cartridges and all Provincial troops are now to receive by applying to the Commanding officer of the Royal Artillery, ammunition sufficient to complete the whole with thirty-six rounds if their horns will hold it and if not they must take no more than their horns will contain and ball in proportion. The whole army to receive provision for seven days. The regular Regiments will receive theirs on the eighth and the seven days will be to the 25th inclusive. The quartermasters to give in tomorrow night the number of men they draw for to Mr. Willistone the Commissary who will fix the hour they draw for their receiving the next morning. The Provincial troops to receive theirs on 19th, sending the quartermaster on the 18th in the same manner as directed for the regulars, and they will receive accordingly and it will be for the 26th inclusive.

Any regiments that arrive who have received provisions to different times to what the troops here have done will complete now to the time as ordered.

John Williams of Colonel Fitch's regiment who was sentenced to suffer death is pardoned. The Commanding officers of Provincial regiments will examine what number of men they which are not marksmen; Some they might have who never fired a gun in their lives. A return to be sent to the deputy adjutant. General to be sent tomorrow morning at nine o'clock of their number that the whole may be ordered out to fire at a mark and any of the damaged cartridges may be allowed for this service which they will likewise make a report of; Adjutant of the day of the Royal.

Continuation of the Orders of the 16th

The first Battalion of General Ruggle's regiment to march at the least notice.

Camp at Ford Edward, Sunday June 17th, 1759
Parole, London

Colonel of the day tomorrow, Colonel Ruggles. Field officer of the piquet this night, Major Campbell. For tomorrow Major Ball.

The first Battalion of the Massachusetts troops to strike their tents at 2 o'clock this afternoon if they receive no order to the contrary. Three ox teams will be allowed to carry their tents and a fourth if necessary.

The Royal and New Jerseys to be ready to march on the least notice. All the species of provisions which the contractors have engaged to furnish the troops for to be delivered when the several species are in store, but if the men's necessary demand for carriages should prevent the most bulky articles from being brought to the army or that the contractors of stores may not at all have in his power to furnish a sufficient supply of every specie in either of these cases, if the regiment chooses, they may receive one article in lieu every time of another in the following proportions: if pease are wanting if one half of the quantity of rice or a pound of bread or flour or a third of a pound of pork may be received in lieu of pease or rice. If any pease, rice and butter are wanting one pound one quarter of pork or three and a half of bread or flour may be received in lieu thereof. If the above provisions be taken in lieu of these species that may not be in store. The regiments will then give receipts of their full rations.

General Guard, first regiment of the Connecticut, Adjutant of the day, Montgomery; the first Battalion of the Massachusetts will receive their provisions at Halfway Brook.

Continuation of Orders of the 17th, 1759

Surgeon McCalm of the Royal having represented to the general that his health will admit of serving the campaign, Mr. Bray Surgeon, mate of the hospital, to return to the hospital.

Whenever a flag a truce or drum may arrive from the enemy with whatsoever party may be sent, they are to be stopped by the first sentry of whatsoever advanced post they come to, which sentry will give notice to the guard that the officer commanding at the post may be informed of it. The officer will send the letter or letters to the general and will keep the drummer or party with flag a truce, so that they cannot see any of the post outworks or camps till the answer from the general is returned. If any officer should be sent with a letter who may say he has orders to deliver his letter or dispatch to the general himself, and will not give them to anyone else, he is not on any account whatsoever to be permitted to advance through any of the outpost, but shall be kept till he delivers his dispatches and remains there for an answer; if he persist and in not delivering them he is to be kept and the officers commanding the post to send a report of it to the general. A proper guard always to be given from the post for the security and protection of those that may be sent.

After orders for the first Battalion of Massachusetts being under orders for marching to strike their tents at reveilles beating and march half an hour after to the Halfway Brook, where the commanding officer will put himself under the command of Colonel Grant. They are to take under their escort the wagons which are to set out very early.

All the men returned by the Provincial regiments not to be marksmen, are to assemble tomorrow morning in the front of their regiment They will then march to the left to the ground where the Massachusetts fired this evening and will fire five rounds a man; Major [Robert] Rogers will take care the grounds in front is clear. Officers of each regiment to attend to see that the men level well.

Camped at Halfway Brook, Monday, June 18th, 1759
Parole, Westminster

The Massachusetts troops with officers to give 100 men at six o'clock tomorrow morning to clear the roads above their camps toward the lake. Lieutenant Rope of the 55th will give them directions.

All the guards and piquet to be under arms about half an hour before day break and remain so until it is clear daylight until the morning scout returns; the officers to be very alert on their outpost and to allow about their men to lay down to a time; the sentries to be relieved every hour.

The officers of the piquet to make their rounds very regularly.

No man is allowed upon any account to go beyond the sentries of the outpost for which the officers are to give their sentries strict charge and whatsoever person is found disobeying these orders shall be severely punished. Twenty men to assist the men of artillery in sorting their tools at six o'clock.

Regimental Orders
Camp Halfway Brook, June 18th 1759

No person on whatsoever account to pass the brook this and the other encampments to them, without liberty from the commanding officer of the Battalion present. If any person is found disobeying this order he shall be punished without privilege of a court martial. Arms to be viewed and returns to be made agreeable to former orders. One subaltern, one sergeant, twenty-four men for piquet; one subaltern, one sergeant, twenty-four rank and file for the quarter guard.

Continuation of the Orders of the 18th

The detachment of the Provincial troops at this post to receive three days provisions at 12 o'clock tomorrow to the 22nd inclusive and the Massachusetts regiment to receive provisions at four o'clock this afternoon for four days to the 22nd inclusive. The Indians to receive three days at 11 this day till the 22nd inclusive, the Rangers four days till the 24th inclusive.

Camp Halfway Brook, Tuesday 19th of June 1759
Parole, Gravesend

A return to be given in this day signed by the commanding officer of the strength of the Provincial regiment and detachment. The commanding officer of the Light Infantry to give in a return of the numbers under his command specifying the number of those on duty and where general Predeaux regiment the Rangers and Indians to hold themselves in readiness to march with the Royal under the command of Colonel Foster as soon as they arrive at this camp.

Continuation of the Orders of the 19th of June 1759

A part of the Connecticut regiment to parade at six o'clock tomorrow morning consisting of one captain, two subalterns, three sergeants, hundred rank and file for mending the roads betwixt this and three mile post. As also two subalterns, two sergeants, forty rank and file with arms to cover the working party.

Massachusetts troops to take the redoubt guard by their camp by the end of the bridge and relieve the guards. those of the Royal Highland regiment by daybreak tomorrow but the old and new guards that remain at the post until near sunrise every day for that guard to mount daily, one sergeant, one corporal and thirty men. The above guard to take the care of the battoes on this side the river and the care of the front of the camp in general.

Camp at Halfway Brook, Wednesday June 20th, 1759
Parole, Southwark

Field officer of the day Colonel Ingersoll. Field officer for the day tomorrow Major Graham.

A captain, two subalterns, as a picket from each of the Provincials and the Connecticut regiment to mount every evening at the tattoos beating, which piquet are to be under arms every morning at the days breaking and remain so until sunrise; Field officer of the day to visit the piquet before they are dismissed in the evening and the guards once a day at the hours they think proper and see that the sentries from the outpost are properly placed after the tattoos beat.

The detachment of the Provincials commanded by Colonel Pearson to be employed as soon as the fort is finished in clearing round it all the brush wood &c for about 400 yards; they are to be covered by the piquets and some Rangers and Light Infantry a detachment of four captains, thirteen subalterns and 500 men. at six o'clock tomorrow morning they are to lay upon the road from this to the three mile post to keep the communication clear and cover the convoys to this place, and on the return of the carriages until they arrive back to the three mile post, one subaltern, 1 sergeant, one corporal and thirty rank and file for the redoubt; one subaltern, one sergeant, one corporal and thirty rank and file and ten sentries, a sergeant and twelve for camp and other necessaries one captain, two subalterns, and fifty men for the piquet.

After Orders

The Royal Highlanders to be in readiness to march tomorrow morning covering parties countermanded for the piquet.[1]

---

1. Three mile (or sometimes called four mile) post I think must have been situated between Glens Falls village and Sandy Hill. E. Hoyt.

CAMP AT HALFWAY BROOK,[2] THURSDAY JUNE 21ST, 1759

Regimental orders for the first Battalion of Colonel Ruggles Regiment that the captain or commanding officers of companies take particular care that their men keep their arms in good order and see that their flints are fast in their locks as I have observed that a great many flints are loose. In all parties it is further ordered that all great hats are cut so that the brims be two inches and a half wide and that no man wears a cap under his hat and more especially when on duty. This order to be strictly observed.

GENERAL ORDERS
CAMP HALFWAY BROOK, JUNE 21ST, 1759
PAROLE, HARTFORD

Field officer for the piquet tomorrow Major Hawks. The piquet from Lieutenant Colonel Ingersoll, consisting of one captain, two subalterns, two sergeants, a corporal and fifty men two piquets to be raised this evening; they are to be paraded at the retreat beating. The captain of each piquet each is to give their men strict charge to have their arms in good order and to be ready to turn out on the shortest notice. All guards to be relieved as usual. All guards of the redoubt are at six o'clock in the morning to advance their sentries as far out as the Royal Highlanders did and to remain till retreat beating and then to come into their post. Whatever person is found guilty, either of the Provincials or Rangers, to fire his piece without order in this camp will be severely punished all orders to be strictly obeyed.

GIVEN ORDERS AT LAKE GEORGE, JUNE 21ST, 1759

Colonel of the day tomorrow Lieutenant Colonel Babcock, Field officer of the piquet, Colonel Smedly; for tomorrow Lieutenant Colonel Saltinstole.

---

2. The works at Halfway Brook must have been erected in the campaign of 1758; the ground is level and rather low, but the brook furnished good water. It was so called from being half way from Fort Edward to Lake George. I believe there was a fort on each side of the brook, on opposite sides of the road; their remains were to be seen in 1817. Soon after General Amherst took part at Lake George in 1759, they were abandoned and demolished. E. Hoyt.

For the officers guard to be advanced a small distance in the front of the old lines, the sentries during the night to be pitched double. The officers of the piquet are to be particularly careful to inspect their men's arms and go the rounds and see the guards and sentries are all alert.

The general expects at all times that every regiment will mount a piquet consisting of one captain, one subaltern, one ensign, two sergeants and fifty rank and file. The general guard tomorrow to be mounted by the Rhode Islanders.

Halfway Brook, Friday June 22nd, 1759
Parole, Richmond

Lieutenant Colonel Ingersoll Field Officer of the day tomorrow. All reports to be made to the commanding officer until further orders. Captain Galord and Captain Humphrys of the Connecticuts are immediately to strike their tents and to take possession of the stockades.

Captain Galord on the right of the gates and commands the north-east angles. Captain Humphreys on the left and to command the S. West angle. They are to mount a corporal and six men for guard.

Whosoever is found guilty of making any disturbance in camp or stockade after retreat beating, either by singing or swearing, or any other noise whereby the guard may be disturbed and the sentries not well able to distinguish any approach of the enemy if any should be lurking in order for a prisoner, they will be severely punished. For the same a captain from the line four subalterns, eight sergeants and hundred men in order to rebuild some fort and to make some new they are to parade precisely at five o'clock this afternoon with out fail; and that sergeant that is found guilty of disobeying orders and have not his quota on the parade where the adjutant shall order, shall be tried for neglect of duty and reduced to the ranks; and non-commissioned officer or soldier that is found to be beyond the sentries on any account whatever, without an order in writing from his commanding officer shall be severely punished.

The retreat to beat ten minutes after sunset. All the guards to be mounted as last night. The piquet is to turn out on any alarm, one in the front of the lines the other on the left in the line in front, and there to wait for orders from me and upon any party being discovered, every man to turn out in the front and there to wait with their acquirements and to be very silent so that they may receive orders without any noise; hundred men from the line with proper officers to parade at six o'clock to morrow morning on the front of the sentry line and there to receive orders.

N. Pearson

Lieutenant Colonel

P. S. these orders are expected to be punctually obeyed by officers as well as men when it is their tour of duty and acquainted by the adjutant. One piquet, consisting of one captain, four subalterns, eight sergeants and hundred men Colonel Ingersoll is to find a piquet consisting of one captain, four subalterns, eight sergeants and hundred men to turn out on any alarm on the least notice and wait for orders; Corporal Backster of Captain McDaniel's Company in the Jersey regiment is found guilty of neglect of duty and is to do duty in the ranks.[3]

---

3. The country about Halfway Brook, which is now (1840) open ground, was in some places fenced into fields, but it seems not to have been inviting to sutlers. The land is not very valuable. Some distance north of the brook the road rises to a pine plain, and woods continue most of the way to Lake George, with the exception of an opening near the south end of French mountain, where there is a small village once a travern half a mile or more south of the ground of Colonel William's ambuscade, Sept. 8, 1755. About half a mile north of the brook, a considerable number of our Provincial troops were cut off by the Indians, July 20, 1758, among whom were three captains, Lawrence, Dakins, and Jones, with one lieutenant, one ensign and fourteen privates. Captain Lawrence was from Groton and the grandfather of General Langley of Hawley on his mother's side. The affair took place near what is called Indian or Blind Rock, near the present road. A party of workmen on the road were first attacked and a detachment sent from the brook defeated on advancing to the spot. The men being panic stricken deserted their officers. Soon after the close of the war, in 1763, a few settlements were commenced in this quarter, and Abraham Wing built a house and barn at Glens Falls which were standing in 1777, the time of Burgoyne's invasion, but were afterwards burnt by Major Carlton, in 1780, who made an incursion from Canada.—E. Hoyt.

Camp Halfway Brook, Saturday June 23rd, 1759
Parole, Shrewsbury

Lieutenant Colonel Ingersoll Field Officer of the day tomorrow. The breast work to be finished by 5 o'clock and the redoubt to be thrown down of the north-west of the stockades. Two piquets to be raised for night consisting of two captains, six subalterns, eight sergeants and two hundred men. These piquets to lay on their arms to be ready to turn out on the least notice and to be extremely silent that they may hear the orders of their officers; they are to parade tomorrow at day break and to wait the commanding officer's orders. Lieutenant Check and his guard is to parade tomorrow at 7 o'clock to load battoes till they are ordered to be relieved; two subalterns, and fifty of the party that was with Captain Bancroft as soon as returned are immediately to get themselves ready and the victuals dressed this night to guard the King's oxen on the west side of the road towards the four mile post and one half of Colonel Pearson's piquet for that purpose; the other three guards as usual.

N. Pearson
Lieutenant Colonel

Camp Halfway Brook, Sunday June 24th, 1759
Parole, Dorset

The quarter guards to be mounted tomorrow morning at break of day without fail. Two captains, four subalterns, eight sergeants and two hundred men to lay on their arms and to be ready to turn out on the least alarm and to form on the two fronts as they were ordered last night to be. For the future if any is found sleeping on his post when on duty, he will not be passed by but must expect to suffer the martial law, in such case provided, as there has been complaint made of some companies of not being alert in turning out their number of men ordered. For the future it is expected they will punctually obey or otherwise they must expect to answer for their neglect.

If any person is found to ease himself within hundred yards of the lines only in the necessary hole provided for that purpose and they be found guilty of disobeying the same, will without doubt be punished.

A working party to be ready tomorrow morning from the lines consisting of one subaltern, one sergeant and twenty privates to be ready at 7 o'clock to load wagons and carts with provisions; Major Hawks, Field Officer of the day.[1]

Camp Halfway Brook Monday June 25th, 1759
Parole, Portsmouth

Lieutenant Colonel Ingersoll Field Officer of the day.

Two piquets to be raised consisting of two captains, six subalterns, eight sergeants and two hundred privates. They are to lay on their arms as usual and to turn out on any alarm at the place that hast been ordered and to wait for further orders. All the fires for cooking are to be made in the front of the lines and not in the rear of the officers tents. All men off duty this day on the lines and also the reserved piquet, are to turn out at four o'clock this afternoon to have their arms examined and their ammunition by the commanding officer and their return to be given in to the commanding officer after viewing the state and condition and they are also to exercise one hour. A party to be paraded at 12 o'clock to load carriages consisting of one captain, two subalterns, four sergeants, fifty men.

N. Pearson
Lieutenant Colonel

Camp at Halfway Brook June 26th, 1759
Parole, Edinburgh

Lieutenant Colonel Field Officer of the day.

Two piquets to be raised consisting of two captains, six subalterns, eight sergeants and two hundred men. The redoubt

---

1. Several baggage wagons were cut off near Halfway Brook, September 8, 1755, the day that Dieskau attacked Johnson at Lake. The two have been confounded by historians. The first was near Sandy Hill Village. Old Mr. Abraham Way of Glens Falls gave me particulars of this affair; and I have accounts of it in several journals by officers and soldiers who were in the campaign of 1758.—E. Hoyt.

guard and the quarter guard to be raised tomorrow at break of day; the drum major is to beat the reveille at break of day tomorrow morning and the piquet are to turn out to their lines. The orderly sergeants are to turn out when they parade their men for guard or piquet and deliver their names when on the parade in writing to the sergeant major and he is to deliver them to the commanding officer who is to mount the guard or piquet so that the officer may know the men and company they belong to, that if any be absent they will be able to confine them for neglect of duty. The officers commanding the piquet or any other guard are to be on the parade at the reveilles beating. For the future the soldiers to keep under arms and they are to be so watchful of their duty that if they do not turn out without calling, they may expect to be confined for such neglect of duty, as they must be sent to the lake to headquarters for trial. Whosoever is found in the camp guilty of playing cards after the publication of this order must expect to suffer for disobedience of orders. It is expected that after the tattoos beat in camp that there is no noise to be made as hast been for some evenings past. If any should be found guilty of disobedience of this nature will be took as a despiser of the martial law.

Continuation of the Orders of the 26th

It is reported unto me that some of the men are lousy, therefore, it is expected that the captains or commanding officers of companies enquire into the affairs and if there is any that is so to order them cleansed otherwise they will louse the whole. It is further expected that the officers see the men cook their victuals properly and not to broil pork on any account whatsoever and to examine the men's tents and see that they are kept clean and to see the men wash their shirts and stockings as often as needful it is expected this order to be obeyed as a standing order. Per order Jos. Ingersoll, Lieutenant Colonel

Camp Halfway Brook, Wednesday June 27th, 1759
Parole, Dublin

Major Hawks Field Officer of the day. The piquet and guards to be raised as yesterday as there is but little duty this day in the camps that it is expected that every captain or commanding officer of companies will set all the men that are off duty to wash their cloaths as perhaps this will be the only leisure they will have all former orders to be obeyed.

It is General Amherst's orders that all the troops at Halfway Brook are victualled up to the 3rd July inclusive. The Rangers included.

Camp Halfway Brook June 28th, 1759
Parole, Hartford

Colonel Ingersoll Field Officer of this day.

All the guards to be mounted as usual and the number that was ordered yesterday. Each commanding officer are by 10 o'clock to see that all the men off duty to draw their charge and wash their pieces clean and have them very dry before loaded; officers likewise to see their ground is occupied today and all the filth cleansed out and buried and new earth covered over.

A sergeant and twelve men is immediately to get all the axes and spades in the camp and return them under the care of the sentry for that purpose and after all is collected they are to be given out by order of the quarter master; all former orders to be obeyed.

Camp Halfway Brook, Friday June 29th, 1759
Parole, Colchester

Major Hawks Field Officer of the day. Captain Whitlesse's piquet. Fifty of them is to join fifty of Colonel Ingersoll's battalion with thirty rangers to drive a number of King's oxen to the Four Mile post. The Rangers are to take their orders from the commanding officer. The piquet and quarter guards to be mounted as usual. The redoubt guard on the east of the artillery is this day to make a guard house as the tents are wanted. Orders reported: It is expected that no party goes without the leave of a commanding officer on any pretence whatsoever. The out sentry are to stop all and suffer none to pass without an order in writing from an officer of the company belonging to this camp.

A court martial to set this day at 9 o'clock to try such prisoners as may be brought before them. Captain Baldwain, president, Lieutenant Seamore, Lieutenant Carole, Lieutenant Tupp members; The court to set at the president's tent; All former orders to be obeyed. The officers are to see that all the men of duty to turn out and exercise from eight to ten and from 4 to 5 o'clock.

Camp at Halfway Brook June 30th, 1759
Parole, Richmond

Lieutenant Colonel Ingersoll Field Officer of the day.

All guards to be mounted as usual. A working party for tomorrow consisting of one captain, two subs, two sergeants, and fifty rank and file. The Connecticut Regiment to be under arms at 3 o'clock this afternoon. All that are off duty the adjutant is to exercise them in platoon firing, two deep. This order respecting exercise is to be continued after this day from the hour of seven until nine in the forenoon and from four until six in the afternoon. Per order, N. Pearson, Lieutenant Colonel

Regimental orders: That every officer commanding a company to give in a return of their company setting forth where all their men are that ever was in their companies as well as those on duty.

To be given tomorrow morning by 7 o'clock and to be signed by the commanding officer of each company on the spot. It is expected that they are made very correct as they will be kept to examine each others by. Per order, N. Pearson.

Camp at Halfway Brook, Sunday July 1st, 1759
Parole, Colchester

Major Hawks Field Officer of the day.

All guards to be mounted as usual. All former orders to be strictly obeyed. A court martial to be set this day at nine o'clock to try such prisoners as may be brought before them. Captain

Whitlesse, president Lieutenant Emblem, Lieutenant Carole, Lieutenant Chease, Lieutenant Pell members. Per order N. Pearson, Lieutenant Colonel

Camp at Halfway Brook, July 2nd 1759
Parole, Colchester

All guards to be mounted as usual. After these orders are published there is to be no fire or smoke in the mouths of the tents or within the lines of these encampments after the tattoo is beat. What ever person is found guilty of disobeying these orders may expect to be confined and tried for open contempt of orders; All former orders to be obeyed. The return is to be given in to the adjutant of all those men which were in the artillery service last campaign.

N. Pearson
Lieutenant Colonel

Regimental Orders
Camp at Halfway Brook, July 3rd 1759

That no officer perfume to give leave for any party to go without the sentry without the leave from the commanding officer of the regiment on any pretence whatever. It is further ordered that no non-commissioned officer or private perfume to go without the sentries, as they will be reported deserted if they are found thus guilty and will be punished accordingly. I would have the officers examine the men's arms and ammunition and see that they are in good order.

Jos. Ingersoll
Lieutenant Colonel

Halfway Brook July 3rd, 1759
Parole, Colchester

Colonel Ingersoll Field Officer of the day; All guards to be mounted as usual, the working detail to be paraded immediately, consisting of one captain, two subalterns, three sergeants, and fifty privates for working at the magazines; all former orders to be obeyed. The commander of the stockades to make a return this day by 3 o'clock of the numbers of the men, their names and their company to the commanding officer of this fort.

Nathan Pearson
Lieutenant Colonel

Camp at Halfway Brook, July 4th, 1759
Parole, Shrewsbury

Major Hawks Field Officer of the day.

A sergeant and twelve men from the lines to cut and burn all the logs and brush that are within the lines of sentries. A working party to be paraded immediately, consisting of one captain, two subalterns, two sergeants, fifty privates without arms. All guards to be mounted as usual. As there seems to be some negligence in exercise for the future it is expected it will be more punctually obeyed.

As it is notoriously true that profane cursing and swearing prevails in the camp. It is not only very far from the Christian soldiers duty and very displeasing to the Lord of Hosts and God of Armies but dishonourable before men.

It is, therefore, required and expected, that for the future the odious found of cursing and swearing is turned into a profound silence. If after the publishing these orders, any is found guilty in the violation of these orders they may expect such punishment as A court martial judge for disobedience; All former orders to be obeyed.[1]

N. Pearson
Lieutenant Colonel

---

1. From the tenor of these orders it is evident that much confusion and disorder prevailed in the Provincial camps. It is often repeated that "the orders are to be obeyed or the men punished." In a camp of regulars little of this is necessary; their punishment generally precedes threats, and all know the consequence of disobedience from experience. In an order issued at Lake George June 22, 1759, notice is taken "of some officers making themselves very familiar with sergeants and even privates, which greatly injures the service; and it is expected for the future that that levelling temper will no longer subsist." Our republican militia would think this aristocratical.—E. Hoyt.

Camp Halfway Brook, July 5th, 1759
Parole, Dublin

All guards to be mounted as usual. All axes and spades this day to be returned to the quarter master whosoever in order to have the exact number that was left for the use of this camp. If wanted after they may have them again by applying to the quarter master. Whosoever is found to secret one will be looked upon as an embezzler of the King's stores and must answer it accordingly.

Lieutenant Colonel Ingersoll officer of the day. He is to see the piquet parade and give them their orders in going the rounds, as some nights it has been neglected; All former orders to be obeyed.

N. Pearson
Lieutenant Colonel

Regimental Orders
Camp at Halfway Brook, July 6th, 1759

It hast been practised some time past amongst some of our officers for to wrangle and dispute with the adjutant on the parade and before the men concerning duty, whereas it is very unbecoming the part of gentlemen as well as against all rules and discipline of war. It is for the future desired that there may not be any wrangles or disputes arise in any such like manner. If the adjutant doeth his duty wrong so that an officer think himself wronged or any of his men, their business is to apply to the commanding officer of the regiment where they will get justice done. It is ordered that the men turn up the flaps of their tents to air and sweep them clean immediately.

Jos. Ingersoll
Lieutenant Colonel

General Orders for the 6th of July, 1759
Parole, Edinburgh

Major Hawks Field Officer of the day. All guards to be mounted as usual. As there was last night a very riotous noise in the camp till one o'clock this morning which is contrary to the orders of this camp and the rules in the army, it is, therefore, required of all officers of guards that for the future that they especially take the greatest precaution after the tattoo is beat, that there be no hallowing or singing in the camp. The officers of the several guards will immediately after the officer of the day hast given them their charge go through the camps and if they find any person making any noise or disturbance they will order them to be still and silent. After that if should be any noise or disorderly behaviour the officer will send and confine them for disobeying and in contempt of orders and they will be punished accordingly agreeable to the martial law.

The working party that is falling trees on the road are to continue until 10 o'clock and then to be relieved by a party from Colonel Ingersoll who are to work till after two and then be relieved by the same. All former orders to be obeyed.

N. Pearson
Colonel

Camp Halfway Brook July 7th, 1759
Parole, Herefordshire

Lieutenant Colonel Ingersoll Field Officer of the day. All guards and parties to be mounted as usual. The working party to be paraded continually two captains, four subalterns, four sergeants and one hundred men. All former orders to be obeyed; a court martial to set to try such prisoners as may be brought before them. Captain Whitlesse president, Lieutenant Seamore, Lieutenant Smith, Lieutenant Hunter, Ensign Gillet, Members; to set at the presidents tent immediately.

Camp at Halfway Brook, July 8th, 1759
Parole, Wools

Major Hawks Field Officer of the day. All guards to be mounted as usual.

The officer of the quarter guard to take especial care that all of the oxen belonging to the King which will be brought inn this night and put under care. If any should get out of sentries, they must be answerable for this neglect; No soldier is upon any account whatsoever either to sleep or sit down when upon sentry; If any one should be found disobeying these orders for the future all those who are found sleeping will be sent to headquarters for trial and they will be severely punished; these orders to be read this night to each officer of the guard so that it may be given in charge not only to all the soldiers that are on duty this night but to continue from officer to officer when they are relieved. All former orders to be obeyed.[1]

N. Pearson
Lieutenant Colonel

Camp Halfway Brook July 9th, 1759
Parole, Portsmouth

Lieutenant Colonel Ingersoll Field Officer of the day; All guards to be mounted as usual; All the troops are to hold themselves in readiness to march at the shortest notice. All former orders to be obeyed.[1]

N. Pearson
Lieutenant Colonel

Camp Halfway Brook, July 10th, 1759
Parole, Southwark
Major Hawks Field Officer of this day.

All the men off duty are immediately to get their arms clean and set out in the fun; they are also to turn out and parade and they are likewise to keep their arms clean and in good order.

N. Pearson
Lieutenant Colonel

General Orders for the 11th of July 1759

A standing order: The Grenadiers and brigades of Royals and Late Forbes during the campaign are to be drawn upon all sur-

---

1. During the campaigns of 1755, 1758, 1759 and 1760 the road from Fort Edward to Lake George was almost constantly occupied by troops, and in the revolutionary war it again became a line of military operations. In passing it, a man of military taste will find much to occupy his mind and useful lessons in strategy.—E. Hoyt.

veys two deep. This makes no alteration in posting the officers or settling the battalions in grand divisions, subs division, one platoon in the front and flank and rear and flank platoon. When the battalions are told off in platoons on the parade the whole battalion is to be three deep, the two centre platoons close and their intervals of half the front of the platoons left between its platoon from the one on the right of the centre to the platoon on the right of the battalion, the same to be observed from the platoon on the left of the centre to the platoon of the battalion. The commanding officer will then order the officers commanding platoons to form them two deep, which they will do by commanding the rear rank and those on the right of the column facing to the right and those on the left facing to the left and halting in the interval the first half forms on the right of the front of each platoon on the right of the column and on the left of the front rank of each platoon on the left of the column the second half forms in like manner on the right and left of the second rank. If there is an odd man the officer take what one he pleases as a second; The method is always to be practised, that every officer commanding a platoon may have the men of the third rank next to him that in case the service requires it the whole battalion may be formed three deep in one instant by the officers of platoons forming the rear rank, as they were, which is never to be done unless the officer commanding the battalion orders it; the men to be acquainted that this is ordered, as the enemy has very few regular troops to oppose us that no yelling of Indians or fire of Canadians can possibly be at two ranks. If the men are silent and attentive and obedient to their officers who will lead them to their enemy and their silence will terrify them more than any huzzahing or noise they can make which the general strictly forbids; And their attention and obedience to their officers who commands platoons will ensure success to his Majesty's arms.

 The general court martial of which Colonel Ruggles is president is dissolved. The general has been pleased to approve of the following sentences of the above court martial: George Deforty of the Inniskillen Regiment accused of suspicion of breaking up a trunk is found not guilty of the crime laid to his charge; he is therefore acquitted. Wm. Harper, of Brigadier Gage's Regiment of Light Infantry, accused of theft is found guilty of the crime laid to his charge and is to receive 400 lashes with a cat of nine tails. John Cotter, soldier in Brigadier Gage's Regt of Light Infantry accused of desertion is found guilty of the crime laid to his charge and is to receive one thousand lashes with a cat of nine tails.

Regimental Orders
for the 11th of July 1759

All men that are not on duty to be paraded this afternoon at three o'clock and the officers will see their arms are drawn and cleansed in good order and see them exercise one hour and a half in firing platoons. If an officer of any one company is not acquainted with platoon firing let them apply to some other for learning so that he may be able to instruct his men. The commanding officers of companies are to see that their men boil their fresh meat and make soup as it will be much more for their health and go much further. A weekly return to be given in of the number of men we have upon these lines immediately.

Joseph Ingersoll
Lieutenant Colonel

Given Orders
Halfway Brook July 11th, 1759
Parole, Shrewsbury

Colonel Ingersoll Field Officer of the day.

All the troops at this place except the garrison and Captain Sheppard's Company to have three days' provisions, two of fresh meat and one of salt. One hundred axe men from this line and fifty from Colonel Ingersoll the piquet to cover them. They are to be paraded at 2 o'clock.

A court martial to set this day at nine o'clock to try all prisoners that shall be brought before them. Captain Whitlesse, president, Lieutenant Emblem, Lieutenant How, Lieutenant Johnson, Lieutenant Tripp, members. All former orders to be obeyed.

Camp Halfway Brook July 12th, 1759
Parole, Dartford

Major Slapp Field Officer of the day. All guards to be mounted as usual.

Captain Robinson and Captain Bancroft and Lieutenant Ingersoll are to survey any provision shown them by the quartermaster and the quantity making a return of the same so that the deficiency may be made up. The adjutant is to order all the men off duty in General Lyman's Regiment to turn out and exercise three hours in the forenoon and three hours in the afternoon the major to exercise them. All former orders to be obeyed.

Nathan Pearson

Camp at Halfway Brook, July 13th, 1759
Parole, London

Major Hawks Field Officer of the day.

All guards to be mounted as usual. A sergeant and sixteen men to grind axes; The quarter master will collect all axes that come from the lake so that they may be well ground and fit for use as there will be no working party this forenoon. It is expected that every officer of duty will see that all their men off duty save one man to a tent to wash and be clean with their coats on; so that they may appear well under arms. They are to turn out at 7 o'clock and exercise till ten and from four till 7 o'clock. All former orders to be obeyed.

N. Pearson

Camp Lake George, July 14th, 1759
Parole, Guilford

Colonel for the day tomorrow Colonel Montgomery; Field officer for the piquet this night, Regular Major Graham, Provincial Lieutenant Colonel Putnam, Regular Major Dugglas. For tomorrow Regular Major John Campbell, Provincial Lieutenant Colonel Miller and Major Whiting.

The regiments to pay tomorrow in the afternoon in the same manner as they did the last time for what spruce beer they have received since that payment. The Rangers and Indians to fire off their pieces tomorrow morning at 5 o'clock in the front of their camps at marks. They will afterwards put them in the best manner they can. It is expected the men on no account whatsoever to touch the five days' bread they were ordered to receive.

The surgeons of the several regiments to meet Doctor Monro at the general hospital at 4 o'clock this afternoon who will direct what proportion of medicines each of them are to furnish for the Light Infantry. Each is immediately to be given into the surgeon that take the care of that corp.

Regimental Orders
No wrestling for the future will be allowed of.

After Orders
General Ruggles' Battalion and Lyman's Regiment as well as the detachment that marched in with them are to be out tomorrow morn at 5 o'clock to fire two rounds in the same manner as the others have done, Colonel Townsend to attend them; the general observed several arms of both these regiments and the detachment was much out of repair. The regiments will send in a return to Major Monypenny of the return of the men not under arms upon that occasion, and they are to repair such arms immediately and when repaired they are to be out to fire. The above two regiments after firing will receive a proportion of flour for five days' bread which they are to get baked and keep in the same manner as the rest of the army and are to receive provisions to the 16th inclusive, to which time all the rest of the Provincial regiments are completed. 450 workmen and two covering parties as usual for the use of the engineers. Hundred men for the artillery, thirty workmen for Captain Loren.

Camp at Lake George, July 15th, 1759
Parole, Croydon
Colonel for the day tomorrow Colonel Schayler; Field officer of the piquet, Regular Major John Campbell, Provincial Lieu-

tenant Colonel Miller; Major Whiting for tomorrow; for tonight Lieutenant Colonel Darby, Regular Provincials Lieutenant Colonel Pain, Major Ball. General Guard to morrow Montgomery.

Regular Regiments to receive three days' provisions beginning at 5 o'clock with the Light Infantry then Grenadiers, Inniskillen and Royal Highlanders and Forbes Royal Artillery, Gage the battalions Ruggles and Lyman and detachments that marched into camp last night will send this evening at 5 o'clock to Mr. Willson, commissary, a return of their effective that marched in; and they will receive tomorrow morning at 5 o'clock, three days' fresh provisions beginning with Ruggles and Lyman and detachments of the regiments; the regiments that have baked bread for five days must now expend it that it may not be spoiled and they will continue baking the flour they receive that they may always have five days of bread ready when the army embarks. The Rangers and Provincial Regiments that fired this day are to complete their ammunition applying to Major Orde commanding the Artillery.

All shells and shot that may have been left by the enemy during the campaign will be of use in sending back again; the following prizes shall be allowed to those that pick them up on their delivering them to the commissary stores at the Artillery Park; for a thirteen inch shell, one dollar; for an eight inch and a quarter ditto; for a large shot shall be paid at 2d each a pound and small shot 1d; all arms taken from the enemy are to be brought to headquarters. The men that take such arms will be allowed each 5s for each good or repairable firelock.

Battoes and whale boats to be wanted by the battalions of Ruggles and Schayler.

		Men
Ruggles	5 battoes for the general and his family	35
	4 Whale boats for the general and his family	32
	7 Battoes for the commissary	49
Schayler	7 Battoes for the General	49
	4 Whale Boats for the General	32
	3 Battoes for hospital	21

Continuation of the Orders of the 15th

One captain, two subalterns, sixty volunteers to be instantly raised to parade at the head of the regiments half an hour after nine with their arms and ammunition and to carry their blankets and to take spruce beer with them and one days bread. They will march down to the waters side where they will join the detachment of the Light Infantry and follow such orders as they shall receive from Colonel Townsend. The detachment Montgomery that marched into camp this day to receive fresh provisions tomorrow for three days at the same time; Ruggles ditto; the quarter master will send to Commissary Willson the effective number of the detachment. This detachment likewise; the reserved men of the Provincials that marched into camp this day are to fire two rounds of ball tomorrow morning at 6 o'clock at the place where the Provincials fired this day. The adjutant of Montgomery's and Babcock's to parade tomorrow morning at reveilles beating at the head of their camps. They will march to the right and join Babcock's piquet from whence they will be marched by Lieutenant Colonel Miller, Field Officer of the piquet, on the west side of the lake, where he will be conducted by an officer of the Rangers and will be joined by 150 Rangers. The general will send further orders to the colonel. The men will take one days provisions and march in their waistcoats and blankets, 450 working men and two covering parties for the engineer tomorrow; hundred men ditto for the Artillery, Captain Loring, forty for Lieutenant Colonel Putnam to finish the garden and to what tools he directs; one captain, two subs, two sergeants and sixty-four men.

Camp Lake George, July 16th, 1759
Parole, Norwalk

Colonel Lyman, Colonel of the day tomorrow; Field officer of the piquet this night, Regulars, Lieutenant Colonel Darby, Provincials, Lieutenant Colonel Pearson; for tomorrow night Major Ball, Regular, Major Alexander Campbell; Provincial, Lieutenant Colonel Goff, Major Waterbury.

The Regiments of the Brigades of the Royal and Forbes and the Provincials will find an officer and twenty men with arms a party sufficient to cut fascines which they are to put into the battoes that when they are loaded that none of the provisions is spoiled. these parties to be sent out immediately in battoes to the west side of the lake but none must attempt to pass the post. The five pickets are to march to the commanding officer of the Provincial battalions to attend Brigadier General Gage at 12 o'clock this day. The Provincials to receive three days provisions tomorrow morning at 5 o'clock. Following Fitch's, Worcester, Schayler, Lovewell, Willard, Ruggles and Whiting they will send a return of their effective number to the commissary this evening and will be observant of the orders of yesterday in relation to bread. Captain Loving will deliver whale boats this evening to Gages and to the Light Infantry tomorrow morning at 5 o'clock.

Continuation of the Orders of the 16th

Orders for the first Battalion that every officer and man of duty turn out to clean their camps of all the stumps and rubbish and put fresh earth over the burnt ground and pitch their tents regular in straight lines. It is ordered that after any officer or sergeant has received details from the adjutant or sergeant major for any guard or fatigue or detachment of any kind whatsoever; that they are not at the time appointed on the parade without fail without any hallowing or calling in camps if any sergeant be guilty of hallowing turn out they shall be confined and tried by a court martial.

A regimental court martial to set immediately to try such prisoners as shall be brought before them. Captain Nixon, president, Lieutenant Ingersoll, Lieutenant Marten, Lieutenant Farrinton, Ensign Samuel Ward, members.

Continuation of the General Orders of the 16th

Eight of the Provincial battalion gives thirteen men each and two of the Provincial battalions fourteen men each for the Ranging Service. The men to be told they will be paid the difference between theirs six that of the Rangers. Commanding officers of the battalions to turn out all volunteers willing to serve in the Rangers. Tomorrow at one o'clock Major Rogers will attend and choose the number that each regiment is to furnish out of such volunteers.

A general court martial of the line to set tomorrow morning at eight o'clock at the president's tent to try to of the late Forbes regiment.

Colonel Whiting, president, Lieutenant Colonel Putnam, Major Alexander Campbell, five captains from the Regulars, Do. from the Provincials, Lieutenant George Burton, Deputy Judge Advocate 450 working men and two covering parties as usual for the engineer. twenty men for the fatigue for Captain Loring; hundred working men for Major Arde, as usual. 500 Provincials with axes to parade tomorrow morning at 5 o'clock in the front of the Grenadiers. Mr. Neild to command this party. Lieutenant Gray will attend. One captain, two subalterns, two sergeants, hundred men at 5 o'clock; two subalterns, two sergeants, sixty men at 6 o'clock and the piquets to cover them.

Camp at Lake George, July l7th, 1759
Parole, Philadelphia

Colonel of the day tomorrow Colonel Ruggles; Field officer for the piquet this night, Regular, Major Gordon; Provincial Lieutenant Colonel Goff, Major Waterberry; tomorrow night, Regular, Major Graham; Provincial Lieutenant Colonel Medly, Major Moore.

Colonel Ruggles' Regiment to receive eight muskets to complete their number and they will likewise change fourteen returned defective for which they will apply to the commanding officer of the Royal Artillery; All the men that have joined the Provincials they are to assemble tomorrow morning at 5 o'clock on the ground where the Provincials fired before. They are to fire two rounds at marks. Brigade Major to attend them to see them fire their ammunition, must afterwards be completed. The whale boats to be marked by the corps they are given to in the same for the battoes; the Grenadiers to receive theirs as soon as the whale boats are ready for which they will apply to Captain Loring. The Rangers are to receive theirs after the Grenadiers. All the whale boats to be kept in the crick or they will otherwise be subject to be spoiled. The proportion of whale boats and battoes: for the Rangers, forty-three whale boats, one battoe; Gage's Regiment one flat bottomed boat, forty-one whale boats, four battoes; Light Infantry for the regiments forty-three whale boats, five battoes; Grenadiers, forty-three whale boats, five battoes. The sutlers must provide men for their battoes allowed them as the general will not permit the men of the regiments to do it.

Continuation of the General Orders of the 17th

The Regular Regiment will receive five locks and bayonets as by their return tomorrow at 5 o'clock. at the park of the Artillery 500 men with axes, 100 with bill-hooks, under the command of Major Willard and conducted by Lieutenant Gray, are to take their tools tomorrow at the reveille beating at the Artillery and march directly; A covering party will be ordered which party must be out at the reveilles beating and they will return to camp by one o'clock or perhaps they may not return until night; 450 working men and two covering parties as usual; for the engineer tomorrow forty men for fatigue for Captain Loring, two hundred men for the fatigue for the Artillery, Gage's regiment to be out tomorrow morning to discharge their pieces by 5 o'clock. General guard tomorrow, first Battalion of Ruggles.

Wednesday July 18th, 1759
Parole, Half Moon

Colonel of the day tomorrow Colonel Worster; Field officer of the piquet this night, Regulars, Graham; Provincials, Lieutenant Colonel Smedly, Major Moore; tomorrow night, Regulars, Major John Campbel; Provincials Lieutenant Colonel Hunt, Major Slap.

The Regular Regiments to receive fresh provisions for three

days to morrow morning, by 5 o'clock, beginning with Gage's, following Royal Artillery, Late Forbes, Montgomery, Royal Highlanders, Inniskillen Grenadiers, Light Infantry of Regiments These complete them to the 21st inclusive. The Provincial regiments to send in a return to the brigade major of arms and ammunition or anything else wanting to complete them; as it is supposed that the men that have joined may not have everything complete as fast as they comes, the commanding officer will immediately have them received and with out delay report to the major brigade everything that shall be wanting. Every man to have a good flint in his firelock and a spare one in his pocket which the officers must take care is not wanting.

They will receive them by applying to Major Arde Commander of the Royal Artillery. A boat for a brigade will be allowed for the surgeon of each of the Regulars and one battoe for the surgeons of the five Provincial battalions, of Ruggles, Willards, N. Hampshire, Babcock, one to those of Schayler, Worster, Fitch, Whitting, and Lyman. those battoes must be received from Captain Loving and be kept by the eldest of each. All the regiments to return their tools to the Artillery and take up their receipts at 5 o'clock this afternoon and each Provincial regiment will send their return to Brigade Major Moneypenny this evening of the number of axes or any other tools they may have that belong to the regiments If the regiments who have companies that have lately joined them since the orders for battoes, should want more than have been ordered will apply accordingly.

The men that have been choose to serve with the Rangers are to join them this evening at 5 o'clock and follow such orders as they shall receive from Major Rogers. They are not to take tents but live in huts in the same manner as the Rangers do. They must take the provision which they have for tomorrow inclusive and they will afterwards draw their provision with the Rangers and they are not to be included in their returns of their respective regiments.

After Orders for the 18th, 1759

Thos. Burk, wagoner, tried by a court martial of the Line for abusing and offering to strike an officer at Halfway Brook, is found guilty and is to receive 400 lashes. The general hast been pleased to approve of the sentences and orderest that the above said Thomas Burk is marched tomorrow morning at 5 o'clock by the provost guard from regiment to regiment and that he receivest thirty lashes at the head of each four Regular Regiments, beginning at Forbes, and so on to the rest; that he also receive thirty lashes at the head of each Provincial Battalion and forty at the head of Schayler. He is afterwards to be marched back to the provost guard and remain there until further orders.

A detachment of 600 Provincials with axes under the command of Major Willard and conducted by Lieutenant Gray to parade tomorrow morning at reveilles beating at the Artillery where they will receive axes. They will set out at the same hour this day that they might finish their work betimes a covering party will be appointed; 200 working men for the Artillery at the usual hour, 450 working men and two covering parties will be appointed; for the engineer thirty for Captain Loving; Josiah Allen, mason, Thomas Caile and Wm. Hail and Joseph Hadcock, Lime burners all of Colonel Willard's Regiment are to attend Colonel Montorse at 5 o'clock tomorrow morning. Every regiment to haul their battoes half out of water immediately.

Camp Lake George, Thursday, July 19th, 1759
Parole, Soupe

Field officer of the day, tomorrow Colonel Fitch; Field officer of the piquet, Regular, Major Campbel; Provincials, Lieutenant Colonel Hunt, Major Slapp; tomorrow night, Regulars, Lieutenant Colonel Darby, Provincials Lieutenant Colonel Saltenstol, Major Hawks; General Guard tomorrow, and Battalion of Colonel Ruggles.

The Provincials to receive three days' fresh provisions tomorrow morning at 5 o'clock beginning at Whiting, following Ruggles, Willard, Lovewels, Schayler, Worster, Fitch, and Babcock which completes them to the 22nd inclusive. The Battalions of Ruggles Willard, Lovewel, and Babcock will each change their defective arms and view their ammunition, flints and bayonets this day at 12 o'clock by applying to Major Arde Commander of the Royal Artillery according to the returns sent in this day.

Regimental Orders
Thursday July 19th, 1759

The commanding officers of each company will examine the state of the men's arms of the Battalion every evening of all the deficiency and how the deficiency happens. This order to be punctually obeyed. All the officers and soldiers of duty to turn out and exercise at 3 o'clock this afternoon and Captain Nixon will attend to teach them. Per orders of Colonel Ingersoll.

After Orders: The general court martial of which Colonel Whiting was president is dissolved; the General hast approved of the said sentences of the above Court martial: Phineas Duggles, of Colonel Ruggles' Battalion, tried for desertion is acquitted; John Monilly, of Late Forbes regiment tried for desertion is found guilty and sentenced to suffer 1000 lashes; Thomas Bailey, of Late Forbes tried for robbery and being a notorious offender is found guilty and is sentenced to suffer death. John Williams, Elias Ludwick, of Colonel Ruggles, first Battalion, tried for robbery; Captain Hesgell of Colonel Babcock's regiment accused of disobeying orders is adjudged not guilty of the crime laid to his charge and is therefore acquitted; The regiments of Schayler, Lyman, Whiting and Worster Fitchs' will receive their arms &c agreeable to their return they have given in by applying to Major Orde tomorrow morning.

The piquets of the line to be out tomorrow morning at 7 o'clock and will march to the front of the Grenadiers drawing up in the same manner as the last day they were out for the execution of Thos. Bayly of late Forbes regiment at the head of the piquet he will be marched by the provost guard in the same manner as the last criminal was. The colonel of the day will attend.

A platoon of Late Forbes will be drawn up in the centre for the execution.

Ten battoes will be delivered to Colonel Lyman's regiment on applying to Captain Loving; A general court martial of the Regulars to set tomorrow morning at 6 o'clock at the present's tent, Colonel Montgomery, president, Lieutenant Colonel Darby, Major Graham, Late Forbes, two captains Inniskillen, one Royal Highlander, one Gage's, one Grenadier, two Light Infantry, two captains for that duty, Lieutenant George Burton, Deputy Judge Advocate, 450 working men and two covering parties for the engineer, as usual 200 men for the Artillery, thirty for Captain Loving.

The regiments to load at 5 o'clock in the following manner agree able to the order of the 11th *viz*: Forbes, flour; Montgomery, pork; Royal Highlanders flour; Inniskillen pork; Predeaux flour; Royal pork.

Ruggles and Willard must follow the Royal Highlanders and the Inniskillen are to load Ruggles pork and Willard, flour, Lovewell pork, Babcock's flour, Whiting pork, Fitch flour, Worster pork, Lyman flour; two regiments are to load at a time one for flour and one for pork and to be allowed an hour for loading and when loaded to return to their station and the boats to be taken of as usual. If any found to be leaky they must be changed before night. Mr. Willson will attend to see that each regiment loads a proper quantity and the quartermaster of each regiment to give him a receipt for the provision they receive. The Connecticut boats now on the beach before the provisions to be moved to the east shore and remain till the last where they will load at their station.

Lake George, Friday, July 20th, 1759.
Parole, Godolphin

On landing Colonel Grant to take the command of Late Forbes' brigade and Colonel Foster the brigade of the Royal. All artificers that have been employed by Colonel Montscone who are now to join the Regiments are to be paid by Colonel

Montscone this afternoon; Orders for the army passing the Lake guard is to consist of Gage's Light Infantry with the flat bottomed English boat in the front of the centre, their whale boats drawing up abreast covering the heads of the columns from right to left; the army to row in four columns, the right and first column to consist of Rangers, the Light Infantry of the Regiments Grenadiers, Willard, Ruggles, 2nd Battalion to be drawn up and row the boats two deep. The commanding officers in a whale boat on the right of the Battalion to the front rank in the boats on the right the rear rank on the left, as the whole of the column marches and embarks by the left in which order they will land. When this column lands Colonel Bradstreet to take care of the whale boats the Rangers and Light Infantry and Grenadiers are to leave only what men are absolutely necessary to take care of their tents and baggage in their battoes; the 2nd column is to consist of the 2nd Brigades of Regiments marched and embarked by the left, beginning at Late Forbes, their front rank in the boats on the right and their rear rank in the boats on the left rowing two boats abreast. The 3rd column is to consist of all the Artillery the radow[1] ahead followed by the rafts all the carpenters boats with the tools Schayler's regiment 1st Battalion of Ruggles with artillery stores &c embarking from the right, rowing two boats abreast, their front rank on the left, and rear rank on the right, the commanding officers in whale boats on the right of the battalion on the left of Ruggles regiment will be followed by the boats belonging to the quartermasters, then engineers, surgeons, hospitals, commissaries, and sutlers large boat with the provisions, floats with horses. The 4th and left column is to consist of Lyman, Worster, Fitch, Babcock, and Lovewel. They are to march and embark by the right rowing two battoes abreast the front rank on the left the rear on the right commanding officers in whale boats on the right of the Battalion; Whiting will form the rear covering the rear of the 4th column from right to left and their right to the 4th column and left to

---

1. Radeau a flat-bottomed boat a scow. E. H.

the 1st column their rear ranks to the column and front ranks to the *Halifax* sloop; The *Halifax* sloop will cruise close to the rear of the whole; All the battalions except Whiting's are to have neither more nor less than one sergeant per regiment and one man per Company for the care of the battoes tents and baggage and officers for brigade of the Regulars one for the five regiments on the left of the Provincials and one for the four on the right. The officers, sergeants and men to be fixed on and their names to be returned to the major of brigade; The Rangers Light Infantry of Regiments and Grenadiers are to be commanded by Colonel Flouellon Lieutenant Brewer to attend Colonel Flouellon, Willards 2nd Battalion of Ruggles commanded by Colonel Ruggles, Lieutenant Gray to attend the two last battalions to receive fifty axes each by applying to Mr. Russel which with those they already have may do for what work may be required of them. The two columns will be commanded by Brigadier General Gage; Colonel Schayler will command the two regiments of the third column which will have each one hundred axes delivered to them by applying to Mr. Russel that they may be ready to clear the roads the moment they are ordered.

Lieutenant Rose will attend Colonel Schayler; The column on the left will be commanded by Colonel Lyman and will be ready to land on the left side or where ordered; the columns to row on the same height the battoes to keep clear of each others oars, and signals to be made on board the *Invincible* Radow or the *Halifax* sloop a small Union flag for brigades and adjutants to come for orders. A red flag is for to sail or row and when struck is for halting. When the red flag is taken down every boat must then dress in its proper place immediately. A blue flag is for the right column to land when replaced for Gage's Lieutenant Infantry, and 2nd column to land if replaced; the 3rd time for the left column to land; the Artillery will land after the 2nd column; Whiting's regiment to have the guards of battoes a 12 pounder on the left of the Rangers an 18 pounder on the right of Lyman. Great care must be taken of arms and ammunition. The men to land in their waistcoats and go as light as possible, carrying only their blankets and provisions, no hurry no huzzahing on any account whatsoever; no man to fire without orders from his officer; the officers appointed to command will receive particular orders from the general and in whatsoever situation the regiments may be in when landed and night comes on, no motions are to be made in the night; each regiment will secure their own ground. Firing in the night must be avoided. The enemy must be met with fixed bayonets, And the regiments not to quit their ground even if the enemy could break through. The regiments are never to get up in heaps but keep their ranks on all occasions. Silence amongst the men must be kept. No password to be regarded or orders to be obeyed unless sent in writing by Deputy Quartermaster General Edy, camp's majors of brigade deputy quartermaster general or engineers. No man is to go back when landed to fetch provisions tents or anything else till there is a general order for it. They must expect to lie one night or two on their arms.

All the empty provision barrels to be sent to Colonel Monttosone. Barrels belonging to the brewery to be sent there. Eight barrels of spruce beer to be allowed to each regiment and one barrel to each company of Grenadiers and Light Infantry a proportion to the Artillery that must be taken into the whale boats and battoes; The regiments to pay to Sergeant Eary this afternoon for their beer or the quartermasters to give their notes for what is due. Everything to be put on board this day that the regiments may be ready to strike their tents in the night or when ordered that the whole may embark as fast as possible. The men must row in turns. No pressing forward. The whole will move on gently. The men that are not employed in rowing must go to sleep that the men may be alert and fit for service when landed.

CAMP AT TICONDEROGA, JULY 23RD 1759
PAROLE, CUMBERLAND

Colonel for the day tomorrow: Regular Colonel, Grant; Provincial Colonel, Schayler; for the piquets this night, Regular,

Major Graham; Provincial Lieutenant Colonel Putnam, Major Whiting; tomorrow night, Major Weft Lieutenant Colonel Pearson, Major Waterford.

The regiments to march and encamp as soon as the ground is marked out for them. The regiments who are to defend the breast work must erect immediately to raise a battery in the front of the centre of each regiment with logs and earth, so that the piquets of each regiment can stand upon it to defend the breast work without pulling any part of it down as it covers the camp from the shot of the place; The men may boil their pots as soon as they will; The camp may be marked out for Lyman, Worster and Fitch in the wood, to be marched facing outwards and advancing their piquets in the front that no straggling Indians may pick of their people; Schayler's Regiment to encamp on the left of Late Forbes. As Fitch's Regiment by mistake have not received their provisions as was ordered they must send to the landing place for three days' provisions.

Camp at Ticonderoga, July 24th, 1759

The piquet of the line to be out tonight in the same manner as last night except the piquet of Montgomery's which will be ordered; All the drums of all the regiments are to beat the retreat without waiting for the evening gun taking it from the Royal. The first brigade to send tomorrow for three days' provisions at retreat beating, they will only receive two days beefcake in the lieu of flour and three days' pork which completes with all species to the 28th inclusive.

Schayler, Lyman, Fitch, Worster and two battalions of Ruggles will receive four days provisions after it is gave out to the Regulars and beefcake instead of flour which completes them with provisions to the 29th inclusive. As Colonel Babcock's Regiments is ordered to the landing place the four battalions of Schayler, Lyman, Worster, and Fitch will furnish a guard of two hundred men to be commanded by a field officer who will take post halfway betwixt the camp and saw mill, which guard is to be relieved daily by the said four regiments.

After Orders of the 24th

The general would on no account have the men fire in the night unless they are very sure of their shots, but receive the enemy with their bayonets.

Camp at Ticonderoga, July 24th, 1759
Parole, New York

Colonel of the day tomorrow, Regular, Colonel Foster; Provincial, Colonel Fitch; Field officer for the piquet this night, Major West; Provincial Colonel Pearson, tomorrow night, Regular, Major John Campbell; Provincial, Major Waterberry.

The commanding officer of the Regular Regiments will choose an intelligent sergeant that they judge will best answer for assisting the engineer or overseers; they will likewise send their names to the major of brigade and order the sergeant to attend immediately upon Lieutenant Colonel Eyre, the houses of office to be made in the rear of the camps and wells to be dug for each regiment, that the men might get water as easy as possible; when a working party is ordered into the trench they must take their arms with them; when they work to the right they will order their arms to the right; and when they work to the left they will lodge their arms to the left; an account to be given in by each corps of all the accidents that happened on the 22nd, 23rd and 24th to the adjutant general at orderly time; If any officer have letters to send by the New York post they will send them in to head quarters this night; Sergeant Monney, of the Royal Highland Regiment is appointed to oversee the people appointed to make fascines and taking account of the number that is made; adjutant of the day tomorrow Late Forbes.

Camp at Ticonderoga, July 25th, 1759
Parole, Kensington

Colonel for this day, Colonel Montgomery; for tomorrow, Regular Colonel, Grant; Provincial Colonel, Schayler; Field officer for the piquet this night, Regular, Major John Campbell;

Provincial, Major Waterberry; tomorrow night Major Alexander Campbell Lieutenant Colonel Smedly.

The general can't but be surprised that such brave and good troops should be subject to be alarmed in the night and that any of the men should fire after the orders given them, without the command of the officers to do it, by which if they dost they will be liable to kill their comrades on their not obeying orders; If their receiving the enemy in the night with their bayonets fixed will cost us more men than the enemy can bring against us and he hopes that no more alarms of this fort will happen.

The piquet of the Royal to be relieved by a piquet of Forbes, this day at 12 o'clock and to be under the command of Major West, Field Officer of the piquet; The Battalion of the Royal is to mount in the trench at retreat's beating, at which time the piquet will return to camp; Six companies to mount on the left and three on the right and one in the centre the whole will mount by the right; they will leave their colours with the guard in camp; the Inniskillen Regiment will furnish a guard of fifty men for the right; when the piquets of the Royal is posted, the Light Infantry and Grenadiers to send to the landing place immediately and to receive three days' provisions, two days beefcake one day of flour which completes them to the 28th inclusive. Whitney's, Willard's and Babcock's Regiments will receive four days' of provisions tomorrow and beefcake instead of flour which completes them to the 29th inclusive; The general hospital is by Worster's Regiment near the road coming into camp where any wounded men may be sent to be dressed. Adjutant for the day tomorrow, Inniskillen.

Camp at Ticonderoga, July 26th, 1759
Parole, Springfield Centre
Countersign, London

Colonel for the day tomorrow, Regular Colonel, Foster; Provincial Colonel, Lyman; Field officer for the piquet this night, Regular, Major Alexander Campbell; Provincial, Lieutenant

Colonel Smedly; tomorrow night Major Hambleton, Lieutenant Colonel Hunt; Adjutant of the day tomorrow.

Royal Highlanders, Late Forbes to mount the trench this night, the Royal will march in by the right, three companies by the trenches on the right, and five to the trenches on the left of Brigade Gage's. Lieutenant Infantry will give one captain, two subalterns and hundred men for the centre; The regiments that mount the trenches will leave on the quarter guard sufficient for the care of the camp, the four Connecticut Regiments to add to their men to replace the Hampshire Regiment, one subaltern one sergeant and thirty men; Massachusetts, one subaltern, one sergeant, twenty men; Rhode Island one sergeant, ten men to join the Artillery tomorrow morn at 5 o'clock the Royal Artillery to complete their provisions to the 28th inclusive being the same day to which the Regular Regiments are completed.

Regimental Orders

That no officer or soldier leave his post on any account without leave from his commanding officer as they will be answerable for it as breach of orders and when any hast leave of absence they will let the commanding officer know when they return. It is required of the commanding officers of companies to give me a return of the number of men they have at this post after retreat beating this night without fail. Per me Jos. Ingersoll, Lieutenant Colonel

After General Orders July 26th, 1759

As there hast been some Indians firing in the rear this day the general depends upon the regiments not being alarmed if they should hear some. firing in the night.

Counter sign this night, London.

The regiments will not set fire to any of the woods in the rear of the camp except what they immediately use to boil their pots which must be separate from the rest.

CAMP TICONDEROGA, JULY 27TH, 1759
PAROLE, KING GEORGE

Colonel for the day, tomorrow, Regular, Colonel Montgomery; Provincial Lieutenant Colonel, Hunt; tomorrow night, Major Graham; Lieutenant Colonel Putnam; adjutant for tomorrow, Predeaux.

The quartermasters and camp colourmen for the two brigades of regulars to assemble at the front of the regulars to attend Lieutenant Colonel Robinson to mark out the camp as soon as possible when the Provincials arrive. The approaches of batteries to be immediately levelled. The regiments will have orders when they will move their camps. The arms and ammunition to be carefully inspected into; The Rangers must complete their ammunition sending the report to the major of brigade the number of rounds that they want. One hundred and thirty men of Montgomery's Regiment lately come up to be completed with thirty-six rounds of ammunition the commanding officer of the Artillery to send a report of what guns he finds in the fort.

AFTER ORDERS FOR THE 27TH

The two brigades of regulars to encamp this night within the breast work at the first ruff and to assemble by the second. The brigades on the left will march by two on the left through the sally port of Montgomery's; The brigades on the right will march in like manner by the right through the sally ports in the front of Predeaux and will pass in front of the 2nd Brigade. The piquets to be as usual. An evening gun to be fired; The first ruff of the drum on the parties returning from the fort to the camp to take the beating from right to left. The right encampment in the rear of the sally port are to let no man out or in but those whose business may call them. The Rangers, Light Infantry, Grenadiers, Lyman and Worster Regiment will instantly destroy the road they have made by laying logs across and cutting down trees so as to make it impassable from Lake Champlain to the road leading to the saw mill to the post, that the brush may grow up and no appearance of the road may remain; they will begin this early tomorrow morning and finish it as soon as they can; when the great road is all stopped as ordered the above mentioned corps will march to the rear through the woods and draw up in front of the lines; from whence the quartermaster and camp colourmen will attend on Lieutenant Colonel Robinson who will mark out the camp. Major Rogers will send a Company of Rangers tomorrow morning at reveilles beating with all the boats to the front; The companies on the left of Colonel Haviland's Corp. will join their corp. at reveilles beating after which Major Rogers will cut trees across the footpath that hath been made by the lake side; the major will receive his orders from the general. All the tools that these corps have with them must be collected. Lieutenant Colonel Robinson will mark out a park for the Artillery.

Camp at Ticonderoga July 28th, 1759
Parole, Ticonderoga

Colonel for the day tomorrow, Regular Colonel, Grant; Provincial Colonel, Schayler; Field officer for the piquet this night Major Graham; Provincial Colonel Putnam; tomorrow night Major Weft, Major Slapp and adjutant for the day tomorrow Montgomery.

The Rangers are to be posted beyond the saw mill on the right to Major Rogers; the Light Infantry of Regiments will encamp on the ground where Colonel Worster's Regiment is at present encamped on the right of the road leading to the saw mill and the Grenadiers will encamp at the entrance of the woods leading from the fort to the saw mill where Worster's Regiment was at first encamped; The commanding officers of each of those corps will report all accidents to the general. Thirty men of the Light Infantry of Regiments and thirty grenadiers with two subalterns to go immediately to the hospital without arms to carry the wounded to the saw mill; an officer and twenty men of the Light Infantry with arms to go with them and escort the party back.

Colonel Whiting will apply to Colonel Bradstreet for battoes and will send a sufficient number to row them to Fort George two mates of the hospital to go with them.

The hospital to change their ground and move to the rear of Forbes. The second brigade of regulars are to give an officer and thirty men as a guard in the fort. A sergeant and twelve on the garden a subaltern and thirty on the right of the lines by the lakeside where the Grenadiers was posted; a sergeant and twelve halfway between that and the Royals; A corporal and six to lay in the trench at the bottom of the hill between the Royal and sergeant post.

The guard of the fort will take care that no boards or any utensils whatever are taken away by stragglers as they will be of service to repair the fort and use of the hospital. Schayler, Lyman, Fitch and Worster's Regiments are to give no guards only what will be for the safety of the camp and those regiments must furnish what working men may be wanted for repairing the fort with the utmost expedition.

Regulars to receive tomorrow four days' provision beginning half an hour after reveilles beating by the Royal, Predeaux, Inniskillen, Royal Highlanders, Montgomery, Forbes, Grenadiers, Light Infantry Regiments and Gage's to complete them to the 1st of August inclusive.

Divine service tomorrow at 11 o'clock to return thanks for the success of his Majesty's arms. Forbes Regiment to face to the right and join the Royal Brigade to have service done by the chaplain of the Royal the other regiments will be attended by their own chaplain. Grand parade for the regulars in the rear of the Royal.

After Orders of the 28th

The brigades they are to furnish sentries on the lines facing the right; the piquets are not to lay out. The men are to receive the provision tomorrow at the saw mill; the regiments to bake their bread at the ovens by the fort by applying to Lieutenant Colonel Robinson who will see what ovens different regiments are to have.

A general court martial of the line to be held at the president's tent at 8 o'clock tomorrow, Colonel Grant president, Major Alexander Campbell, Major Hambleton, Royals one captain, Forbes one captain, Inniskillen two, Predeaux one, Royal Highlanders and Montgomery three, Ten captains for that duty, Lieutenant George Burton, Deputy Judge Advocate.

Camp Ticonderoga, July 29th, 1759
Parole, Gage

Colonel for the day tomorrow, Regular Colonel, Montgomery; Provincial Colonel, Lyman; Field officer for the piquet this night, Regular Major; West Provincial, Major Duggles; adjutant for the day tomorrow Royals.

The Provincials to receive four days' provisions tomorrow beginning at Ruggles, Schayler, Fitch, and Lyman, Worster, Willard and Babcock and Whiting. Lieutenant Colonel Eyre will make a disposition for the different employs of the work to be carried on by the four Provincial regiments on repairing the fort which his Majesty's services requires shall be done with the utmost expedition. Each regiment will make a return to the major the number of lime burners, masons, and carpenters they have.

Colonel Schayler is to have the superintendency of the work under the direction of Lieutenant Colonel Eyre and Colonel Schayler will appoint such field officers and other officers as he judgest best for the oversight of the work.

The commanding officer of corps will take all opportunities of exercising the men. Montgomery to be out to fire tomorrow morning at 6 o'clock; the troops on the communication not to be alarmed ; The general hospital in the rear of Forbes.

The ovens to be given for the life of the troops, No 1 on the right of the Royal; No 2 on the Inniskillen and Royal Highlanders; No 3 to Montgomery and Forbes; No 5 to Grenadiers and Lieutenant Infantry; No 6 to Gages; No 7 to Lyman and Worster; No 8 Schayler and Fitch. No baker but such as those corps employed to bake in any of these ovens. Every corps in the army to send immediately to Mr. Russel at the Park of Artillery the intrenching tools now in their possession. Reserving such quantities as is necessary for the clearing of the encampments.

Camp at Ticonderoga, Monday July 30th, 1759
Parole, Windsor

Colonel for the day tomorrow, Regular Colonel, Foster; Provincial Colonel, Worster; Field oficer for the piquet this night, Regular Major, John Campbell; Provincial Major, Dugglas; tomorrow night Lieutenant Colonel Darby, Major Waterberry; adjutant of the day tomorrow Late Forbes.

The regiments and corps to keep four days' of bread the that quantity may be always ready when the troops embark and they will apply to Mr. Willson the commissary for such a proportion of flour which will be allowed when the provisions are afterwards received.

After Orders for the 30th

It is forbidden to make use of the whale boats unless particularly ordered as they will be rendered unfit for service. The corps who have had arms spoiled by shot or shells from the enemy may give them in unto the Artillery and they shall receive others in their room and send a report to the major of brigade of what they exchange.

Any fire-locks that have been a great while loaded must be drawn; they may blow some powder out of them tomorrow at 6 o'clock and then all arms to be put in thorough good order; Montgomery's additional to be out to fire at marks tomorrow at 6 o'clock in the swamp on the right.

Camp at Ticonderoga, Tuesday, July 31st, 1759
Parole, Marlborough

Colonel for the day tomorrow, Regular Colonel Montgomery; Provincial Colonel Schayler; Field officer for the piquet this night, Regular Colonel, Darby; Provincial Major Waterberry; for tomorrow night adjutant of the day tomorrow of the Inniskillen. Captain Skean of the Inniskillen is appointed Major of Brigade.

Camp at Ticonderoga, August 1st, 1759
Parole, Carolina

Colonel for the day tomorrow, Regular Colonel Foster; Provincial Colonel Lyman; Field officer for the piquet this night, Regular not asserted; Provincial Lieutenant Colonel Pearson; tomorrow night Lieutenant Colonel Smedly; adjutant for the day tomorrow Predeaux.

As a number of shoes are come up intended for the use of the troops and will be delivered to them at prime cost in England which is 3s 6d a pair, The regiments may receive in the following proportion or as many of that proportion as they like to take by applying to Mr. Tucker agent to Mr. Kelby at the landing place; Royals 284; Forbes 276; Inniskillen do; Royal Highlanders 376; Predeaux 276; Grenadiers 288; Light Infantry do; Gages 276; Royal Artillery 56. The quarter masters must pay for them at the above mentioned rate.

After Orders for the 1st of August 1759

The general court martial of which Colonel Grant was president is dissolved, the general approved of the following sentences of the said general court martial: that Captain Russel of Late Forbes Regiment is to make the following submission to Lieutenant Colonel Darby on the parade before the officers of the regiment: "Sir I am sorry I have been guilty of disrespectful behaviour to you as my superior officer and therefore I ask your pardon."

Captain Howard is found not guilty of the crime laid to his charge and is honourably acquitted.

Thos. Bayly a soldier in the 17th Regiment accused of theft is found guilty and is to receive 1500 lashes with a cat of nine tails.

William Ray of Gage's Light Infantry accused of insolence and threatening language is found guilty and is sentenced to receive 500 lashes with a cat of nine tails. Samuel Whittoe, Corporal in Gage's Light Infantry accused of insolent behaviour is found guilty and sentenced to be reduced to the ranks. Samuel Merrum, of Colonel Ruggle's Regiment, accused of shooting a man of the Royal is adjudged to have done but his duty and is therefore acquitted. Thos. Reed and John Reese of Late Brigade Forbes' Regiment accused of mutiny.

Thos. Reed is found guilty of the crime laid to his charge and is, therefore, sentenced to suffer death but in consideration of Sergeant Hartford striking John Reese three or four times without any provocation John Reese is to receive 500 lashes.

The regular Corps to receive provisions tomorrow beginning by break of day with Forbes following Montgomery, Royal Highlanders, Inniskillen, Predeaux, Royals, Gage's Light Infantry. They will receive for four days and these men will receive two pints of pease apiece, the provisions to be immediately dressed as the men will carry it with them. This completes the regulars to the 5th inclusive. Babcock and Willard to be ready to march when ordered. They will immediately receive of provisions and two pints of pease a man which they will dress and this completes them to the 6th inclusive. Captain Reed is appointed Major of the Highland Regiment.

Camp at Ticonderoga, Thursday August 2nd, 1759
Parole, Shenactady

Colonel for the day tomorrow, Regular Colonel, Montgomery; Provincial Colonel, Worster; Field officer for the piquet this night, Regular Major Hambleton; Provincial Lieutenant Colonel, Smedly; tomorrow night Major Gordon, Lieutenant Colonel Putnam; adjutant for the day tomorrow Montgomery.

The Rangers Light Infantry and Grenadiers and Gages will take whale boats to the saw mill river and put them immediately to the nearest place to their encampments provided they do not obstruct the passage of any boats going down and that the boats will be safe. these Corps are desired to take no more whale boats than what are absolutely necessary to carry their number; The Royal and Forbes will load the battoes with the provisions that are on the beach. The major of brigade will send the proportion that each is to take. The corps to have the same number of battoes *viz*: two per regiment as allowed in coming from Fort George. If the battoes are over as expected the Regiments will embark this night so that everything must be ready but none of the guards relieved till ordered; The Regiments to send a return immediately to the major of brigade of what number of battoes they want to complete them and must have parties waiting at the saw mill to receive them as soon as they come. Mr. Naper director of the hospital will send for a battoe; And the commissaries are to have one battoe. Mr. Willson and Tucker will either proceed or send two of the commissaries forward. The regiments will cut as many boughs immediately as will be necessary to cover the bottoms of the battoes for the security of the provisions.

Noon Orders

As the army is under orders for marching for the reduction of all Canada; The general is willing to give an opportunity to the following persons under sentence of the court martial to wit Thomas Bayly, Thomas Reed, John Reese of Late Forbes corporal Whitway and William Bay, of Brigade Gage's Regiment to wipe off their crimes by their future good behaviour and they are hereby pardoned.

Willards Regiment to remain at the landing place; Ruggles 2nd Battalion and Schaylers to receive provisions immediately to complete them to the 6th inclusive. If Ruggles 2nd Battalion should have any men working with Captain Loring, that are absolutely necessary, they are to be left with him. The lawyers and carpenters furnished to Captain Loring by the regulars are to remain along with him as long as he absolutely wants them.

After Orders

Colonel Fitch is to leave Sergeant Edy with the masons of his regiment who are at present at work with him for the repair of the fort. He will likewise leave Ensign Waterman and Lieutenant Bishop. Lieutenant Colonel Pearson, Major Slapp, Captain Parsons, Lieutenant Lubner of Lyman's Regiment and Captain Holby of Worster's are appointed to have the care of and inspection of the workmen employed in the repair of the fort; the Provincials are to receive four days' provisions tomorrow at the reveille beating beginning with Whitings, following Ruggles' 1st Battalion, Lyman's, Worster's and Fitch, each to receive two pints of pease, which completes them to the 6th inclusive, as Schayler and Fitch are to be ready to march on the first notice, Lyman and Worster will furnish all the working men for the fort except those by order. Fitch will boil their provisions in the same manner as ordered for the other regiments

Colonel Lyman will have the command of the troops left here and will have particular orders from the General Lieutenant Brigham is to remain here to direct the work in which Captain Whelock will assist and Lieutenant Gray will remain overseer.

Camp at Ticonderoga, August 3rd, 1759

Colonel of the day tomorrow, Regular Colonel Foster; Provincial Colonel Fitch; Field officer for the piquet this night Regular Major, Gordon; Provincial Lieutenant Hunt, for tomorrow night, Major Weft Lieut Colonel Putnam; adjutant for the day tomorrow Royals.

George Edwards a deserter in the 17th regiment is to suffer death.

The piquets of the line is to assemble immediately in the front of Montgomery's. The commanding officer of Forbes will order that regiment to erect a gallows on the battery immediately in the front of Montgomery's where the prisoner George Edwards is to be hanged in his French coat, with a label on his breast, "Hanged for desertion to the French." He is to be left hanged all day and at retreat beating to be buried very deep under the gallows and his French coat with him. This is to be put into execution immediately and if the provost martial doth not find a hangman the commanding officer of the piquet will order that the provost master doth it himself.

Lyman's and Worster's Regiments are to change their camps. A quartermaster and camp colourman to assist Lieutenant Colonel Robinson who will mark out the ground for them; The regiments to take care that all the battoes are corked that was ordered down to repair those that were leaky.

After Orders for the 3rd of August

A general to beat tomorrow morning at 2 o'clock assembly half an hour after and the regiments will send their tents and baggage to the boats as soon as possible that the whole may be embarked and ready to move off by daybreak. Gage's Light Infantry will cover the right of the front columns in the same manner as at Lake George, dividing their boats with the three pounders to the right and left.

They will as soon as they embark draw up opposite the post where Major Rogers was embarked and remain till the columns joins them. The Rangers and Light Infantry of Regiments and Grenadiers will march by the right and form the columns on the left of the centre; The Artillery will form the columns on the right of the centre; Schayler and Fitch Regiments will march by the left and they are to man the Artillery boats; the rafts will lead the columns for which the signal will be given as on Lake George both for sailing and landing and that column will be followed by the boats of the quarter masters, engineers, generals and staff baggage, hospital stores, commissaries, sutlers and the boats with the tools will immediately follow.

The rest of the columns with Artillery Babcock and Ruggles 2nd Battalion, will form the columns on the right and will march by the left and embark in the morning as soon as they can get their boats. Any provisions that may be left by the saw mill they will take with them. All the columns to have their boats two deep, those that marched by the left have their front ranks to the right, a boat with a 24 pounder on the left of the right column, the other boat with a 24 pounder on the right of the left column and a 12 pounder on the two centre columns. Colonel Ruggles commands the columns on the right; Colonel Haviland on the left, Colonel Schayler the column on the right of the centre, Colonel Grant on the left of the centre; the men will disembark with their coats on unless they will be ordered to the contrary; The Provincial battalions that remain here will receive their provisions for four days and three days as it becomes due.

Colonel Whiting and Lieutenant Colonel Ingersoll will report all extraordinaries to Colonel Lyman at Fort Ticonderoga. The commanding of Montgomery's detachment will mount the following guards from each detachment an officer and twenty-four men at the fort; a sergeant and ten men in the fort by the water side; a corporal and six on the garden and they will obey such orders as they shall receive from Colonel Lyman. All guards from the right ordered to march tomorrow are to join the regiments at the reveille beating of the general.

Camp at Crown Point August 6th, 1759
Parole, New Jersey

Colonel for the day tomorrow , for the Regular Colonel Foster; Provincials Colonel Babcock; Field officer for the piquet this night, Regular Major, Read ; Provincial, Lieutenant Colonel Hunt; Tomorrow night Lieutenant Colonel Darby, Lieutenant Colonel Saltonstall. Adjutant for the day tomorrow Royal Highlander.

As twenty-four barrels of spruce beer are come to the fort the corps may send for seven of the same immediately in the following proportion: The Royal and Royal Highlanders and Montgomery three barrels each late for 61s Inniskilling and Predeaux; two each Artillery Light Infantry Grenadier, Gages Light Infantry two each.

Major Rogers to send a party of men with an officer to take two battoes immediately to Ticonderoga to apply to Sergeant Arey for spruce beer which they are to load with and bring to camp here without loss of time.

The Provincials to receive three days' provisions tomorrow beginning with Ruggles at 5 o'clock, ending with Babcock; this completes them to the 9th inclusive. The three ovens in the fort shall be for their use to bake their bread in. Orders are given for all the sutlers to be permitted to bring cattle over from Fort George, to Ticonderoga and as a road will be finished this day from Ticonderoga to this place the regiments will acquaint their sutlers accordingly that they may bring any live cattle to the camp. Lieutenant Monteries is appointed *Aid Du Camp* during the absence of Captain Prescott.

After Orders

An officer from the line and a corporal and six men from each regiment of regulars to assemble immediately in battoes near the Royal and proceed this evening to Ticonderoga from whence they are to bring all the spruce beer and brewing utensils to this camp All the corps in the lines to send a return of the sawyer, miner and blacksmith that they have to the Major of Brigade Monypenny this evening an officer and fifty rangers to assemble at Gages Light Infantry at 5 o'clock tomorrow morning they will take six battoes and proceed two miles down the lake when they will cut spruce and the officer will take a French deserter with him who will show him where the spruce is and a man who can talk German to be the interpreter. A party of Gage's Light Infantry will go in the English boat to guard the battoes. The officer will deliver the spruce under the care of the sergeant of the guard by the fort.

The regulars are to furnish for the engineer 300 to parade tomorrow morning at 5 o'clock in the front of Royal Highlanders when Lieutenant Colonel Eyre will order them 200 men of the Provincials to assemble tomorrow morning at 5 o'clock in the front of the Royal and are to take with them what tools they want from the magazine by the fort.

Major Rogers will send a captain and two subalterns and sixty men as a covering party with some Indians and an officer with them to show the commanding officer the best place in the wood on the other side of the lake the covering party must not fire any drooping shot at any game they are to take as many men from the Royal as they want and a day's provisions with them and when they return at night they will deliver the battoes to the guard of the Royal where they will reserve them.

Crown Point, 7th of August 1759
Parole, Boston

Colonel of the day tomorrow for the Regular Colonel Montgomery; Field oficer for the piquet this night for the Provincial Colonel Schayler; Regular Lieutenant Colonel Darby;

Lieutenant Colonel Saltonstall; for tomorrow night Major Alexander Campbell, Lieutenant Colonel Putnam; Adjutant for the day tomorrow, Predeaux.

The Light Infantry to change their fire locks they received at the train and to take carbines in the room. The observe that some people are not obedient to the orders of 5th of August which permitted two battoes per regiment to go a fishing and by which we may lose men and if any are found disobedient to that order hereafter, they shall not be permitted to take a battoe out. The arm of the drafts to be examined and every regiment to complete them with what may be wanting.

The Provincials to mount a guard of one sergeant and twelve men in the fort to put a sentry upon the ovens in the fort and to take care that none comes there but what has permission. Colonel Robinson will show them what oven they are to use.

A general court martial of the army to fit tomorrow morning at 3 o'clock at the president's tent. Colonel Fitch president, Major Gordon, Major Dugglas and six captains from the regulars, and Lieutenant from the Provincials. Lieutenant George Burton D.J.A.

After Orders

200 working men from the regulars, at 11 o'clock in the morning for the engineer, 300 workmen from the Provincials, at the same time Captain Firbrook of the Jersey Regiment, and fifty of the men that work with him, this day to be of the number, who are to finish the work in the rear of the Grenadier hundred by the Light Infantry to throw up a work beginning at 5 o'clock tomorrow morning.

Lieutenant Colonel Eyre will trace it out this evening. Captain Williams to oversee the work.

A captain and sixty Rangers to set out tomorrow morning at 5 o'clock with six battoes General Gages Light Infantry will send at the same time the English boat and to stay out till toward evening. The captain of the Rangers will take the French deserter from the general guard and must go to the place that the deserter will show them where the French have always supplied themselves with spruce. They must bring as much spruce as they can to camp. A corporal and six men point in battoes and march your detachment by land in case battoes can not be furnished you and put yourself under the command of Colonel Haviland at Crown Point.

J. Amherst
Albany
June 1st, 1760

General Orders
Camp near Albany, May 27th, 1760
Parole, Dartmouth

The regiments of 1000 are to be allowed as last year, three ox carts for their sutlers and those of 700 two ox carts; for the corps the are to serve up the Mohawk River; their sutlers will be allowed to have two small battoes instead of ox carts, these are to be allowed without interfering with any intended for the King's service; they are to be marked and numbered. Rum is so pernicious to the soldiers, that no sutler of any regiment will be permitted to take any rum, except by an order from the commanding officer of the regiment who may take what he thinks absolutely necessary for the use of the regiment specifying in his orders to the sutlers, the quantity and the mark of the cask it is in, and no other sutler will be allowed to take any rum into the field as it is forbidden. All the regiments are always to be allowed to carry their baggage on march, one wagon for each company, one for the commanding officer and one for the staff; when the baggage goes by water, they are to be allowed battoes in proportion to the above allowance of wagons.

After Orders

The regiments of 1000 men are allowed three wagons to two companies and battoes in proportion. The second Battalion of Royal Highlanders are to try their arms the day after tomorrow beginning to fire at 6 o'clock the 28th.

Battalion Royal Highlander's regiment and Montgomery to

receive two days' provision to the 31st inclusive, the Rhode Island and Jersey troops, and all that remains immediately to disembark and land in the meadows, where Captain Prescott will meet them and conduct them to the ground where they are to encamp, they will send in returns as soon as possible of their number, that their tents may be provided for them; they will take all the provisions remaining in the sloops for their use in the camp sending in returns to what day they received, the same for the companies of the Massachusetts troops at Green Bush to cross the river and encamp as the regiment is now encamped. No officer whatever to lay out of camp.

Albany, 28th May 1760
Parole, Cambridge

The third regiment of N. York to send in returns of the number of arms they have in their regiment and the number wanting to complete their effectives. For the future every corps to give weekly returns on every Monday morning, as well as repeat monthly returns. Montgomery's to be ready the first notice.

Albany, 29th May 1760
Parole, Yorkshire

The companies of Montgomery's regiment to march tomorrow morning at 5 o'clock. They will receive their wagons in proportion to their number allowed to carry camp equipage and baggage to Schenectady by applying to Colonel Bradstreet. All men on duty of that regiment to be relieved this evening and their colours to be lodged in the fort, in the same manner as the regulars. Major Campbell will receive his orders from the general.

The orders given the 5th of May last year at Albany relating to the Grenadiers and Light Infantry, filling of the battalion and posting of officers, the sergeants taking fire-lock, instead of halberts, and only one drummer allowed per company the rest in the barracks, no women being permitted to go with the regiment or to follow them. The method of marching the regiments are to practice the order for the front and flank and rear platoons are to be all duly observed this campaign and as more baggage than is absolutely necessary for the officers is an encumbrance to officers and men, must be an obstruction to the motion of the army in the country, each officer must take a small tent blanket and bear skin and portmanteau; they will take no sacks into the field; the regiments to have gorgets will wear them when on duty and each officer will take care the men do not load themselves with more than what is absolutely necessary.

The Cognowaga Indian is suspected to be lurking about the town or camp. Officers and soldiers who see an Indian who is not known and can not give an account of himself, will bring him to headquarters. The Massachusetts troops to receive four days' provisions.

Regiment Orders

A return of the strengths of each company to be given immediately As the men that mount the quarter guard suffer for want of tents there will be but one tent per camp at present allowed for the officers as the general will soon provide tents for the officers. A provision return signed by the commanding officer of companies to be given to the quartermaster immediately.

Regiment Orders
Albany, 30th May 1760

A regimental court martial to sit this morning at the president's tent to try such prisoners as shall be brought before. Captain Russel, president. Lieutenant Peck, Ensign Stafford members.

General Orders
Parole, Albany

The general court martial ordered this morning to fit at the orderly house rooms so soon as the prisoners is marched in for a trial accused of burning Mr. Tenbrook's outhouse Major Greyham, President. Captain Muntiness, Deputy Judge Advocate. All evidences to attend in case the court martial should not be over by the time.

Sir Allen Mclean's Company is to march at 2 o'clock this after noon, evidences are to remain here, and a corporal and six men to march the prisoner.

The commanding officers of the companies of Montgomery's regiment having desired to take their colours into the field are to take them accordingly. All the regiments are immediately to clear their men to the 24th of April afterwards at the end of every two months. Agreeable to former orders one sergeant and two corporal guards of six men each to be posted by Lieutenant Coventry along the fence which runs at the bottom of the hill to Hallam's house to prevent the fence from being destroyed and the cattle getting out. Two sergeants and thirty-six men to be ordered from the Provincials for the service of the scows and to remain till further orders.

After Orders

Captain Batun Captain Hawkins and Captain Platt Companies of the N. York regiment to be completed with arms according to the returns given in the afternoon by applying to Col Williamson tomorrow morning at 5 o'clock. The first and third Regiments of N. Yorkers to be completed with arms tomorrow morning according to returns given in by applying to Colonel Williamson first regiment to receive theirs at half after five the 3rd at six.

General Orders
Camp Near Albany, 31st May 1760
Parole, Berlin

The field officers of the Provincials who are arrived here and have companies to send a return of their ranks and date of their commissions to the adjutant general tomorrow at orderly time. Colonel Thomas, an officer commanding the Massachusetts troops, will send a report from what companies the several detachments of the Massachusetts sentry the Hudson River are taken, as the companies are not formed into battalions. He will give in his returns at 5 o'clock this evening. The general will see what

Provincial troops are in camp, at the head of their encampments. At 5 o'clock this evening they are to be drawn up in two ranks all those that have arms are to appear with them and that have bullet pouches and powder horns will likewise put them on.

A court of enquiry consisting of one major and four captains of the N. York troops to set at the court house at—clock tomorrow morning to examine into the accusation against Peter Mackay who is confined by lieutenant on suspicion of heaving a man over board and drowning him.

The general court martial ordered yesterday will assemble the moment the prisoner is marched into town.

The 2nd Battalion of the Royal Highland regiment to receive three days' provisions at 5 o'clock tomorrow morning which will complete them to the 3rd day of June inclusive.

The troops on no account to pull down or destroy any of the fence. Extraordinaries in camp to be immediately reported at headquarters.

Regimental Orders

Commanding officer of each company will take care that their men appear clean and no man whatever to be absent from camp this afternoon.

After Orders

The Massachusetts regiment to furnish three sergeants, three corporals and sixty-seven privates for the quartermaster general those parties to be sent to Lieutenant Coventry's quarters at 6 o'clock tomorrow morning and the Rhode Island troops to furnish two sergeants, two corporals and thirty-three privates for the Artillery.

The first N.York regiment to furnish one sergeant and twelve privates The second, one corporal and seven, the third, one sergeant and seventeen for the Artillery. those parties to march from the several corps to the parade near the church where a man from the artillery will receive them.

General Order
Albany, Sunday 1st June, 1760
Parole, Hanover

Three hundred of the Rhode Island regiment are to march at 3 o'clock this afternoon according to the orders sent to the Lieutenant Colonel of the regiment One battoe or two if necessary, to be allowed to carry their tents and necessaries. Captain commanding this detachment will receive orders in writing.

All the Massachusetts troops that are encamped to strike their tents tomorrow morning at day break and march down to the meadow below the town. They are to take all their camp equipage and camp necessaries with them, and are to receive boats with provision to go up the river with. Colonel Thomas will receive orders from general.

Lieutenant Colonel Ingersoll is to remain here to receive the Massachusetts troops as they arrive. The regiment of 1000 will be allowed the provisions or the four pence in the lieu of it for four women per company. This allowance shall be paid to the women by Lieutenant Coventry at Albany. The commanding officer is to send a list of the women of each company who are recommended for the provisions which he will sign and transmit to the major of brigade who will give this to Lieutenant Coventry and give in their names to the matron of the hospital, yet if they should be requested for the attendance of the sick, they may attend or otherwise they will be struck off the allowance.

The general court martial of which Major Graham is president is dissolved, and Donald McKinnim, private soldier of Montgomery's Regiment tried on suspicion of having maliciously and wilfully set fire to Mr. Tenbrook's outhouse, is found not guilty of the crime laid to his charge and is acquitted. Captain Cameron will take him to join the regiment

General Orders
Albany 2nd June 1760
Parole, Aberdeen

The guard at Loudon Ferry to be relieved tomorrow as usual.

One sub, two sergeants and twenty-eight men of the New York Regiment is to march this afternoon at 3 o'clock at Loudon Ferry to relieve the lieutenant and thirty men of that corps who are posted. That subaltern and sergeant will take all the orders that have been delivered to that lieutenant, which he will obey and he will remain there till further orders. The lieutenant, when returned will march into camp here to receive their bounty, money arms, etc. One captain, two subalterns, sixty men of the New York and Jersey troops without arms to parade this afternoon at 3 o'clock just where the Massachusetts troops were encamped, where will be delivered to them, and a person will show them where to cut timber for mending the road. When they leave off work the axes to be delivered to the provost guard if they are not ordered to be brought back to town The two companies of Massachusetts troops arrived at Green Bush are to cross the water and encamp immediately. The New York, and New Jersey and Rhode Island troops to receive provisions tomorrow morning at 5 o'clock which completes them to the 6th inclusive.

General Orders
Albany, 3rd June 1760
Parole, Dresden

The three companies of the Massachusetts to receive provisions to the 7th inclusive are to strike their tents at 2 o'clock this afternoon and send them down to the meadows below the town, where they will have one battoe and two if necessary, to take their tents up the river. The company will march at 3 o'clock. The captain commanding them will receive his order in writing.

A general court martial to set tomorrow morning at 8 o'clock at the orderly room in the barracks, for the trial of all the prisoners in the provost guard. One colonel, one lieutenant colonel, one major, Lieutenant Campbell of the 2nd Battalion of the Royal Highlanders Deputy Judge Advocate, all evidences to attend.

The Massachusetts to leave the evidences against the men of their corps confined yesterday for desertion. one captain, three subalterns, one sergeant and two privates of the New York, New

Jersey and Rhode Island troops, to parade without arms tomorrow morning at 5 o'clock in order to work upon the road. A person will be appointed to attend to direct them all. The Provincials as they arrive in camp are to send returns of the number of arms they have and the number wanted to complete them; they will also find returns of the number of horns and bullet pouches they have.

The 2nd Battalion of the Royal Highland Regiment to receive four days' provisions tomorrow morning at 5 o'clock which completes them to the 7th inclusive.

General Orders
Albany, 4th June 1760
Parole, Copenhagen

When any of the troops Regulars or Provincials during the campaign are employed as artificers or labourers they will be paid for the same at the following rates in New York currency; all artificers *per diem* 1/3; to mortar makers and labourers workers of the kind 1/-; Other labourers in work such as building storehouses or barracks or hospitals 19d. All other works such as entrenchments, making of forts, or parties mending of roads, they are the soldiers duty and never paid; a gill of rum per man is not to be allowed for any of those works unless they should be employed in wet work, or that the weather be wet and bad, that may make it necessary for the soldiers to have rum, for as the men will be always supplied with spruce at very reasonable price; rum will be of more disservice than good to them. Where any work is carried on by artificers or labourers the accounts of the several workmen must be kept by the commanding officers and the persons who direct from which account only the men will receive their wages.

When any regiment or any part of them are going from one camp or quarters to another that they take battoes and provisions, they are not to be paid for it, but when the corps are sent on purpose for the battoe service, they will be paid at the following rates New York currency. Captain *per diem* 4/; Non-commissioned officers and private men per battoe 3/.

The men will have rum given them in such manner as for other service, that when the weather is bad, the service may require it, and circumstances permit otherwise they are not to expect it.

The commanding officers of all the parties ordered on that service are to keep a lift of the names of men, the camp the regiment who they belong to, and the time they work which list they are to certify and to give into the major of brigade who will deliver it to the deputy quartermaster general that it may be approved of and paid.

After Orders

One captain, three subalterns and four sergeants to hundred privates of the New York, New Jersey and Rhode Island to parade without arms tomorrow morning at 5 o'clock at the provost guard in order to work upon the roads. A person will be ordered to direct them, one field officer, three captains, six subalterns twelve sergeants and 288 privates of the New York and New Jersey to parade in the road by the Massachusetts encampment without the fire locks or cartouche boxes, to carry only bayonets with troops. Two subs, with forty men to form two platoons to parade the same time with them; with their arms and accoutrements. Ammunition will be delivered them at the rendezvous, the whole to march without tents, taking provisions with them.

The field officer will have his orders in writing from the general. The arms and things left behind them will be taken care of by the regiments The field officer for the command tomorrow Lieutenant Colonel Vanseaack.

General Orders
Albany, 5th June 1760
Parole, Thornhausen

All the Connecticut troops that may arrive this day will be ready to move to Loudon Ferry and Schenectady, the commanding officer will have his orders in writing. The provost to go his rounds in camp frequently to destroy all rum that may be selling in the huts near the camp; All the Provincial Regiments to send in a return of what Swiss or Frenchmen are enlisted in any of the companies; specifying where they have served before or whether this is the first campaign. The commanding officer to make inspection themselves into their several companies that their returns may be exact.

GENERAL ORDERS
ALBANY, 7TH JUNE 1760
PAROLE, BRUNSWICK

The Connecticut troops that are returned from Schenectady arc immediately to encamp. Thos. Rowland, Wm. Massey and George Not, of the Royal regiment and Daniel Carrey, of Captain McClean's Independent Companies returned by the sergeant of the hospital fit to go into their regiments are to be marched by a corporal from post to post until they join their respective corps.

The second Battalion of the Royal Highland regiment to receive three days' provisions tomorrow morning at 5 o'clock which completes them to the l0th inclusive, The Connecticut troops in camp to receive four days' provisions immediately, which completes them to the l0th inclusive.

GENERAL ORDERS
CROWN POINT, 18TH JUNE 1760
PAROLE, NORWALK

A return of each, field officer for the day tomorrow Major Campbell.

General Amherst his orders that the amount of the molasses that has been used at the several posts as likewise the quantity that is at present remaining and the money that has been (topped for the payment of the molasses that is issued according to the orders of Nov. 22nd at Crown Point; to be reported to Lieutenant Colonel Robinson or Lieutenant Coventry at Albany the l5th.

The baggage and forage money, as likewise the winter allowance of 4/ in lieu of provisions will be paid immediately to the staff officers of the regiments and independent companies. The two battalions of the Royal Highlanders and Ogdens will receive theirs at Albany. The other regiments are not to send for it. Lieutenant Colonel Robinson will take the money for the regiment to the westward and Major Christian for the regiments and independent camps to the northward. No firing money is allowed but to the garrison at Albany and Schenectady the who will be paid their usual allowance by applying to Lieutenant Colonel Robinson.

As some battoes were stove by the carelessness of those who brought them for the engineer it is expected they will for the future obey the orders they have had for carrying the battoes around the point as soon as they are unloaded, no person to quit his battoe till they are unloaded, and his order be complied with though the hour of work should be over as they ought to be certain of punishment through their negligence.

It is hoped for the future no mistake will be made in the evening for the workmen breaking off sooner than the gun firing. The engineer will order the alarm beat when the men are to quit work, for their breakfast and dinner likewise. For the different assembly at different hours appointed at work except at 5 o'clock will be done by the officers of the fort guard.

FATIGUE TOMORROW
PAROLE, STANFORD

	C	S	S	R.V.F
Regulars	1	2	5	140
Mass	2	4	6	390
R. I	0	2	3	70
Total	3	8	14	600

A return of the Massachusetts and Rhode Island with the names of the field officers of the dates of their commission to be given in tomorrow morning at orderly time. George Penter of the 17th regiment to attend the brewery.

General Orders

For the day tomorrow Major Gordon. A return of the artificers in the Royal Regiment to be given to the Engineer this evening at 5 o'clock. The Royal and Rhode Island to take their proportion of their duty tomorrow.

Fatigue Tomorrow

	C	S	S	R.V.F
Regulars	1	2	5	140
Provincials	3	8	12	560

Captain Senior Lieutenant Rossy Captain Cross and Stafford for fatigue tomorrow

General Orders
Camp Crown Point, 20th June 1760
Parole, New Haven

For the day tomorrow Major Campbell. The general court martial of which Lieutenant Colonel Derby was president is dissolved. Colonel Haviland approves of the said court martial. The Joseph Cavendish, John Macintosh, John Lee, John Guest of the 17th regiment John Leslie, James Magruske of the 2nd of the Royals, John Robinson of the Independents all tried and found guilty of desertion are to be punished as follows *viz*:

	lashes
John Cavendish	1000
John Macintosh	500
John Lee	1000
John Guest	1000
John Leslie	1500
James McGrath	1000
John Robinson	1000

But as he is just come to the command of his Majesty's forces in the Northern district that the above persons sensible of their crimes that they will for the future behave as good soldiers he, therefore, pardons them; that, their crimes merit many and he does assure them and the rest of the army this is the last time he will pardon any of that fort.

The artificers of the Royals to attend the engineer at 5 o'clock. John Rogers, of the Inniskilling regiment to attend the engineer.

Fatigue Tomorrow

	C	S	S	R.V.F
Regulars	1	2	5	140
Provincials	3	8	12	560
	4	10	17	700

General Orders
Crown Point Saturday, 21st June 1760
Parole, Guilford

For the day tomorrow Lieutenant Colonel Derby. Divine service to be at tended tomorrow morning at 10 o'clock at the head of the 17th as usual.

General Orders
Parole, Fairfield

For the day tomorrow Major Gordon.

The regulars to receive two days' fresh and two days' salt provisions tomorrow, beginning with the Royal Artillery at 6 o'clock following 17th Inniskilling and Royal allowing one hour for each regiment The Provincials to receive four days' salt beginning with Rhode Islanders and so following Massachusetts and Rangers. This completes the army to the 26th inclusive. Returns of the number victualled to be given in this evening at 5 o'clock to the commissary. Monthly return to be given in tomorrow at orderly time to the major of brigade.

The engineers to pull down the huts in the forest tomorrow.

The following men to attend the engineer tomorrow morning at 5 o'clock: James Caaly, John Jobson, Cain Conners, Joseph Arthred, John Nep, miners. Edward Mantle and Richard Leed, mortar makers of the Inniskilling Regiment

Return of the number of men now in the Provincials who have served as gunners here or elsewhere to be given in this evening to the major of brigade. The commanding officer of each corps to order the different companies to make hand-barrows or other carriages for carrying their spruce beer and other provisions, if they do not provide them in a reasonable time they will not receive spruce beer, as rolling the casks damages them. those that do not return the casks in good order must not expect to be served. It is recommended to the officers and sutlers to give to the spruce brewery any cask they may have fit for that use. The Massachusetts to receive twenty-one tents from the quartermaster of the 27th regiment for the two first detachments that arrived of that corps.

General Orders
Crown Point, Monday 23 June 1760
Parole, Milford

For the day tomorrow Major Campbell. those men returned by the Massachusetts and Rhode Island Regiments as gunners to join Lieutenant Colonel Orde immediately. Fatigue tomorrow as usual.

General Orders
Parole, Seabrook

For the day tomorrow Lieutenant Colonel Derby.

The prisoners lately come from Canada not to do duty with arms until they are exchanged, those of them who belong to the corps here are to join them as soon as those that are on board the vessels come up to Crown Point. The rest are to go to Albany under the care of the officers that come with them. Such privates as are here belonging to the corps at Quebec are to have their account fettled, arms and accoutrements taken in that they may proceed to New York under the care of those officers who are not exchanged. Any of the sailors that have to stay here shall be employed in a peaceable way until they shall be exchanged. The inhabitants belonging to our colonies are likewise to go with this party that they may be supplied with provision. The Grenadiers and Light Infantry not to be put on duty or fatigue tomorrow morning as they will encamp in separate corps.

The eldest captain in each will have the command. The Light Infantry fort guard to be augmented to one sergeant, one corporal and eighteen men. The re-enforcements to join at 4 o'clock this after noon. Fatigue as usual.

After General Orders

All the masons belonging to the different corps to be sent to the engineer tomorrow morning at 5 o'clock. Sergeant Franklin of the Inniskilling regiment is to attend the same hour.

Morning Orders
Crown Point, Wednesday 25th June

The Grenadiers' Companies of the 17th and Inniskilling Regiments to remove their encampments at 10 o'clock this morning. Sir. John Blackney will shew them the ground.

Parole, Branford

The Provincials to erect hospital for their sick as soon as they possibly can. A return of the artificers in Captain Morris' detachment of Massachusetts to be given in this evening at retreat beating.

General Orders
Crown Point, Thursday 26 June 1760
Parole, Killingsworth

For the day tomorrow Major Campbell. Colonel Ingersoll, and Major Willard three captains, nine subalterns, nine sergeants and 300 of the Massachusetts to go up to Putnam's encampment tomorrow where they are to be employed in getting timber for the fort. Colonel Ingersoll will receive his directions from Captain Garth, engineer and get fifteen battoes from the major brigade which he must be answerable for.

All arrears of spruce money to be immediately paid to Mr. Frasier the barrack master. For the future no spruce beer will be delivered till paid for. The army to receive four days' salt provisions tomorrow, beginning at Rhode Islanders following Massachusetts the Royals 17th and 27th Regiments Rangers and Royal Artillery allowing one hour for each corps. The account of the Regulars to be settled to the 24th inclusive. They are not to be paid their balance till orders. The Grenadiers to furnish the guard at the Light Infantry Fort. one corporal and six men of the Regulars tomorrow to mount as a guard on the provisions.

Working Party
Regulars 140
Provincials 560
700

General Orders
Crown Point Friday 27 June 1760
Parole, Pemberton

For the day tomorrow Lieutenant Colonel Derby. One captain, three subalterns, four sergeants and one hundred and fifty Provincials to join Lieutenant Ord including those he has already. They are to take with them their proportion of tents. A list of the prisoners that came lately from Canada and have joined the corps here to be given in this evening at 5 o'clock. The rest of those prisoners to be paraded at 9 o'clock at the Artillery walk in order to embark for Ticonderoga. Men belonging to the corps at Quebec to assemble at the same time. The recruits and awkward [squads] of the regulars to practice with powder and ball at a mark as often as the commanding officer of corps thinks it fit between the hours of 5 and 8 in the morning. They may likewise practice the battalions at marks not exceeding twelve rounds per month till further orders.

WORKING PARTY
Regulars   140
Provincials   560
               700

Sergeant Grant of the Regulars to attend Captain Grath, Engineer.

GENERAL ORDERS
CAMP SATURDAY 28TH JUNE 1760
PAROLE, DARBY

For the day tomorrow Major Gordon.

WORKING PARTY TOMORROW

	C	S	S	R.V.F
Regulars	1	2	5	140
Provincials	3	10	12	560
	4	12	17	700

As complaint has been made to Colonel Haviland that the Provincials do not come to work regularly after breakfast and dinner. It is, therefore, ordered that the officers parade them at the above times and to be answerable that their numbers are just.

GENERAL ORDERS
CROWN POINT, SUNDAY 27TH JUNE 1760
PAROLE, NEW LONDON

For the day tomorrow Major Campbell, one captain, two subalterns, two sergeants and hundred Provincials to parade at 5 o'clock tomorrow morning and to take sixteen battoes and proceed to the saw mills where eight are to be loaded with provisions and eight with boards and returned as soon as possible. The provisions to be unloaded here as usual, and the boards at the point where battoes are repairing, and are to be delivered to Mr. Marshal who has charge of them.

Working Party Tomorrow

	C	S	S	R.V.F
Regulars	1	2	5	140
Provincials	3	10	12	560

Command to Ticonderoga Lieutenant Trip 1.

Fatigue Captain Marshal 1

Lieutenant Walson, Lieutenant Rose and Ensign Fenner, Lieutenant Kembell Quarter Guard.

General Orders
Parole, Providence

For the day tomorrow, Lieutenant Colonel Derby.

The French prisoners in the Grenadier guard be removed to Gage's Light Infantry Fort and the soldiers barracks of Light Infantry of Regiments to be given to Lieutenant Colonel Ord. The army to receive two days and four days' salt provisions tomorrow. Beginning at 6 o'clock with the Royals, following the 7th Inniskilling, Royal Artillery, Rangers, Massachusetts and Rhode Islanders allowing an hour for each regiment. Returns to be given in the evening to the company. If the Provincial sutlers do not put their rum into the casements agreeable to former orders, will be stove and they will be turned out of camp.

Working Party Tomorrow

	C	S	S	R.V.F
Regulars	1	2	5	140
Provincials	9	10	12	560

Any one that offers to take a painter, oar or anything else belonging to a battoe or displacing them shall have hundred lashes without a court martial and the June punishment for any person who shall steal hay or grass or corn intended for the army. 'Tis expected Provincials officers will be more regular in reading orders to their men.

GENERAL ORDERS
CROWN POINT, JULY 1ST 1760
PAROLE, WOODBRIDGE

For the day tomorrow Major Gordon.

Two subalterns, four non-commissioned officers and fifty-eight privates of the Provincials to assemble this evening at 3 o'clock in order to go down the lake to relieve the same number of Regulars on board the sloop.

WORKING PARTY TOMORROW

	C	S	S	R.V.F
Regulars	1	2	5	140
Provincials	9	10	12	560

GENERAL ORDERS
CROWN POINT JULY 2ND, 1760
PAROLE, STONINGTON

For the day tomorrow Major Campbell. One captain, three subalterns, three sergeants and hundred privates of the Massachusetts to parade tomorrow morning at 5 o'clock to take six battoes and proceed to Colonel Ingersoll's encampment and put themselves under his command, and they are to take their tents and provisions with them. Captain Silas Brown for the above party. The Rangers to be formed into companies agreeable to a list his excellency General Amherst has sent.

The Provincials every two or three days if the weather permit, to strike tents in order to air and sweeten the ground, a little earth to be thrown into to prevent noisome smells. The Light Infantry to encamp this afternoon at 5 o'clock on the left of the ground they had last year. They are not to give men for the works tomorrow. The Grenadiers to give their proportions for the works tomorrow. The Grenadiers and Light Infantry each to appoint a sergeant to attend for orders and to keep the details for corps. Working party: Regulars 140. Provincials 560.

After Orders

No liquor of any sort to be fold to soldiers by sutlers or people after gun firing. Any soldier found in the market after that hour will be sent to prison. For that purpose a patrol to go at different hours through the market from the quarter guard of 17th and Inniskilling Regiment which they will take night about. The sutlers of the Rangers as well as the other sutlers in camp, and market people to meet quartermaster Blakney and the barracks master in the fort to morrow at 11 o'clock.

General Orders
Camp Crown Point 3rd July 1760
Parole, Staten Island

For the day tomorrow Lieutenant Colonel Derby.

A sutler of the Rangers, and George Morris of the market who had their liquor stove this day to quit Crown Point immediately. If they are hereafter found in camp or any post between this and Albany they will be whipped and drummed out. All sutlers and market people are desired to take notice they will be served the same way or worse if they are found to make soldiers drunk or doing anything else contrary to orders.

The barrack master to acquaint all sutlers and market people with all orders concerning them, and he is hereby ordered to search and examine any huts, tents and cellars belonging to those people and see if any spirituous liquors they have contrary to orders. Any of the camp or garrison guards are to furnish him with a file when he demands it for the above service. Working as usual. The artificers of the Provincials to encamp on the left of their corps, that they may be in greater readiness to turn out.

General Orders
Friday, Crown Point 4th July 1760
Parole, Elizabeth Point

For the day tomorrow Major Gordon.

The Massachusetts and Rhode Islanders to furnish four men

that they have had the smallpox they are to take one tent and pitch it where the timer lies in the rear of the Light Infantry. They will receive one battoe which they will take care of at the place in order to ply between the camps and the smallpox hospital. They are not to come into camp on any account and are to receive their directions from Dr. Monroe. The following quota of the Massachusetts are to attend the engineer tomorrow morning at 5 o'clock. Thos. Neal, Caleb Flow, Wm. Varnish, Wm. Smith, Nathl. Hardy and Lewis Martin. The men employed in rafting timber not to be included in the engineers number of 500. Working party as usual.

Regimental Orders

The commanding officer of companies will have their men strike their tents every fair day at 10 o'clock and to remain in that position until 2 in the afternoon that the ground may air. The orderly sergeants will make a report every morning at 10 o'clock of the sick and lame in each camp.

Fatigue tomorrow, Captain Russel, Lieutenant Bennit and Ensign Gardiner. Quarter Guard Lieutenant Pullon.

General Orders
Crown Point, Saturday 5th July
Parole, Trenton

For the day tomorrow Major Campbell. The men to work for the future from reveilles beating until 8 o'clock when the the retreat will beat for them to go to breakfast. The prisoners march at 9 o'clock when they are to return to work. Retreat at 12 for dinner, the prisoners to march at 4 o'clock and to continue to work until gun firing. Working party as usual. Divine service tomorrow at 10 o'clock in the front of the 17th regiment Fatigue tomorrow Captain Fry, Lieutenant Warren and Lieutenant Watson, Quarter Guard Lieutenant Willcox.

General Orders
Crown Point, July 6th, 1760
Parole, Brunswick

For the day tomorrow Lieutenant Colonel Derby. One captain, two subalterns, four sergeants and hundred privates of the Provincials to parade tomorrow morning at 5 o'clock. They are to take sixteen battoes and proceed to the saw mill where they are to load them with provisions and return as soon as possible. Sixty men are to be added to the engineer tomorrow. Nicholas Hide of the Rhode Islanders to attend the Engineer tomorrow.

Working Party Tomorrow

Regulars	140
Provincials	560
	700

The Light Infantry to give their proportion to the work tomorrow. The army to receive two days' fresh and four days' salt provisions tomorrow morning beginning at 5 o'clock with the Rhode Islanders and following the Massachusetts, Rangers, Royal Artillery, Inniskilling, 17th Royals allowing one hour for each corps. They are to give in the number to the commissary this evening at 5 o'clock this completes the whole to the 12th inclusive.

General Orders
Crown Point July 7th, 1760
Parole, Frankford

For the day tomorrow Major Gordon. As Major Christian is arrived here and Deputy Quartermaster General he is to be obeyed as such. A return is to be made to Major Christian by the quartermaster of the names of the sutlers belonging to each regiment All bakers to save the flour casks for the quartermaster general. Each regiment to appoint a man to attend to their cows. those found with out a person to take care of them, will be taken for the use for the hospital Fifty men are to be added to the engineer tomorrow.

Work Tomorrow
Regulars   220
Provincials   590
              810

Regimental Orders
Camp at Lake George, July 5th, 1760

That the party be ready to embark, in order to cross the lake, by the break of day tomorrow morning. That Major Hawks lead the front; Captain McFarland bring up the rear. That one officer go in each battoe and the remainder to be under the conduct of some trusty man. That five well men be appointed to each battoe. The sick or invalids be distributed at discretion. That officers take special care to equalize the strength of boat crews to the best advantage.

Sir John Hawks Major

Sunday the 20th of July 1760
Parole, Prince Town

For the day tomorrow Major Campbell.

Spruce beer not exceeding one barrel per company at the usual price to be delivered by Mr. Francis tomorrow morning at 5 o'clock to the Regular troops who are to receive the same under the directions of their respective quarter masters, who are likewise to give receipts from time to time for the quantity received and to be answerable that the barrels are returned the following morning; if neglected that regiment or company will be struck off the allowance for one week, the quarter master to take care that the barrels are never rolled either full or empty. Any man detected disobeying these orders will be severely punished.

On Tuesday morning the same hour the Provincial troops, Rangers etc. may receive spruce beer at the brewery, entirely on the same footing and observing the orders under the same penalty as above directed for the regular troops. The delivery of spruce beer to be continued daily to the Regulars, Provincials and Rangers, if barrels enough can be provided. Beginning as above directed a return to be sent in by the respective quartermasters this day to Mr. Francis, barrack master, who has the direction of the brewery of the number of the barrels per company which will make the brewing and issuing more regular. In the same return may be mentioned what quantity regimental sutlers will want for officers. The quantity of molasses of what was expected and what did arrive and on the road prevents any double price being made for the present. The money for the beer to be collected from the respective regiments in consequence of the receipts before mentioned as often as Mr. Francis applies for the same. A general court martial of the Provincials, consisting of one colonel, one major, four captains and eight subs, to assemble tomorrow morning at the president's tent to try all prisoners brought before them. Captain Pringle of the Inniskilling Regiment Deputy Judge Advocate. prisoners names, crimes, evidences names to be given in to the deputy judge advocate at 5 o'clock this evening. A court martial of the line to assemble tomorrow morning at 8 o'clock at the president's tent, Kennedy's tent, of the 7th Regiment Royals, one subaltern Inniskilling two members. president for the above court martial Colonel Ruggles, members Lieutenant Colonel Saltonstall, Major John Hawks. For the General Court Martial tomorrow Captain Lieutenant Benj. Byum.

Morning Orders
Monday July 21st, 1760

The general court martial ordered to assemble that day is not to meet till tomorrow at 8 o'clock as the judge advocate is ill.

Crown Point, July 21st, Monday
Parole, Piscataway

For the day tomorrow Lieutenant Colonel Darby.

The general court martial of the lines held this day is approved of by Colonel Haviland. The piquets of the regulars to assemble in the front of the 17th regiment this evening after gun fire where the sentence of the court martial is to be put in execution. The drummers of the regulars to attend. 150 men of the lines to go for provisions tomorrow morning at reveille beating to Ticonderoga or Sawmill as Major Christe will order it to be delivered. For this duty one captain and two subs of the Regulars, one captain and three subs of the Provincials and two subs of the Rangers with a proportion of sergeant and corporal. The whole to be under the command of the captain of the Regulars. This detachment is expected back tomorrow night. They will receive their battoes at the landing point as usual. As in yesterday's orders concerning spruce beer. The master workmen or those who have the direction of them send a return to Mr. Francis of their number, spruce beer will be delivered to them at the same rate and in the same proportion as troops; gabions and fascine makers and who are employed by Captain Lieutenant Williams are to do duty in the lines until further orders. Working party for the fortress as usual. John Farnal of the Massachusetts to attend the engineer tomorrow at 5 o'clock.

Tuesday, 22nd of July 1760
Parole, Upper Malboro

For the day tomorrow Major Gordon. Morning orders: The general court martial orders to assemble this day not to meet till tomorrow morning at 8 o'clock. The same number of regulars, Provincials and rangers as this day ordered to parade at reveille beating and proceed to Ticonderoga sawmills for provisions as Major Christe will order to be delivered. They will receive their battoes as ordered yesterday. The three prisoners tried by the court martial of the lines are pardoned at the request of their commanding officer.

The men that was employed by Captain Williams engineer to deliver.

Crown Point, August 11th, 1760
Parole, Oswego

The Massachusetts and Rhode Islanders to be under arms this afternoon at 5 o'clock that the engineer may know their exact number. A return of all the Regulars to be given in tomorrow morning to Mr. Stuart. Wm. Foster, Colonel

After Orders

The working party to turn out tomorrow morning at beating of the "Pioneer's March". The Massachusetts to give for the working party one subaltern, one sergeant and fifty men. The Rhode Islanders to give two subalterns, two sergeants and hundred men. A sergeant and six men of the Rhode Islanders are immediately to mount as a guard on the garden and not to allow anybody to take anything out without an order from the commanding officer and a corporal and six men to mount as a guard on the battoes.

Crown Point, August 12th, 1760
Parole, Canada

Any of the sutlers that are found feeding in the meadows shall immediately be sent for, for the use of the hospital. All the Regulars who are returned to Colonel Foster as invalids to attend roll calling at troop beating and tattoo. Any that are found absent shall be severely punished for disobedience of orders.

After Orders

That Colonel Hawks shall order a working party as follows: the Rhode Islanders to give two subalterns, two sergeants and hundred men, the Massachusetts to give one subaltern, one sergeant and fifty men and to parade tomorrow morning when the "Pioneer's March" begins to beat. The Provincials were all to eat this morning. D. Stuart.

Regimental Orders
August 12, 1760

It is expected that the gentries be alert upon their duty and suffer none to pass after 9 o'clock without hailing. The vaults are to be covered every morning and no man is to ease himself in any other place. Tomorrow a new vault is to be dug against the encampment near the garden. It is expected that there be no disturbance in camp after night and that all who are able are to turn out at reveille. It is particularly expected that every man washes himself constantly and keep himself clean. The barks are all to be taken up from the vacant tents and carried to the guard forthwith. The streets must be cleared at the front of the encampment. John Hawks.

Crown Point, 13th August 1760
Parole, Boston

The working party tomorrow as usual: it is recommended to Colonel Hawks and the officers under his command that the arms of their men may be inspected and kept in good order and particularly the arms of the artificers so that they may be in good order when wanted.

Crown Point 14th August 1760
Parole, Montreal

It is Colonel Foster's positive orders that no man shall go a mooting about the block houses in the woods. The first that is found in disobeying these orders shall be severely punished. Colonel Hawks is to appoint an officer to act as adjutant who is to receive orders from Mr. Stuart every day at 12 o'clock at the Royal encampment. Colonel Hawks is to give in a return to Colonel Foster of all the Provincials that are here present, mentioning those that are fit for duty and those sick in the general hospital and those sick in camp. This return to be given in as soon as possible and likewise a return of the artificers of Captain Ingersoll's Company that came in yesterday.

Crown Point 14th August 1760

Mr. John Leberview is to act as a adjutant and be obeyed as such until further orders. Lieutenant Geo. Freeman is to act as quarter master until further orders and be obeyed as such. Jess Teague is to act as sergeant major and be obeyed as such. As it is unwholesome to cook within the encampment it is expected that fires for the future are made without. All the soldiers of the Massachusetts that have not received money of the pay master and stand in need, may apply to him tomorrow at

12 o'clock with the officer who commands them, but none are to receive money that have received already. No man is to go out from the camp to fire upon any pretence whatever. John Hawks, Lieutenant Colonel

CROWN POINT, AUGUST 15TH, 1760
PAROLE, PORTSMOUTH

The working party as usual tomorrow. The Provincials to give in an exact return of the deficiency they have in arms and ammunition.

CROWN POINT, AUGUST 16TH, 1760
PAROLE, DARTMOUTH

The working party tomorrow as usual. Colonel Foster is very much surprised that Colonel Hawks don't give in a return of all the Provincials here upon the spot according to orders of the 14th.

CROWN POINT, AUGUST 17TH, 1760
PAROLE, PHILADELPHIA

The working party tomorrow as usual. The following sawyers to attend the engineer tomorrow morning at reveille beating. Eben. Gutten, Elijah Harvey, James Ross and Elijah Dunning, Eben Taw, John Bagett all of the Massachusetts. A court martial to sit tomorrow morning at 10 o'clock. Captain Hag president. Lieutenant Newland, Ensign Foster, Ensign Shaw and Ensign Grant.

Crown Point August 23rd, 1760
Parole, Brunswick

It is Colonel Foster's order that no sutler or woman offer to go down the lake in any of the battoes that may have occasion to go with out written pass and signed by him. If any is found disobeying this order they shall be drummed out of camp.

Crown Point, August 24th, 1760
Parole, Glasgow

The working party tomorrow as usual. The Provincials to furnish for the new fort guard tomorrow and men who are to parade at the front of the Royal encampment tomorrow morning at half an hour after seven with their arms. An officer to visit the new fort guard whenever he pleases in the daytime but particularly after retreat beating to see the prisoners are hand cuffed according to orders and if the officer misses any of the guards, absent without leave from the sergeant he is to confine them directly. The sergeant of the guard is to make his report as usual.

Crown Point August 25th, 1760
Parole, London

The working party tomorrow as usual. The Provincials to furnish twelve men tomorrow for the new fort guard, and parade at the front of the Royal the same time as this day. Officer for this day Ensign Foster; tomorrow Ensign Shaw.

Crown Point, August 26th, 1760
Parole, Manchester

The working party tomorrow as usual. The Provincials to send the same number of men as this day for guard. Officer of the day tomorrow Ensign Grant. A court martial to sit tomorrow at 10 o'clock to try what prisoners may come before them.

Regimental Orders
Crown Point August 27th, 1760

It is Colonel Hawk's positive orders that those who have taken bark from the old hospital shall immediately return it there again and not any more be taken from thence upon any account. those that are detected breaking this order will be severely punished. If any are found easing themselves in the old guard houses or anywhere out of the vaults they will be punished. The officers are to see these orders duly executed.

CROWN POINT AUGUST 30TH, 1760
PAROLE, SPRINGFIELD

The working party and guards tomorrow as usual. One sergeant and seven private men of the Provincials to parade tomorrow morning at 6 o'clock at the head of the Royal encampment in order to escort an express to the army. Officer of the day tomorrow Lieutenant Newland.

CROWN POINT, AUGUST 31ST, 1760
PAROLE, DARTMOUTH

The working party and guard tomorrow as usual. For the future when any boat is going down the Lake express, the party is always to take a fortnight's provisions with them. To visit the guard to morrow Ensign Foster.

CROWN POINT, SEPTEMBER 1ST, 1760
PAROLE, ISLE AUX NOIR

The working party and guard tomorrow as usual. One sergeant and twenty-four private men of the Provincials to hold themselves in readiness tomorrow morning at 7 o'clock in order to export some battoes to Ticonderoga, they are to take two days provisions with them. Officer for the day tomorrow Ensign Grant. A court martial to set tomorrow at 10 o'clock to try what prisoners may come before them. Lieutenant Newland, president, Ensign Grant and Foster members.

CROWN POINT, SEPTEMBER 4, 1760
PAROLE, MANCHESTER

The working party tomorrow as usual. It is Colonel Foster's orders that the officer of the day is to visit the French prisoners at 12 o'clock in the day and at retreat beating at night, and see that none of the prisoners is absent. The Provincials to send sixteen private men for the fort guard tomorrow morning at 6 o'clock at the head of the Royal encampment in order to export four French prisoners to Ticonderoga. The party to take two days provisions with them. Officer for the day tomorrow Ensign Grant.

Crown Point, September 5th, 1760
Parole, Aberdeen

The working party and guard tomorrow as usual. Officer for the day tomorrow Lieutenant Newland. One corporal and sixteen men of the Provincials to parade tomorrow morning at 6 o'clock in order to export a battoe with provisions to the Isle Aux Noir. The party to take seven days provisions with them. One corp. and four men to attend every morning at six o'clock at Mr. Stewart's hut and receive his directions concerning a chimney that is to be built. This number of men to continue till the work is finished.

Crown Point September 6th, 1760
Parole, Chester

The working party and guard tomorrow as usual. Officer for the day tomorrow Ensign Foster. One captain, two subs, four sergeants and hundred and twenty men of the Provincials to parade tomorrow morning at reveille beating, in order to go across the lake to the wood for the engineer. The party to take seven days' provisions with them. The working party to have but half a hour at breakfast and two hours at dinner.

Crown Point, September 7th, 1760

Officer for the day tomorrow Ensign Grant. The Provincials to furnish hundred men for the engineer. Tomorrow the guard as usual.

Crown Point, September 8th, 1760
Parole, Philadelphia

The working party and guard tomorrow as usual. Officer for the day tomorrow Lieutenant Newland. No sutler or soldier are to presume to take away any of the old battoes; if any is found in disobeying this order they shall be severely punished.

Note

To a traveller unacquainted with the history of the country from Fort Edward to Lake George, the route will present nothing very interesting. Professor Silliman, who passed over it in 1819, says, "It is an uninteresting country, partly of pines, barren and partly of stony hills"; and excepting the villages of Sandy Hill and Glens Falls, it will so appear. But to me every mile brings up reminiscences of military events of a most interesting nature in which officers and soldiers of my acquaintance have a share. On the low ground a small distance west of Sandy Hill village the baggage teams and escort were cut off in July, 1758, in an Indian ambuscade. At the east part of Glens Falls village was a small field work at the time, and at Halfway Brook the remains of two field forts are seen, one on each side.

Here considerable bodies of troops were posted in 1758 and 1759, and many of the orders in the preceding pages are dated. About half or three-quarters of a mile north of the brook, where the road rises to a pine woods, at what was called Indian Rock, a party of Provincial troops were attacked, defeated, and a considerable number killed, on July 20, 1758, among whom were Captains Dakin, Jones, and Lawrence, two lieutenants, and one ensign. Captain Lawrence was from Groton, Mass. About two miles from there the road passes a defile formed by morasses on each side and a brook called Five Mile Run.

Near this defile Montcalm passed with the advance party during the siege of Fort William Henry, August, 1757. About a mile north of this defile is the south point of French Mountain and a small village near the place where Baron Dieskau encamped the night before his attack on General Johnson, September 8, 1755, and also the place where Captain McGinniss and Folsom (?) attacked Dieskau's troops after their repulse at the lake. At the distance of half or three-quarters of a mile from this place on the road is the ground where Colonel Ephraim Williams with 1000 Provincials and 200 Indians was ambuscaded by Dieskau on the morning of the same 8th of September, and defeated with the loss of many officers and men of his detachment and he himself slain. The ground is somewhat elevated, with a ravine and a swamp on the east side. Passing this spot the road descends to lower ground to a small brook and within a quarter of a mile passes the west side of Bloody Pond.

The ground south of this place where Colonel Williams fell is generally open, but at the time of the action was covered with woods. The principal part of the action was fought some distance south of the pond. A small distance north of the pond the road has recently been turned to the right into low ground and intersects the old road about a mile south of the lake. By following the old road from the pond the traveller will pass over other places where attacks occurred. At the south end of the lake and the ruins of Fort William Henry and Fort George the ground is now mostly open, and on that south of the latter is the place of the battle between Johnson's and Dieskau's forces, September 8, 1755.

The village of Caldwell occupies the ground where Montcalm carried on his operations in August, 1757, at the siege of Fort William Henry and the entrenched camp of Colonel Monro, the latter on the rocky eminence south east of William Henry, where Fort George is now seen. Several skirmishes occurred south of this entrenched camp during the siege, as well as at other times and places on the old road, and on the same ground the massacre of Monroe's garrison happened. The ground where Williams was first attacked is still covered with wood, but a small cottage is seen on the open ground south of Bloody Pond. On this battle ground about 140 men were found and buried the second day after the affair, and among them Colonel Williams, at a large rock within a few rods of the present road. The ground now presents a solitary aspect.

In the journals of officers and soldiers written during the campaigns of 1755 the arm of Lake Champlain extending from Ticonderoga to White hall is often called South Bay; but the name was more properly applied to the bay spreading to greater width south-west of that at Whitehall, and here the Rangers and detachments from the armies at Lake George were often sent to watch the enemy in their incursions by that channel. In the War of the Revolution, subsequent to Burgoyne's expedition, a post was maintained at Fort Ann village. E. Hoyt. September 7, 1842.

ALSO FROM LEONAUR
AVAILABLE IN SOFTCOVER OR HARDCOVER WITH DUST JACKET

WELLINGTON AND THE PYRENEES CAMPAIGN VOLUME I: FROM VITORIA TO THE BIDASSOA by *F. C. Beatson*—The final phase of the campaign in the Iberian Peninsula.

WELLINGTON AND THE INVASION OF FRANCE VOLUME II: THE BIDASSOA TO THE BATTLE OF THE NIVELLE by *F. C. Beatson*—The second of Beatson's series on the fall of Revolutionary France published by Leonaur, the reader is once again taken into the centre of Wellington's strategic and tactical genius.

WELLINGTON AND THE FALL OF FRANCE VOLUME III: THE GAVES AND THE BATTLE OF ORTHEZ by *F. C. Beatson*—This final chapter of F. C. Beatson's brilliant trilogy shows the 'captain of the age' at his most inspired and makes all three books essential additions to any Peninsular War library.

NAVAL BATTLES OF THE NAPOLEONIC WARS by *W. H. Fitchett*—Cape St.Vincent, the Nile, Cadiz, Copenhagen, Trafalgar & Others

SERGEANT GUILLEMARD: THE MAN WHO SHOT NELSON? by *Robert Guillemard*—A Soldier of the Infantry of the French Army of Napoleon on Campaign Throughout Europe

WITH THE GUARDS ACROSS THE PYRENEES by *Robert Batty*—The Experiences of a British Officer of Wellington's Army During the Battles for the Fall of Napoleonic France, 1813.

A STAFF OFFICER IN THE PENINSULA by *E. W. Buckham*—An Officer of the British Staff Corps Cavalry During the Peninsula Campaign of the Napoleonic Wars

THE LEIPZIG CAMPAIGN: 1813—NAPOLEON AND THE "BATTLE OF THE NATIONS" by *F. N. Maude*—Colonel Maude's analysis of Napoleon's campaign of 1813.

BUGEAUD: A PACK WITH A BATON by *Thomas Robert Bugeaud*—The Early Campaigns of a Soldier of Napoleon's Army Who Would Become a Marshal of France.

TWO LEONAUR ORIGINALS

SERGEANT NICOL by *Daniel Nicol*—The Experiences of a Gordon Highlander During the Napoleonic Wars in Egypt, the Peninsula and France.

WATERLOO RECOLLECTIONS by *Frederick Llewellyn*—Rare First Hand Accounts, Letters, Reports and Retellings from the Campaign of 1815.

AVAILABLE ONLINE AT
www.leonaur.com
AND OTHER GOOD BOOK STORES

ALSO FROM LEONAUR
AVAILABLE IN SOFTCOVER OR HARDCOVER WITH DUST JACKET

CAPTAIN OF THE 95th (Rifles) by *Jonathan Leach*—An officer of Wellington's Sharpshooters during the Peninsular, South of France and Waterloo Campaigns of the Napoleonic Wars.

BUGLER AND OFFICER OF THE RIFLES by *William Green & Harry Smith* With the 95th (Rifles) during the Peninsular & Waterloo Campaigns of the Napoleonic Wars

BAYONETS, BUGLES AND BONNETS by *James 'Thomas' Todd*—Experiences of hard soldiering with the 71st Foot - the Highland Light Infantry - through many battles of the Napoleonic wars including the Peninsular & Waterloo Campaigns

THE ADVENTURES OF A LIGHT DRAGOON by *George Farmer & G.R. Gleig*—A cavalryman during the Peninsular & Waterloo Campaigns, in captivity & at the siege of Bhurtpore, India

THE COMPLEAT RIFLEMAN HARRIS by *Benjamin Harris as told to & transcribed by Captain Henry Curling*—The adventures of a soldier of the 95th (Rifles) during the Peninsular Campaign of the Napoleonic Wars

WITH WELLINGTON'S LIGHT CAVALRY by *William Tomkinson*—The Experiences of an officer of the 16th Light Dragoons in the Peninsular and Waterloo campaigns of the Napoleonic Wars.

SURTEES OF THE RIFLES by *William Surtees*—A Soldier of the 95th (Rifles) in the Peninsular campaign of the Napoleonic Wars.

ENSIGN BELL IN THE PENINSULAR WAR by *George Bell*—The Experiences of a young British Soldier of the 34th Regiment 'The Cumberland Gentlemen' in the Napoleonic wars.

WITH THE LIGHT DIVISION by *John H. Cooke*—The Experiences of an Officer of the 43rd Light Infantry in the Peninsula and South of France During the Napoleonic Wars

NAPOLEON'S IMPERIAL GUARD: FROM MARENGO TO WATERLOO by *J. T. Headley*—This is the story of Napoleon's Imperial Guard from the bearskin caps of the grenadiers to the flamboyance of their mounted chasseurs, their principal characters and the men who commanded them.

BATTLES & SIEGES OF THE PENINSULAR WAR by *W. H. Fitchett*—Corunna, Busaco, Albuera, Ciudad Rodrigo, Badajos, Salamanca, San Sebastian & Others

AVAILABLE ONLINE AT
www.leonaur.com
AND OTHER GOOD BOOK STORES

Printed in the United Kingdom
by Lightning Source UK Ltd.
130937UK00001B/65/P